Charles
Edward
White

STUDIES IN CULTURE
& COMMUNICATION

Martin S. Dworkin, General Editor

The series is devoted to education in its most comprehensive meaning, embracing the activities of formal instruction and learning carried on in schools, and all the forces of social influence upon the development and behavior of individuals and groups. Drawing upon a broad range of literatures, in many languages, the series presents new and rediscovered works, focusing closely on critical studies of the arts, educational implications of courses of thought and behavior, and tactics and instruments of profession and persuasion. No partiality of doctrine or expression is intended or imposed, the selections following a sovereign purpose to stimulate and inform the continuing critique of ideas, values, and modes of communication that is the growing tissue of education, and perennial flowering of culture.

MODERN AESTHETICS: AN HISTORICAL INTRODUCTION
The Earl of Listowel

JEFFERSONIANISM AND THE AMERICAN NOVEL
Howard Mumford Jones

THE RISE OF THE AMERICAN FILM: A CRITICAL HISTORY
With An Essay
EXPERIMENTAL CINEMA IN AMERICA 1921–1947
Lewis Jacobs

MAN AND HIS CIRCUMSTANCES: ORTEGA AS EDUCATOR
Robert McClintock

GRAHAM GREENE: THE FILMS OF HIS FICTION
Gene D. Phillips, S.J.

STUDIES IN CULTURE
& COMMUNICATION

GENE D.
PHILLIPS, S.J.

GRAHAM

GREENE:

TEACHERS COLLEGE PRESS
Teachers College, Columbia University
New York and London

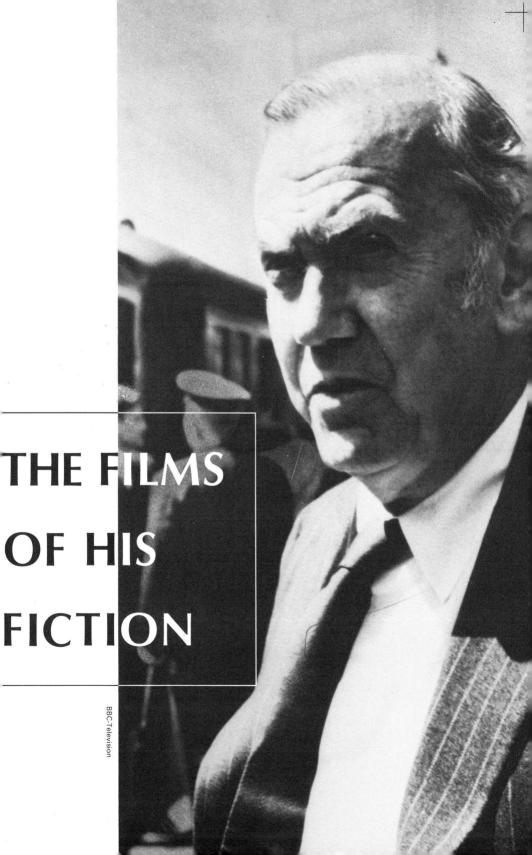

THE FILMS
OF HIS
FICTION

© 1974 by Teachers College, Columbia University
Library of Congress Catalog Card Number: 73–85252

Art Director: Hanns L. Sperr

Cover Art: Carl Wester

Manufactured in the United States of America

To
William K. Everson

GENERAL EDITOR'S FOREWORD

THE WRITING ON THE SCREEN*

"The movie writer does not need to know how to write; he does need a talent for plot contrivance and a sense of colloquial dialogue. This has been true of the movies since the beginning." So saith Leo Rosten, in his *Hollywood: The Movie Colony; The Movie Makers*,[1] a work applying methods of sociology where "possible," in an attempt to make ". . . the difference between social science and gossip, between systematic analysis and casual journalism,"[2] in studying what was the world center of film production at its height of power and glory. Rosten later shows sufficient respect for screenwriters, even quoting Samuel Goldwyn on the "author" as the "indispensable requirement" of a good film, as ". . . a picture can't rise higher than its

---

*This essay draws on research and writing being done under auspices of the Institute of Philosophy and Politics of Education, Teachers College, Columbia University.

[1]New York: Harcourt, Brace & Company, 1941. Reprinted in *The Literature of Cinema* series, New York: Arno Press and The New York Times, 1970; page 313.

[2]*Ibid.*, p. vi.

story."[3] The implied denigration nevertheless remains, as Rosten stresses the limitations of the writer's rôle, and his inevitable frustration and bitterness, in what is essentially and traditionally a collaborative process, producing salable merchandise for the entertainment market place.

Whether or not it has been "true . . . from the beginning," the notion itself is a persistent one, since the earliest efforts to do more in films than record action for its own sake. And it was surely more "true" in the years before the addition of simultaneous sound reproduction to the images on screen, when it was the function of the director that was established as principal in the reality of film making—and in its mythology. Writers provided story outlines or scenarios, then continuities for directors to bring to cinematic life. The writing had no being, as matter to be read, apart from what was there to cue or inspire the director's imagination. Only in the usually separate craft of doing titles to accompany the pictures on screen did writing convey meaning directly to audiences. The rest was silence, if almost always with musical accompaniment, and often with sound effects. The public saw what the director created for the screen, even the new gods and goddesses of movie stardom seeming to have burst from his forehead in a cinematic cataclysm.

This view, putting the writer in his place, is purveyed, for but one appropriately curious example, in a popular detective novel of the early 1920s, one of an already sizable genre of books and stories inventing a brash new world of miraculous movie making and magical movie people. *The Film Mystery*, by Arthur B. Reeve,[4] in a series featuring "Craig Kennedy," redoubtable practitioner of crime detection as exact science, has to do with a couple of suitably ingenious murders, via envenomed pins and botulin toxin, during the shooting of *The Black Terror*, being made, significantly, at a mansion at Tarrytown, near New York City, then still in the running with Hollywood as a production center. At one point, the producer scoffs at a question as to the whereabouts of the script writer:

---

[3]*Ibid.*, p. 316.
[4]New York: Harper & Bros., 1921.

"An author on the lot at the filming of his picture, to bother the director and to change everything? Out! When the scenario's done he's through. He's lucky to get his name on the screen. It's not the story but the direction which counts, except that you've got to have a good idea to start with, and a halfway decent script to make your lay-outs from."[5]

The narrator, a character in the story, vaunts his movie knowledge in remarking that the producer may have known he was exaggerating, "going counter to the tendency to have the author on the lot." But the decisive commentary may be in the *denouement* itself (there being no mystery that books are written by writers). It is the screenwriter, after all, who is discovered to be the murderer, having done in . . . yes, the star actress *and* the director!

To run down the writer in film making, of course, is to raise up the director, first and most of all, leading to what looks to some, notably writers, as an "extravagant critical cult of the director," in the phrase of Terence Rattigan. This cult, "a legacy, and a bad legacy, of the days of silent film," he has said, is perpetuated by "responsible film critics," who persist in giving the public "the impression that it is the director and not the screenwriter who writes the script." This may have been true before sound, when "the status of the pre-Jolsonian screenwriter was often merely that of translator, stenographer, and general hack."[6] But it is time for the screenwriter to

". . . throw off the shackles of the director (and the camera) and remember that the screenplay is the child not only of its mother, the silent film, but also of its father, the Drama; that it has affinities not only with Griffith, De Mille and Ingram, but also with Sophocles, Shakespeare, and Ibsen."[7]

Reeve's fictional producer disdains the "story" in film making as but a step on the way to the images conceived by the director, prepared for and captured by the camera, and selected and joined in the editing process. Rattigan raises a working writer's banner on behalf of a dramatic and literary integrity of the written script, at once independent of the intended filmic outcome, yet ineluctably vital to it. Both posi-

[5]*Ibid.*, p. 43.

[6]"A Magnificent Pity For Camels," in John Sutro, editor, *Diversion: Twenty-two Authors On the Lively Arts.* London: Max Parrish, 1950; p. 181.

[7]*Ibid.*, p. 185.

tions are overstated, the former, perhaps, only slightly more than the
latter. But both continue to be maintained, with appropriate exaggera-
tions, in arguments among film industry people, critics, and audiences
—as is surely evident in the often savage snarling over the *auteur* theory
of film "authorship," that developed in Paris in the 1950s and '60s.
Future scholars may in puzzlement ascribe the confused bickerings of
critics and packs of critics there, and later in Britain and the U.S.,
as much to contending political ideologies, or to opportunism of rival
self-publicists bidding for some new kind of movie stardom, as to
any differences over film theory and practice. The forces of ambient
politics, and the drive of individual motivations aside, however, what
made the controversy possible, and probably inevitable, was a conver-
gence of two complex factors: the one, a rediscovery of the history
of motion pictures; and the other, a renewed urgency to establish
the credentials of cinema as "art" among the traditionally accepted
arts.

The new awareness of film history had much to do with the
growth of serious study of popular culture in general, but it was especially invigorated and informed by a new and increasing availability
of the ancient movie artifacts. These, although once and for so long
treated as ephemera by the film makers themselves, were now lovingly
pursued, collected, and belatedly preserved, with all the furious dedi-
cation of Poggio Bracciolini and the Humanist scholar-sleuths, searching out the manuscript remnants of classical culture. Not only an
affection for silent films, but a veritable mystique of their "purity"
as cinema and as folk culture, became essential elements of intellectual
apparatus after the turn of mid-century. Not least affected were new
waves of film makers, nostalgic for a halcyon era of the movies before
most of them were born.

Notions of the nature of film creation idealizing silent film techniques were renovated, often subordinating or even eliminating the
scriptwriting function, going so far as to permit—nay, to *demand*—
spontaneous conception on the part of the director, and improvised
action and dialogue by actors. And, it was no mere coincidence that
there were available new, highly portable cameras, sound recorders,
and lighting equipment, as well as hypersensitive film materials, that
allowed not only a release from dependence on studios, with their
elaborate installations, but also a kind of careful, sophisticated imita-

tion of what were seen as unencumbered techniques of early cinematography.

All this was happening, to be sure, at a time of general upheaval in the motion picture industry. The great studio complexes, after being forced under anti-monopoly regulations to disengage their radiating chains of theaters, were being disintegrated, or transformed into manufactories for television. Film production could now be "independent" of studio control and the programming requirements of established networks of distribution and exhibition. That this industrial system had usually worked to restrict film makers, including scriptwriters, was an old and real complaint among those who look first to the artistic and informational potentialities of the screen. However true this may be, there ought to be puzzlement, if not embarrassment, for the more doctrinaire of these critics in the current rediscovery of so many of those slick products of the high days of the movie studio system as works of authentic cinematic style and preëminently popular entertainment.

In any event, the more the movies are taken seriously, the greater the tensions between what must be regarded as individual and creative, and what is inescapably collaborative, technical, and industrial, in their production and provision for audience participation. The opposing forces, exhibiting a Heraclitean dynamic in balance, affect interpretations of the history of motion pictures, as well as judgments of particular films, and inevitably come to issue in all the arguments over "authorship," the rôle of writers, and what screenwriting in general has to do with writing, an established "art," and with cinema, a parvenu of uncertain pedigree.

A good case can be made for screenwriting as a special, privileged function in film making, with unique problems and relationships to all other operations involved. But in the contentions over the importance of writers there are elements of what are in some ways periodic urges to assert the distinctive contribution of one rôle or another in the complex of crafts and activities having to do with making films and bringing them to audiences. These claims for recognition, at the very least, have their own justifications, but are also clearly punctual in a time of heightening disaffection with depersonalized processes of mass production and anonymous services, and of radical ventures to assert a sense of participation in the making of things of value. In this

case, questions of worth of contributions have the more power to
raise banners of passionate advocacy, as the making of films implicates
so many essential functions in all its stages. There can be talk of what
is done by directors, producers, actors, cameramen, editors, com-
posers, designers, and a score of others, as well as of writers, that could
not go on in discussions of any other medium—saving, of course,
television, which, for all its many differences, is near enough in nature
to cinema: nearer, say, than is live-performance theater.

Even those working in the logistical and commercial phases of
motion pictures may claim some creative involvement in what happens
in the theatrical transaction that is vital to the realization of a film
before audiences. And the assertions are made not only by trade
groups, or orators at conventions of industry people, celebrating the
indisputable leadership of this or that part of the movie business. In
fact, it was an artist, a maker of highly subjective, abstract expression-
ist films, who made the point most clearly and forcefully, without
pretension, in an interview some years ago.

He had come to films from painting, which had already gained
him recognition by museums and collectors, in order, he told this
writer, to fulfill the latent cinematic implications of his graphic art.
But, while persisting in working alone or in close direction of others,
trying for as much control over techniques and outcomes in his films
as he had sought in his painting, it was not he who completed his
work, he insisted, but his distributor: the agent-entrepreneur—albeit
one plainly concerned with more than commerce—who took his films,
sought out their potential audiences, and arranged for them to be *seen*,
to come alive as cinema in theaters, auditoriums, and classrooms.
What was on the reels, he implied, had only potential reality, and this
far less than, and far different from that of a painting in a closet, say,
or on an easel in an empty room; or of a book on a shelf; or even of a
musical score awaiting performance.

The argument is not at all new, to any who have thought seriously
about the special nature of this quintessentially modern *techné*, in
which all individuality must be mediated by an intricate technology
and an immense industry, functioning to create experiences for audiences of multitudes at once—so that still pictures appear to move,
figures of light and shadow seem to speak and sing, and distances of

time and space to be bridged in an absolute velocity of illusion. The lesson, however, always needs renewal, and never more urgently than when defenders of cinema as "art" misappropriate criteria of creativity from the established aesthetics of older media, themselves often more conventional and historically variable than philosophically coherent.

In the belated eagerness of intellectuals to recognize the qualities and powers of the cinema, as, indeed, of modern "popular art" in general, many curiously misunderstand and diminish the essential differences that make simple identification with traditional "fine arts" misleading. Past and present are thereby falsified, in forgetting that, as in the wise observation of the eminent historian of ideas Paul Oskar Kristeller:

> ". . . the various arts (in the course of history) change not only their content and style, but also their relations to each other, and their place in the general system of culture, as do religion, philosophy, or science. . . ."

and, further to the point being made here,

> ". . . the moving picture is a good example of how new techniques may lead to modes of artistic expression for which the aestheticians of the eighteenth and nineteenth century (sic) had no place in their systems."[8]

This is by no means to support the aggressive naïveté of know-nothings, including fanatic audio-visualists as well as miners of "underground" ideologies, who disconnect cinema from all antecedent culture, talking as if seeing is somehow opposed to thinking, and there is possible a critical, yet somehow non-intellectual rhetoric that is valid only for judging films. As was said by no less a prophet of the visual in cinema than Sergei Eisenstein—while asseverating the fundamentally intellectual nature of *viewing*:

> ". . . our cinema is not altogether without parents and without pedigree, without a past, without the traditions and rich cultural heritage of the past epochs. It is only very thoughtless and pre-

---

[8]"The Modern System of the Arts: A Study in the History of Aesthetics." *The Journal of the History of Ideas*, XIII (1952) 1. Reprinted in Philip P. Weiner and Aaron Noland, editors, *Ideas In Cultural Perspective*. New Brunswick, N.J.: Rutgers University Press, 1962; p. 205.

sumptuous people who can erect laws and an esthetic for cinema, proceeding from the premises of some incredible virgin-birth of this art!"[9]

What *is* argued is, or ought to be, a commonplace: that the "art" of cinema may not be reasonably considered as prior to or separate from its *techné*, involving the essential industrial technology, collaborative creativity, complex logistics, and social transformations that are the very stuff of the "dreams that money (*must*) buy"; that what makes cinema new and unique among the arts is precisely what must be always recognized, in order to discuss films meaningfully in ways that are coherent with our critical understandings of all other aspects, media, and individual creations of culture.

In this light, it becomes possible to regard as archaic and irrelevant, as well as exaggerated, both Rosten's view (whether this be "social science" or "gossip") of the screenwriter as a kind of skilled illiterate, and Rattigan's idealization of him as an embattled *littérateur*. To begin with, writing as *writing* is not one, but many, many things—and long may they flourish, in all conceivable diversity of mode and manner! But writing for filming is something else again, for reasons good, bad, and worse, that writers, first of all people, have argued "from the beginning" to explain, or explain away, what they were doing.

Almost to a man (and woman!), writers who have worked for the screen, whether preparing original scripts or adapting existing books, plays, stories, and other materials, have made much of the distinctive nature of their task, both in praise or, commonly enough, in disparagement. The latter attitude, in fact, became quite fashionable among writers in Hollywood, as is testified to in innumerable memoirs, exposés, *romans á clef*, and even films—as well as in more-or-less disciplined studies of the place and industry, led in seriousness and merit by Rosten's and Powdermaker's.[10] Writers for filming elsewhere have

---

[9]"Dickens, Griffith, and the Film Today." in Sergei Eisenstein, *Film Form: Essays In Film Theory.* Edited and translated by Jay Leyda. New York: Harcourt, Brace and Company, 1949; p. 232.

[10]Hortense Powdermaker, *Hollywood, the Dream Factory: An Anthropologist Looks At the Movie Makers.* Boston: Little, Brown & Company, 1950. (See especially Chapter VII, "The Scribes"; Chapter VIII, "Assembling the Script"; and Chapter IX, "The Answers.").

shown more of the same mixture of outraged intelligence, self-destruc-
tive cynicism, and resigned opportunism—perhaps because the emol-
uments for screenwriting in other countries notoriously have been
so much smaller.

The attitude has sufficient justification, as thousands upon thousands of films sadly attest. For themselves, writers have given the
blackest accounts of menial labors on motion picture assembly lines,
chronicling violated literary integrity, enforced anonymity, collective
rape of individual creation, ideological repression, total, demeaning
domination by corrupt authority—and, as may be surprising, usually
precarious livelihood. But there have always persisted the straight
questions as to why the writers have gone on with it all; and whether
there may not have been, and may yet be, despite any limitations and
attendant evils, some realistically worthy opportunities in screenwriting, that may attract the best people, with some hope of honorable
fulfillment. The answers given by writers to both questions are pre-
dictably various, and there are good writers who have had good reasons for both quitting screen work or staying with it. But there must
be a case, after all, for what is surely a sensible professional attitude,
and there has been quite enough good writing for films to bear witness.
Moreover, there are good writers for the screen, Graham Greene for
one, who are careful to preach what they practice, especially inveigh-
ing against the self-fulfilling denigration of screenwriting so often
played-at by the mediocre, or by those good writers who let themselves do less than they can do. Nigel Balchin, for another, has spoken
of what he regards as

> ". . . the greatest pitfall of the novelist-turned-screenwriter; the
> pitfall of thinking of the job as highly paid hackwork in an infe-
> rior medium. It is true that a large number of bad films are made.
> But for that matter a large number of bad novels are written and
> so is a large quantity of bad verse. There are no bad media; there
> are only bad performances *in* a medium. It is fatal to start a script
> from the attitude that however good it is, the resulting film will
> be bad. Bad films are sometimes made from good scripts. But in
> nine cases out of ten bad films originate from bad scripts; and
> one of the most fruitful sources of bad scripts is the author who
> thinks the job too crude and simple for him. I cannot think of
> any novelist now writing whose most subtle ideas are too subtle

for film treatment—if he learns how to handle the medium as carefully as he has learnt to write his books."[11]

Balchin's argument (which can draw support from the statements of Greene, as well as from the example of his screenwriting), must not be taken to intend that books may simply and fully be translated into films. The key word and issue here is the "ideas" contained, and the point is that the two media are distinct, methodologically, for all that a "scene" on a page may be transmogrified to one on screen that is instantly recognizable. And, the old truism means, too, for only one more thing, that the scene on the page remains, its potentiality for the imagination at least provisionally unchanged, even if a filmed version appears utterly different. It is this consideration, of a sustained life for a literary work despite what happens in a movie adaptation, that has comforted so many writers in allowing their books to be made into films, or in participating in the transformation themselves.

Here, it is Greene who may be the most notable, perhaps unique example, having had, it is likely, more to do with screen work, directly and indirectly, than any major literary figure, so far in the century. Indeed, a significant revelation of the Reverend Gene D. Phillips' book, *Graham Greene: The Films of His Fiction*, is that Greene's admiration for the motion picture medium, and his mixed feelings about the film versions of his own work, may finally be based on his certainty that his writing will survive whatever filmic transliteration, good or bad. As to the latter, he told Phillips, ". . . I can only repeat what I have said before: In the long run the smile will be on the author's face. For the book has the longer life."[12] Father Phillips does not concur, arguing that the good films made from Greene's work "will last as long as anything he has written." But this disagreement, if there is any, in no way weakens the insistence of the good screenwriters, such as Balchin and Greene, on the essentiality of good screenwriting for good films— which Phillips in fact corroborates in comparing the film versions of Greene's fiction prepared by other screenwriters with those he did himself.

In any case, it would be foolish to fault Greene for having faith in his literary work, even if it may be too soon—the survival of some-

[11]"Writing In Pictures." in John Sutro, editor, *op. cit.*; p. 154.
[12]See p. 187 in this volume.

thing cultural being always problematical, and of anything photo-
graphic being hardly predictable—to talk of altering Ovid's famous
paean to the permanence of writing, *Scripta* . . . , to *Cinema ferunt
annos*. As to this, it may be worth noting that there is an extra-added
attraction today, for writers turning from print to cinema, an outcome
of the change in public attitude discussed earlier, that has encouraged
study of films as serious works, and has elevated erstwhile merely
popular movies to cultural respectability.

In the event, there has grown a new regard for film scripts—with
which writers, after all, have something to do, for all the frequently
decisive reshaping by directors and others. Whether or not they may
be "read" as are books or plays, film scripts are now published frequently, in what is an established genre of the enormous contemporary
production of printed works on cinema. While still fundamentally
related to what is realized on screen, the published scripts nevertheless
present screenwriting to audiences in ways hardly possible before,
with inevitable consequences for the writers' own notion of themselves
and what they are doing.

And what they are doing, in fact, may not be so clear as is the easy
distinction of printed words and images on screen, that is so decisive
and fundamental, but that can be carried to fearsome oversimplifica-
tions, as in contrasting, usually in polemic, what is given as "purely
verbal" discourse with something called "pure cinema." Even to say,
"to write a film," or "to film a story," implies such integration of media
in the imagination, if not in the tactics of production, as to call for
some revisions, at the least, of conventional separations of the arts—
exemplifying once again the natural dynamism of cultural activity,
that has been remarked before. Printed words, indeed, are involved
with filmed images in ways that, as this writer has elsewhere argued,
"may be the best example for our time of a practical, if not essential
interdependence of the arts—or, at the least, of an integral relationship
among media of mass communications."[13]

The arts once were not separated from each other, or from either
the paramount or the least concerns and activities of the people who
created them and lived their meaning. Even now, their distinctiveness,

[13]"The Printed Screen." In the author's column, "Critic's Rostrum." *The Educational Forum*, XXXIII
(November, 1968) 1; p. 109. Also in *Quadrant* (Sydney), XIII (January-February, 1970) 7; p. 51.

as creative media and as experiences to have and to share, may be more truly a matter of conventional attitudes, or of limited abstraction for philosophical analysis, than of essential differentiation. We may observe this integration, surely, in considering the bearing of music, and its orchestrated silences, on the whole experience of motion pictures. And, returning to the matter of writing and what it has to do with film, we may wonder whether what is happening, when verbal ideas and narratives become particular images and sequences of thought and action on screen, may not be a reassertion of the very nature of writing, rather than evidence of its passing potency.

This, or something not unrelated, may have been in Federico Fellini's mind when he said to me, during a talk in 1957, that he had come to making films precisely because he is a *writer*. Well, precisely what he meant at that moment he could not clarify; it sounded good to him, and somehow right, and maybe, as is the way of the arts, it is a matter of becoming: clearer, for one thing, but truer, for all the rest.

New York City   MARTIN S. DWORKIN
March, 1973

PREFACE

Graham Greene is one of the few major literary talents of our time to show a serious interest in the motion picture medium. Other major novelists like Faulkner and Fitzgerald have written for the screen, but they always considered it hack work which they endured in order to earn enough money to go back to writing serious fiction. Greene, on the other hand, has always taken the cinema seriously. He has written both film criticism and film scripts, often adaptations of his own fiction. His film criticism, some of the best of our age, according to critic Roger Sharrock, appeared between 1935 and 1939 in the *Spectator* and in the short-lived *Night and Day*, of which Greene was co-editor in 1937.

His talent as a screenwriter complements his talents as a fiction writer, for there is a definite cinematic quality about his narrative style, whether on page or screen. As Sharrock has written, "Long before they were made into film scripts, his narratives were crisply cut like cinema montage." Almost all of Greene's novels have been filmed, and we shall see in examining these adaptations that no one can transcribe Greene's vivid prose into visual images and still retain his multiple levels of meaning better than Greene himself.

In taking up each of Greene's novels and short stories that has been filmed, I shall first consider it as a work of fiction, independent of the fact that it was later filmed; for it is only in understanding each work in itself as Greene originally conceived it that we can grasp the relative merits of the subsequent screen version based on it. Greene has divided his novels into what he calls his "entertainments" and his serious fiction, and I shall keep this distinction in dealing with his work. I have placed the short stories of Greene that have been filmed among his entertainments, since they seem to fit into that category best. Because his entertainments are primarily concerned with action, it is not surprising that many of them were adapted to the screen before his serious fiction, which centers more on the nuances of character development and therefore is more difficult to put on film.

Much has been written on the theoretical level about the relation of film and literature, as in Bluestone's *Novels into Film* and Jinks' *The Celluloid Literature*. In examining Greene's association with the cinema over almost forty years, I hope to show how the wedding of fiction and film works out in practice. Like any marriage, there have been periods of disappointment as well as of satisfaction, but when one considers Greene's association with the film medium as a whole, one sees how genuinely fruitful the alliance of fiction writer and of film writer can be—particularly if they happen to be the same person.

GENE D. PHILLIPS, S.J.

ACKNOWLEDGMENTS

First of all, I am most grateful to Graham Greene, who discussed this book with me personally and corresponded with me about it throughout the time that I was preparing it.

Of the many others who helped me I would like to mention the following:

Sir Hugh Greene, Sir Alec Guinness, and film makers John and Roy Boulting, Edward Dmytryk, George Cukor, and everyone else who graciously granted me interviews.

The staff of the British Film Institute of London, in particular Colin Ford and Jeremy Boulton of the National Film Archive, Colin MacArthur of the Education Department, and John Gillett.

Søren Fischer and Brian Baxter, also of the British Film Institute, for allowing me to draw on the Graham Greene filmography which they compiled for Mr. Greene's John Player Lecture at the National Film Theater, February 15, 1970.

Peggy Waterkeyne of the National Society of Film and Television Artists of London; Ronald Browne, librarian of the Farm Street Jesuit Residence, London; Alexander Walker, film critic of the London *Evening Standard;* and Maryvonne Butcher, literary editor and film critic of the London *Tablet.*

Maximillian/Trianon Productions, Nice, for permission to quote from the film script of *The Comedians.*

The Johnson Fund of the American Philosophical Society for a grant with which to pursue this study.

All of the quotations from the books by Graham Greene are copyright © by Graham Greene, 1973, and by the following publishers:

William Heinemann, London, and the Viking Press, New York: *Journey Without Maps* (1936); *Brighton Rock* (1938); *The Confidential Agent* (1939); *The Lawless Roads* (American title: *Another Mexico* (1939); *The Power and the Glory* (1940); *The Ministry of Fear* (1943); *The Heart of the Matter* (1948); *The End of the Affair* (1951); *Twenty-One Stories* (1954); *The Quiet American* (1955); *Our Man in Havana* (1958); *In Search of a Character* (1961); *A Sense of Reality* (1963); The Bodley Head, London, and the Viking Press, New York: *The Comedians* (1966); *The Collected Essays* (1969); *Travels with My Aunt* (1970); *A Sort of Life* (1971); William Heinemann—The Bodley Head, London: Introductions to the Collected Edition of the novels: *It's a Battlefield, England Made Me, Brighton Rock, Our Man in Havana* (1970); *The Confidential Agent, The Power and the Glory, The Heart of the Matter* (1971). Percival Marshall, London: *Why Do I Write?* (1948). William Heinemann, London: *The Third Man* and *The Fallen Idol* (1950). Mercury Books, London: *Three Plays* (1961). Norstedt, Stockholm: *Introductions to Three Novels* (1962). Lorrimer, London, and Simon and Schuster, New York: *The Third Man* (film script) (1968).

CONTENTS

ILLUSTRATIONS

Graham Greene:

The Films

of his

Fiction

1

THE BEGINNING OF
THE AFFAIR:
GRAHAM GREENE AS
CINEMA CRITIC

It was unusually warm for a spring day on the French Riviera. I got off the bus in Antibes, the small town on the Mediterranean coast where Graham Greene lives, and which has served as the setting of some of his short stories. He had agreed to meet with me for a conversation about his work for the cinema. Greene answered the door himself and I was immediately put at ease by his ready smile and his softspoken manner. We settled down in his living room, which overlooks the sea, and began our discussion of his long career in the cinema.

Greene recalled at the outset that he had loved the movies from childhood. The screen adaptation of Anthony Hope's *Sophy of Kravonia*, the story of a kitchen maid who became a queen, was the first film that he remembers seeing. The year was 1911 and Greene was seven years old at the time, but he can still recall "the rumble of the queen's guns crossing the high Kravonian pass beaten hollowly out on a single piano." In his autobiography, *A Sort of Life*, Greene says that the first movie theater was opened in his home town just after the First World

War. His father, who was headmaster of Berkhamsted School, once allowed his senior boys to attend a special performance of the first Tarzan movie there "under the false impression that it was an educational film of anthropological interest, and ever after he regarded the cinema with a sense of disillusion and suspicion."

Nevertheless, Greene became seriously interested in cinema as he grew up, and shared this interest with his younger brother Hugh, who was later to start the Oxford University Film Society. "While I was at Oxford," says Graham Greene, "there was a review, long since defunct, called *Close-Up*, which dealt with all the major directors of the time."[1] He took a bound volume off a shelf and showed it to me. It was dated 1928 and contained articles by leading film makers and theoreticians of the cinema such as Eisenstein and Pudovkin.

Although Greene published his first novel, *The Man Within*, in 1929, and continued to publish novels at the rate of almost one a year in the ensuing decade, his income from writing fiction was not sufficient to support his wife and children. Accordingly he turned to journalism as a way of augmenting his earnings, and in 1935 became a film critic for the *Spectator*. He continued in this capacity until 1940, when he became literary editor. From July through December of 1937, Greene co-edited with John Marks a weekly journal of opinion called *Night and Day*, which had Greene himself as film critic, Evelyn Waugh as book critic, and included Elizabeth Bowen, James Thurber and others among its contributors. With such a distinguished roster, one could almost have predicted that *Night and Day* was too good to last; but the precise reason for its short life I shall mention later.

Although Greene has never articulated a fully developed set of critical principles according to which he judged films, a representative sampling of his writings about the motion picture medium does indicate what he looked for in a good film. For one thing, Greene endorsed the kind of film that is basically entertaining and will therefore appeal to a wide audience. "The cinema has got to appeal to millions," he wrote in an article which he contributed in 1938 to a collection of essays called *Footnotes to the Film*. "We have got to accept its popularity as a virtue, not turn away from it as a vice . . . . The novelist may

---

[1]All ten volumes of *Close-Up* (1927–1933) were republished in 1971 in book form as part of the Arno Press Cinema Program. They have been newly edited by Kenneth MacPherson and Winifred Bryher.

write for a few thousand readers, but the film artist must work for the millions."[2] Later he added in one of his *Spectator* columns (June 16, 1939): "A film with a severely limited appeal must be—to that extent—a bad film."[3] When I reminded him of these remarks, Greene commented, "I think I would stand by that today. By a film with a limited appeal I mean a flop. A good film is seldom a complete flop, whereas a book can be very good and still be a flop. That is, it may never reach its intended audience."

Nevertheless Greene has never felt that box office popularity should be the sole index of a film's worth. "Does reaching the public necessarily mean reaching the biggest, most amorphous public possible?" he asked in another *Spectator* column (November 19, 1937). "Isn't it equally possible to reach a selected public with films of aesthetic interest? . . . The cinema, of course, should be a popular art, but need the popularity be worldwide?" In order to ensure the financial success of a film, Greene pointed out, producers often try to cater to the lowest common denominator in their potential audience by mass-producing escapist entertainment which offers no challenging ideas for the more reflective filmgoer. The average film always has a clearly defined moral, Greene wrote. "The huge public has been trained to expect a villain and a hero, and if you're going to reach the biggest possible public, it's no good thinking of drama as the conflict of ideas; it's the conflict—in terms of sub-machine guns—of the plainest Good and the plainest Evil."

It is in this context that Greene developed in his essay in *Footnotes to the Film* his concept of poetic cinema. By this term he meant films which not only entertain the viewer but challenge him as well, by depicting for him not only life as it is but also life as it ought to be. This description of the artist's theme, which Greene drew from Chekhov, he feels has never been bettered: "Only in films to which Chekhov's description applies shall we find the poetic cinema." Greene went on to say that in discussing poetic cinema he was using the term *poetic* as Chekhov did, in its widest sense, "as the power to suggest human

[2]Graham Greene, "Subjects and Stories," *Footnotes to the Film*, ed. Charles Davy. London: Lovat Dickson, 1938; reprinted in *The Literature of Cinema* series. New York: Arno Press and The New York Times, 1970; p. 64.

[3]I have drawn my citations from Greene's film reviews from the original sources, but the reader will be interested to know that the collected film criticism of Graham Greene has been published in England by Secker and Warburg and in the United States by Simon and Schuster.

values . . . . Photography by itself cannot make poetic cinema. By itself it can only make arty cinema."

Greene today still agrees with these statements: "It is still true that film, and fiction too, should present life as it is and also life as it should be. I still believe, too, that if you excite your audience first you can put over what you will of horror, suffering, and truth. By exciting an audience I mean getting it involved in the story. Once it is involved it will accept the thing the way that you present it."

In his essay Greene chose Fritz Lang's 1937 film *Fury* to illustrate what he means by poetic cinema. (He had already written in his column in *Night and Day* for November 4, 1937, "Occasionally a film of truth and tragic value somehow gets out of Hollywood onto the screen. Nobody can explain it . . . . Jehovah is asleep, and when he awakes he finds he's got a *Fury* on his hands.") *Fury*, Greene explained, was just as exciting as Lang's earlier films, but this time in the course of the exciting action "the poetry had crept in." The attempt of the mob to lynch Spencer Tracy for a crime that he did not commit provided a typical thriller situation; but the effectiveness of these scenes, Greene maintained, was owed in part, at least, to the earlier sequences which depicted the happiness of Tracy and his fiancée which had been shattered by the later events in the film: "Life as it is and life as it ought to be: every poetic image chosen for its contrasting value."

Films like *Fury* helped to reaffirm Greene's faith in the potential of the film medium as an art form. When he was young, he reminisced in the 1958 *International Film Annual*, he saw the possibility of silent cinema developing into a new kind of art.[4] There was, for example, Erich Von Stroheim's classic *Greed* (1923) with its poignant image of the doomed lovers "walking down the long breakwater between the grey seas under the drenching rain." Next came the talkies, "which were a setback, but a temporary one"; at least in isolated scenes if not in complete films they gradually began to manifest a selectivity of sound that was artistically promising.

Then came films like *Fury* to show that the possibility of poetic cinema could be realized on the screen. Another example of a film that Greene prized in this regard was *The Stars Look Down*, directed in 1939 by Carol Reed, for whom Greene was later to write three films. It is

---

[4]Graham Greene, "The Novelist and the Cinema: A Personal Experience," *International Film Annual No. 2*, ed. William Whitebait. New York: Doubleday & Co., 1958; p. 54.

interesting to see what Reed's future collaborator thought of one of his films:

"Dr. Cronin's mining novel has made a very good film—I doubt whether in England we have ever produced a better. Mr. Carol Reed, who began some years ago so impressively with *Midshipman Easy* (1936) and then became involved in the cheap little second features that were regularly churned out by the smaller English studios, has at last had his chance and has magnificently taken it." Greene goes on to mention the authentic flavor of the film, constructed as it is of "grit and slag-heap, back-to-back cottages, and little scrubby railway stations," and then concludes: "Once before Mr. Reed tried his hand at a documentary story—*Bank Holiday* (1937). It was highly praised and was full of 'characters,' but it smelt of the studio. Here one forgets the casting altogether; he handles his players like a master, so that one remembers them only as people" (January 26, 1940).

Reed's film dealt in a straightforward fashion with life in a Welsh mining community. In addition to presenting life as it is, he also implied life as it ought to be, particularly in the character of the young man who gets a scholarship and leaves the pits, and then returns to work for the betterment of the miner's lot. Hence *The Stars Look Down* qualified as well as any film to be poetic cinema.

But unfortunately the examples of poetic cinema over the years have been all too infrequent, Greene has found. When I asked him whether he thought a more recent film like Joseph Strick's version of James Joyce's *Ulysses* (1967) would qualify as poetic cinema, Greene said that, regrettably, it did not: "The first twenty minutes were exciting in the sense in which I have explained that word; but excitement was painfully lacking after that. Since the film failed thereafter to involve me, it likewise failed either to shock or interest me. The poetic, lyrical element simply disappeared. Listen to Siobhan McKenna's recording of Molly Bloom's monologue and then listen to Barbara Jefford's reading of the same lines in the last half hour of the film. Miss Jefford brings the monologue down from the lyrical plane while Miss McKenna does not. *Time* magazine was correct in saying in its review of *Ulysses* that Mr. Strick had illustrated Joyce's prose as one might do in a slide lecture and had not turned Joyce's words into visual images. Moreover, I cannot acquit Mr. Strick altogether of shocking rather than exciting his audience. The shocking passages are spread out over eight hundred pages in the novel; yet all of the shocking material is in the film."

To clarify further Greene's concept of poetic cinema, I asked him if he thought that a popular director like Alfred Hitchcock had produced any examples of this kind of film making. He referred me to an article that he had written for the *Fortnightly Review* (March, 1936). In it Greene noted that Hitchcock's films are melodramas and that melodrama should be exciting. But he complained that Hitchcock often amuses rather than excites his audience. Greene admitted that some of Hitchcock's tricks are good as tricks, such as the scene in *The Thirty-Nine Steps* (1935) in which the scream of the charwoman as she finds the corpse merges with the shriek of a train whistle as the Flying Scotsman is shown rushing north, carrying the hero away from the scene of the crime of which he has been unjustly accused. Hitchcock's tricks are interesting for the moment, wrote Greene, but his films have been amusing when they could easily have been exciting. What Hitchcock and directors like him need, he concluded, is a documentary eye which can transform melodramatic material into something be- lieveable, not to say realistic: "We can't be properly entertained by their stories unless we are excited, and we can't be excited unless we are convinced."

At the risk of oversimplification, one might sum up Greene's theory of poetic cinema by saying that for Greene a good film would be one which possessed the proper blend—according to subject mat- ter—of realism (life as it is) and poetry (life as it ought to be). Looking back on these ideas, Greene says that, while he has never explicitly had the concept of poetic cinema in mind when writing for the screen, it very probably influenced his work subconsciously, just as it in- fluenced his film reviews.

The best way to savor the work of Greene the film critic is to sample a selection of his reviews, and I have chosen most of my examples from the reviews which Greene wrote for *Night and Day*.

To begin with, although in his film criticism Greene advocated realism in motion pictures, he was the first to deplore its presence in a film where it was only in the way, as in the mad movies of the Marx Brothers. In his review of *A Day at the Races* (August 12, 1937) Greene contended that real people, such as the pair of young lovers who are always present in a Marx Brothers' film, serve only to undermine the fantasy world that the brothers work so hard to establish: "When Groucho lopes into the inane, they smile at him incredulously (being real people they cannot take him for granted). No, these revellers of the higher idiocy should not mingle with real people nor play before lavish scenery and an arty camera. Like the Elizabethans, they need only a chair, a painted tree."

If realism was out of place in fantasy and farce, Greene did look for it in thrillers, as we saw above in his treatment of Hitchcock. "Even a thriller cannot thrill unless the characters are established in our imaginations," he wrote of an inferior spy film; "and the packed plot of this film allows them no chance" (December 16, 1937). By the same token Greene was pleased with Humphrey Bogart's performance as the gangster Baby-Faced Martin in William Wyler's *Dead End* because Bogart made Martin a fully-developed realistic character, not a mere stereotype. As Bogart plays him, Martin is "the ruthless sentimentalist who has melodramatized himself from the start (the start is there before your eyes in the juvenile gangsters) up against the truth; and the fine flexible direction supplies a background of beetle-ridden staircases and mud and mist," all of which combine to show life as it is in these circumstances. Unfortunately, life as it ought to be is mirrored, unconvincingly in Greene's opinion, in the person of the virtuous heroine played by Sylvia Sidney "with her driven childish face" (November 25, 1937). Hence *Dead End* just missed being the piece of poetic cinema that it might have been.

Greene usually found his best examples of poetic cinema in documentaries and there were some great ones in the 1930's, such as those made by John Grierson about working-class life in England. Greene was also deeply impressed by the uncompromising realism of Luis Buñuel's searing picture of some destitute Spanish peasants in *Land Without Bread*. He called it "an honest and hideous picture free from propaganda," except for the shot of a church interior which was accompanied by some reference to clerical wealth. "Wealth!" Greene commented. "One smiles at the word in face of the two-penny interior and wonders whether the government has done so much for the people that one can afford to stop up this one hole they have to creep to for cleanness and comfort."

Much of what Greene wrote in his reviews about films of the day, I feel, would stand up even if we were reappraising the same films

now. John Atkins, however, detects in Greene's film criticism "a growing tendency to be irritated by films in general, to criticize shortcom-
ings that might almost be invisible—in fact, to nag."[5] It is true that
Greene does at times betray some irritation with a film that he is reviewing, as when he dismisses a dreary comedy called *Café Metropole*
as one in which the camera was "planked down four-square before the
characters like a plain, honest, inexpressibly dull guest at a light and
loony party." But my own impression of Greene's film criticism is that
his negative judgment of one film is usually balanced by a positive
judgment of another, and that he usually has good reasons for both.
In other words, one does not find Greene's reviews to be a steady
stream of nasty pronouncements, as Atkins might suggest.

For example, in the same issue of *Night and Day* in which Greene
criticized the camera work in *Café Metropole* (September 30, 1937), he
praised the photography in Feyder's *Knight Without Armor*: "To me the
most aesthetically satisfying of all cinematic shots is—in rough script
terms—the medium close shot, and this is the distance at which Feyder
remains consistently from his characters: close enough for intimacy
and far enough for art."

In dealing with Greene the cinema critic, Atkins goes on to accuse
Greene of waging a vendetta against the American film industry in
general and American-born actresses in particular. He points, for example, to Greene's review of Jean Harlow's last film, *Saratoga*, in
which Greene said that Miss Harlow, who had since died, gave no
indication in this film that, had she lived, she would have improved as
an actress. "Her technique was the gangster's technique—she toted a
breast like a man totes a gun," Greene wrote in summing up her career
(August 26, 1937). In this particular case Greene was admittedly unfair.
Jean Harlow gave a poor performance in her last film because she was
woefully miscast as a pseudo-sophisticated "society" type. But in
other films she had already proved herself a fine comedienne if not a
great actress, as when she held her own on the same screen with
Wallace Beery, John and Lionel Barrymore, and the rest of the all-star
cast of George Cukor's *Dinner at Eight* (1933). Hence it was unjust of
Greene to write off her entire career on the strength—or rather the
weakness—of her last film. However, any critic is guilty of an occa-

---

[5]John Atkins, "The Curse of the Film," *Graham Greene: Some Critical Considerations*, ed. Robert O.
Evans University of Kentucky Press, Lexington: 1967; p. 211.

sional lapse of this sort, and when one looks at Greene's criticism as a whole there seems to be little justification for the charge that he was biased against American actresses or American films.

Actually Greene's likes and dislikes seemed to know no boundaries, either of nationality or of sex. He found American actress Carole Lombard charming in the American film *True Confessions* and judged the film itself the best comedy of the year. He thought the young British actor Laurence Olivier's acting was too self-consciously stagey, in contrast to what he considered the seemingly effortless performances of Olivier's older colleague, Robert Donat. Greene was no more impressed by Germany's Marlene Dietrich and Sweden's Greta Garbo, both of whom were imported to make American films, than he was by a home-grown American actress like Jean Harlow. Dietrich does not act, he remarked in reviewing *Knight Without Armor*; "she consents to pose; she is the marble motive of heroisms and sacrifices." In another column Greene objected strongly to "the deathly reverence" with which Garbo was treated in "the dull, pompous films they make for her" (December 23, 1937). One of the most devastating reviews that Greene ever wrote was about British actress Anna Neagle's performance in the British film *Nurse Edith Cavell*. By comparison, he was amiable to Jean Harlow. Greene described Miss Neagle as moving rigidly onto the set "as if wheels were concealed under the stately skirt; she says her piece with flat dignity and trolleys out again—rather like a mechanical marvel from the World's Fair."[6]

But the most significant review of Greene's entire career as a cinema critic is certainly the one which he wrote about Shirley Temple's performance in John Ford's *Wee Willie Winkie* (October 28, 1937). "Infancy with her is a disguise," said Greene; "her appeal is more secret and more adult." He continued, "Her admirers—middle-aged men and clergymen—respond to her dubious coquetry . . . only because the safety curtain of story and dialogue drops between their intelligence and their desire." Greene says laconically of the resulting legal action, "Shirley Temple, aged six, sued me for libel, and *Night and Day* came to a comic, if disagreeable end." *Night and Day* had to pay $9,800 in damages, a financial blow which the fledgling publication could not sustain. Accordingly, six months after its inception,

[6]Greene's review of *Nurse Edith Cavell* was printed in its entirety in the program for his appearance at the National Film Theater in London for the John Player Lecture Series, on February 15, 1970.

Night and Day ceased publication with the issue of December 23, 1937.

Atkins implies that the Hollywood film moguls had entered into some kind of "collective informal decision that Greene must be stopped" because of his negative reviews of American films, and that they pounced on his treatment of the Shirley Temple vehicle to put an end to his career as a critic. It seems more likely, however, that the wrath of Miss Temple's family and financial guardians (whom Greene had called "leaseholders" in the review) would have been quite enough to percipitate a libel suit without any urging from film executives. In any event, after the demise of *Night and Day*, Greene went right on reviewing films for the *Spectator*. In the winter of 1937–38, he took a trip to Mexico to write a travel book, *The Lawless Roads* (also called *Another Mexico*). While there Greene received word that the Lord Chief Justice had taken a severe view of the libel case and, were Greene to return to England, he might be arrested for criminal libel, which could well entail a prison term. Greene therefore stayed on in Mexico longer than he had originally planned and collected enough material for a novel, *The Power and the Glory*, as well as for the travel book.[7]

On his return to England, Greene continued to review films for the *Spectator* until be became literary editor and drama reviewer for the magazine in 1940.[8] He remained with the *Spectator* until he went to work for the Foreign Office during the Second World War. His career as a professional film critic was at an end. However, since Greene would be involved in one way or another in the production of more than twenty films in the years ahead, his association with the cinema was hardly over; it was really just beginning.

[7] The American reader may find the judgment against Greene in the Temple libel suit rather severe. In commenting on the decision for the author, Rev. John Kinsella, S.J., of the Law School of Loyola University of Chicago, pointed out that, although the provisions of English law governing libel were originally incorporated into American legal practice, they have since been modified considerably by enactments of the various state legislatures. These modifications have been in the direction of making it more difficult for the plaintiff to prove his case. "The First Amendment to the U.S. Constitution," says Father Kinsella, "protects freedom of speech and of the press, and this constitutionally guaranteed right has to be balanced against the individual's common law right to his own good reputation in the community." Because of this concern with freedom of the press, therefore, decisions in libel suits are given less frequently in favor of the plaintiff in the United States than in England. "It is unlikely," Father Kinsella concludes, "that Greene would have been fined for his review of the Temple film had the case been tried in America instead of in England." Cf. *Gatley on Libel and Slander*, ed. R. L. McEwen and P. S. C. Lewis. 6th ed. London: Sweet and Maxwell, 1967. [*Editor's note*: The offending review of *Wee Willie Winkie* is not included, perforce, in the new collection of Greene's film criticism, *Graham Greene On Film*, edited by John Russell Taylor, (New York: Simon & Schuster, 1972), but there is an appendix (pp. 276–277) dealing with "The Shirley Temple Libel Action," and an account of the hearing before the High Court of Justice, as published in the Law Reports of *The Times* of London, May 23, 1938.]

BBC-Television

Greene on board the Orient
Express. The toothbrush ?
Perhaps a comment on the
baggage needed by international
travellers-in-intrigue.

THE FALLEN IDOL

London Films Productions

PART ONE

THIS GUN FOR HIRE

Paramount Pictures

THE CONFIDENTIAL A

Warner Brothers

OUR MAN IN HAVANA

Columbia Pictures

J. Arthur Rank Productions, Ltd.

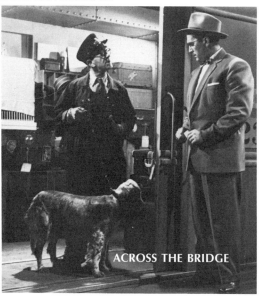

ACROSS THE BRIDGE

THE FILMS OF GREENE'S ENTER- TAINMENTS

Selznick Releasing Organization

THE THIRD MAN

LOSER TAKES ALL

Distributing Corporation of America

2 | THE STRANGERS' LAND: ADAPTATIONS OF GREENE'S ENTER- TAINMENTS BY OTHER SCREENWRITERS

The American novelist James M. Cain once remarked that he had rarely gone to see the screen version of one of his novels. "People tell me, don't you *care* what they've done to your book? I tell them, they haven't done anything to my book. It's right there on the shelf. They paid me and that's the end of it."

When I asked Graham Greene why he had been willing to sell the rights to so much of his fiction to film companies despite what might happen to it in the hands of the movie makers, his reply was similar to the one given by Cain: that the sale of film rights of one's fiction was a source of income. He then directed me to his essay in *International Film Annual No. 2*, in which he expanded on his personal feelings about his work being bought for filming. In it he recalls with gratitude that the sale of *Stamboul Train* to Twentieth Century-Fox in 1932 enabled him "to go on writing without seeking other employment until a second prize came my way in 1934." That was when Paramount purchased *A Gun for Sale*.

Greene concedes, however, that the monetary gain involved in selling a story to the cinema carries with it some degree of sacrifice on the author's part: "Now when you sell a book to Hollywood you sell it outright. The long Hollywood contracts . . . ensure that you have no 'author's rights.' The film producer can alter anything." Nevertheless the author usually agrees to these terms, offering himself the consolation that the smile in the long run will be on *his* face: "For the book has the longer life."[1]

Greene is one of the few novelists who can say that almost all of his novels have been filmed. One of the reasons that film makers have gravitated toward his fiction as a source of material for motion pictures is that his fictional style is really quite cinematic to begin with, a fact which has been noted again and again by literary critics. In reviewing Greene's novel *The Heart of the Matter* (*Commonweal*, July 16, 1948), Evelyn Waugh described the cinematic quality of Greene's narrative style this way: "It is as though, out of an infinite length of film, sequences had been cut," which, once they have been assembled, comprise an integral experience for the reader. "The writer has become director and producer. Indeed, the affinity to the film is everywhere apparent. It is the camera's eye which moves from the hotel balcony to the street below, picks out the policeman, follows him to his office, moves about the room from the handcuffs on the wall to the broken rosary in the drawer, recording significant detail. It is the modern way of telling a story. Now it is the cinema which has taught a new habit of narrative."

In his book, *Graham Greene*, David Pryce-Jones speculates that Greene's work as a screen writer over the years has influenced his writing style. Because Greene has worked intermittently as a script writer since the 1930's, says Pryce-Jones, "plainly his style and construction owe something to the effects of cutting and dissolving from shot to shot learned in this capacity."[2] Greene, however, disagrees with this view: "I don't think my style as a writer has been influenced by my going to the cinema over the years. *It's a Battlefield* is the only one of my novels that was intentionally based on film techniques and it was written in 1934, before I had done any film scripts. It was my only deliberate attempt to tell a story in cinematic terms and it is one of the few novels which I have written that has not been filmed."

Paging through *It's a Battlefield*, one finds several scenes constructed as if for a film. For example, Greene describes a murder in the

---

[1]Graham Greene, "The Novelist and the Cinema: A Personal Experience." *loc. cit.,* p. 58.

[2]David Pryce-Jones, *Graham Greene*. New York: Barnes and Noble, 1967; p. 71.

course of the story in vivid cinematic terms. When the assailant grabs the victim, an old woman, she throws up her hands and screams just as a nearby freight train begins to hoot on a higher note than she can reach, so that her screams go unheard. Greene composed this image, incidentally, a year before Hitchcock used a similar effect, described in the previous chapter, in his film *The Thirty-Nine Steps*.

In addition to the cinematic quality of his fictional style, Greene's work also recommends itself to the film maker because his novels have always been built around a strong story line which can be visualized and acted out on the screen, even when the story is being told from a subjective point of view. Writes critic Vernon Young, "The climaxes of Greene's novels are rarely staged in the mind alone."[3]

The marked affinity which Greene's fiction has with the film medium serves to bring into relief the fact that, in general, cinema has more in common with fiction than with any other form of literature. I would like to take a moment to recall for the reader some corollaries of this concept, in preparation for studying the films made from Greene's fiction. To begin with, one might be tempted to suppose that drama is closer to film than fiction is, since a play, like a motion picture, is acted out. But there the similarity really ends. For both a novel and a film depend more on description and narration than on dialogue, while in a play the emphasis is reversed. Novelist Robert Nathan, in affirming the closeness of fiction and film, calls a movie "a novel to be seen, instead of told." The motion picture, like the novel, "ranges where it pleases, it studies the reactions of single characters, it deals in description and mood, it follows, by means of the camera, the single, unique vision of the writer. You will find, in every novel, the counterparts of long shots and close-ups, trucking shots, and dissolves; but you will find them in words addressed to the ear, instead of pictures meant for the eye."[4]

Nevertheless, in emphasizing the close relationship that undoubtedly exists between fiction and film, one must not forget that they still remain two different media of expression. Hence inevitable differences arise between the way that a story can be presented in a novel and on the screen. Compression becomes an important factor in

---

[3]Vernon Young, "Hollywood: Lost Moments," *Accent*, IX (Autumn, 1948), 124.

[4]Robert Nathan, "A Novelist Looks at Hollywood," in *Film: A Montage of Theories*, ed. Richard Dyer McCann. New York: E. P. Dutton, & Co., 1966; p. 130.

making a motion picture from a novel, since the novelist can take as many pages as he likes to develop his plot and characters, whereas the script-writer has only a couple of hours of screen time at most. One way for the screen writer to handle this problem is to select what he considers to be the key sections of the novel and to develop them in his script to their full dramatic potential, rather than to try to present, survey-fashion, all of the events in the book.

Erich Von Stroheim proved once and for all that the latter method could not be used without producing a film of inordinate length, when he tried to film Frank Norris's *McTeague* paragraph by paragraph as *Greed* in 1923. "I had always been against cutting great chunks out of a novel to fit it into screen time," he once said. "Some of the world's great masterpieces have been hacked in this way." Stroheim consequently came up with a film that would have been close to ten hours in running time had it been released as he made it. So, instead of great chunks being cut out of the novel when it was adapted for the screen, great chunks were cut out of the finished film by the studio.

Screenwriter Edward Anhalt, on the other hand, compressed Morton Thompson's huge *Not as a Stranger* into a manageable length for filming by literally tearing out of the novel the pages that constituted the episodes which he wanted to portray in the film and stringing them along a clothesline. Then he devised expository scenes which would serve as transitions from one incident to the next. In the last analysis, says George Bluestone in *Novels into Film*, what the script writer is really composing is a kind of paraphrase of the novel which he is adapting to the screen. The resulting film, therefore, can never be a replica of the novel on which it is based, for a work of art that was originally conceived in terms of the techniques of one medium always resists, to some extent at least, being converted into another medium, even when the two media in question have as much in common as do fiction and film.

Bluestone continues: "Like two intersecting lines, novel and film meet at a point and then diverge. At the intersection, the book and shooting-script are almost indistinguishable. But where the lines diverge, they . . . lose all resemblance to each other," for each works within the framework of its own conventions."[5] For example, there is no literary equivalent for "getting things into the same shot," as

[5]George Bluestone, *Novels into Film*. Berkeley: University of California Press, 1961; pp. 62–63.

Charles Barr has very perceptively pointed out in his article in Mc-Cann's *Film: A Montage of Theories*. It might take a novelist several phrases to build up a description of a given object or incident, whereas the film maker can show the same thing on the screen in a single image. Vladimir Nabokov notes this in having the narrator of *Lolita* remark that there is no way for him to relay to the reader the impact he felt at seeing his wife lying dead on the street after having been struck down by a car, for he must describe the details of the scene one by one, whereas he saw the whole thing in a single flash of vision. Stanley Kubrick in his film of *Lolita* (1962) was able to show the accident in one shot, just as the husband saw it.

Unquestionably, then, a story must undergo many superficial alterations when it is adapted to the motion picture medium. What must be preserved throughout this transformation from the one medium to the other is the spirit or theme of the original work of fiction. If the basic intent of the original story is somehow mislaid between page and screen, the original author has just grounds for complaint, and we shall shortly see some examples of this in the case of the film versions of Greene's work.

I shall deal first with the adaptations of Greene's entertainments before taking up the films made from his serious fiction since, as a matter of fact, most of the entertainments were filmed first. Within the group of films made from Greene's entertainments I shall begin with those that have been prepared for the screen by writers other than Greene himself before examining more in depth how Greene has coped with the problems of adapting his own fiction for the screen.

Many literary critics have spent a great deal of space in trying to clarify the difference between Greene's entertainments and his serious fiction. Actually Greene himself has provided the simplest explanation of the difference. In the course of a radio interview he defined the two categories of his fiction this way: "In one's entertainments one is primarily interested in having an exciting story as in a physical action, with just enough character to give interest in the action, because you can't be interested in the action of a mere dummy." In the serious fiction, "I hope one is primarily interested in the character, and the action takes a minor part."

Elsewhere Greene has explained why he has taken to writing a lighter type of fiction at times: "The strain of writing a novel, which keeps the author confined for a period of years with his depressive self, is extreme, and I have always sought relief in entertainments—for melodrama as much as farce is an expression of a manic mood."[6] A thriller gives us pleasure, says Greene, because the characters "have so agreeably simplified their emotions" for us. But his entertainments are far from being superficial action pieces, even though they do not possess the same kind of character analysis that one finds in his serious fiction. Indeed, Greene says that he has always disliked "books written without truth," which are designed to be read "while you wait for a bus, while you straphang."

In both his entertainments and his serious fiction Greene often deals with lonely, flawed human beings. He developed this sympathy for failure, he tells us, in adolescence, the age when "one may fall irrevocably in love with failure," because he realized that those who remain always seedy, drab, and unsuccessful continue thereby "to be worthy of God's notice if of no one else's."[7] Even in his entertainments Greene has never been able to bring himself to create handsome heroes of the James Bond variety or to tell a story that offers escapist adventure for its own sake. Greene rather portrays man as God made him, in a corrupt, man-made world, and this dark vision somehow survives in every film based on his fiction, no matter how much tampering has been done with the original story in the course of its metamorphosis from book to movie.

The reason that many of Greene's novels have been adapted to the motion picture medium by writers other than Greene himself is that Greene has always hesitated to involve himself in the film-making process. He has felt that even when he has written a script himself there is still no guarantee that the resulting film will be faithful to the spirit of his original story. "Even if a script be followed word by word," he says in his essay, "The Novelist and the Cinema," "there are those gaps of silence which can be filled with the banal embrace; irony can be turned into sentiment by some romantic boob of an actor. No, it is better to sell outright and not to connive any further than you have to at a massacre."

⁶Graham Greene, "Preface," *Three Plays*. London: Mercury Books, 1961; p. xiii.

⁷Graham Greene, "The Revolver in the Corner Cupboard," *The Lost Childhood and Other Essays*. New York: The Viking Press, 1962; p. 173. cf. *A Sort of Life*. New York: Simon and Schuster, 1971; p. 127ff.

Hence Greene's initial attitude toward turning his fiction over to a movie company was a pragmatic one. The money he earned from the sale of a story would allow him to go on writing without having to take another job in order to support his family. It was only later that he gradually got more and more involved in the production of films made from his work, perhaps spurred on by those happy if somewhat rare occasions when a good story of his was allowed to become a good film as well.

Orient Express, the first film made from a Greene novel, was not one of those occasions. It was based on *Stamboul Train*, the fourth novel which Greene had published and the first to be labeled an entertainment. Greene was delighted to sell the movie rights to Fox, for in 1932, he remembers, "I was down to £30 in the bank, a child was on the way, . . . and I had no prospects." Nor is it surprising that Fox wanted to film the novel. It is a tightly constructed story about a cross section of people making the journey from London to Istanbul, and shows how their lives dramatically intersect before they reach their destination, a kind of *Grand Hotel* on wheels.

Yet the film script was worked over by no less than four screen writers (including Oscar Levant, the late concert pianist and actor) before it was thought ready to go before the cameras. This is curious, since Greene wrote the book as if he was in effect moving a camera from compartment to compartment on the train, developing the story along the way. In fact one critic hazarded a guess that this technique was suggested to Greene by Hitchcock's film *The Lady Vanishes*—something that is hardly possible since *Stamboul Train* was published in 1932 and filmed the following year, whereas Hitchcock released *The Lady Vanishes* in 1938.[8]

Greene ran across the film of *Stamboul Train* in 1938 while he was in Africa writing *Journey Without Maps*. Seeing it again, he found it "a bad film, one of the worst I had ever seen; the direction was incompetent, the photography undistinguished, the story sentimental. If there was any truth in the original it had been carefully altered, if anything was left unaltered it was because it was . . . cheap and banal enough to fit the cheap and banal film." Recalling the advertising for the film, Greene says, "Never before had I seen American ballyhoo at work on something I intimately knew." Fox had been "magnificent in

[8]Cf. A. A. DeVitis, *Graham Greene*. New York; Twayne Publishers, 1964; p. 55.

its disregard for the article for which it had paid." The gaudy posters spoke of two youthful hearts fleeing from life, crashing across Europe on the wheels of Fate. Greene was able to draw some satisfaction from the fact that the film had been a failure: "It might be vulgar but it wasn't successfully vulgar. There was something quite un-Hollywood in its failure."[9]

Despite his keen disappointment with *Orient Express*, Greene sold *A Gun for Sale* to Paramount in 1936 for £2,500, but the studio did not get around to filming it until 1942. Prior to that Greene had published a short story in *Collier's Magazine* called "The Lieutenant Died Last" (June 29, 1940), which was purchased by Ealing Studios in England and expanded into a full-length film entitled *Went the Day Well?* in 1942.

The original story is quite short and simple: During World War II an old poacher is out pursuing his nefarious trade on the day when a little English village is invaded by a small band of German soldiers disguised as members of the British armed forces. At the time the Germans take over the village, the old man is out in the woods poaching and is therefore overlooked by the soldiers who are rounding up the villagers for imprisonment in the village church. He manages to discern what is going on, however, and—with his courage fortified by alcohol—he takes the Germans by surprise and either captures or shoots them all. Because of his heroic behavior the town authorities are willing to overlook the fact that he was poaching when the mini-invasion occurred, and he becomes something of a local hero. Nevertheless, in the midst of all of his bragging he cannot forget that a German lieutenant had died clutching a picture of his family, a reminder that even the enemy is human.

From this brief vignette a full-length film was fashioned, presumably as a morale booster for the British people in the dark days of the war. A patriotic tone is set at the very beginning of the film by an epigraph which reads:
> Went the day well?
> We died and never knew.
> But well or ill,
> Freedom, we died for you.

[9]Graham Greene, *Journey Without Maps*. New York: The Viking Press, 1965; p. 65.

After the epigraph, which refers to the villagers who died resisting the German invaders, the film opens with a prologue which is set in the future *after* the end of the war. We are introduced to an old church sexton who addresses himself to the camera as if to a group of tourists as he points out a gravestone in the church cemetary which is inscribed with German names. "They wanted England," he says, "and this is the only part of English soil that they got." He then begins to narrate the events that led up to the deaths of the Germans who are buried in the churchyard.

In Greene's story a small group of Germans parachute to the ground near the village, giving the villagers the impression that they are British soldiers on maneuvers. In the film the band of Germans is much larger and they arrive in several trucks. They billet in various homes in the village with orders to prepare the way for Hitler's proposed invasion of England. The audience has been tipped off from the beginning to the true identity of the soldiers and to the true nature of their business; and so the film builds suspense by posing the question of how and when the villagers will discover what is happening. When they do, new suspense is created by making the audience wonder how the villagers will be able to notify the outside world of what is going on, since the Germans have cut off all means of communication. The suspense builds as the people try various ruses to send an S.O.S. to the neighboring villages and each attempt fails. For example, a woman writes a message on one of a dozen eggs and gives the box to a lad passing through town to take home to his mother. The lad, however, meets with an accident while riding his bicycle home, falls off the bicycle, and breaks all of the eggs.

At this point the poacher, who is the principal character in Greene's story, finally enters the picture in much the same way as in the original plot. Because he has been out of town poaching, he has escaped the notice of the Germans and is able to help get the news of what has happened to a nearby village. After a shootout with the real British soldiers that have been summoned, the Germans are either killed or taken prisoner and the film ends with a patriotic speech by the church sexton in the graveyard where the film began.

Even though *Went the Day Well?* was obviously made to help the war effort in Britain and its message is only too loud and clear, the film is still in many ways very exciting and suspenseful. A crisp documen-

tary air is supplied for the movie by director Alberto Cavalcanti, the
itinerant Brazilian movie maker who became an important member of
the British documentary movement in the 1930's and '40's. "The
quality that made the British documentary so distinctive was the calm-
ness of its presentation," Arthur Knight has written in *The Liveliest Art*.
"Without resorting to flamboyant techniques or emotion-charged
commentaries, it sustained interest and provoked thought."[10] This is
largely true of Cavalcanti's approach to *Went the Day Well?* Although
its theme is patriotic, the film is still enjoyable as a thriller.

The most thorough analysis of the film that has yet been done is
by film historian William K. Everson, and it deserves to be quoted
here at some length.[11] Everson calls *Went the Day Well?* not only one of
Cavalcanti's finest works, but also one of the best and yet least-ap-
preciated British films of and about World War II. "Rural England is
attractively photographed and its day-to-day life quite realistically
evoked," he has written.

> In a sense, it is an updated equivalent of the World War I anti-
> Hun atrocity movies. It is more restrained, more sensible, and has
> an amiable sense of humor—but the intent is the same. Whereas
> before the Hun appeared as an outright beast, here he appears ini-
> tially beneath a veneer of civilization, which is only gradually
> stripped away—to reveal the same beast beneath! To its credit, the
> film realizes the obviousness of its own device and counters it
> with sly humor.

This humor is evident, for example, in the scene in which one of
the townspeople, trying to soft-soap a German, tells him that she does
not believe all of the propaganda that she has heard about Germans
impaling babies on bayonets. "Babies on bayonets?" muses the
German. "What would be the advantage?" Everson continues:

> Made at the height of the invasion scare in England, the film
> propagandized for vigilance and against careless talk, and added
> the morale-booster of telling the tale in flashback from after the
> victorious winning of the war. Like so many British films of the

---

[10]Arthur Knight, *The Liveliest Art*. New York: New American Library, 1967; p. 213.

[11]William K. Everson, "Program Notes for *Went the Day Well?*" New School Film Series. New York: New School For Social Research, July 20, 1971.

period, and especially the wholly or partially Government spon-
sored ones, it seems to suggest that England was a honeycomb of
Fifth Column activity, with aristocrats and pubkeepers alike
forming an incredible net of espionage.

This last plot device gives rise to several Hitchcock situations in
the film as the townspeople seek to uncover the crypto-Nazis among
their very own neighbors, who are aiding the enemy in their attempt
to take over the town. The final battle scenes provide an exciting climax to the film and are especially effective because Cavalcanti has
filmed them in a straightforward documentary style. "From its *Our
Town* opening through its building of suspense paralleled by laughter,"
Everson concludes, "*Went the Day Well?* is an odd film, yet a powerful
one."

The one noticeable omission in the movie of the material provided by the short story is the compassion that the old poacher secretly
feels in the story for the dead lieutenant who will never return to his
family. Apparently, in the midst of the war effort and with the real
danger of Hitler launching an invasion of Britain, the producers of the
film felt that injecting a note of sympathy for the enemy into the movie
would have been out of place; although, if it were handled in the same
subtle and skillful way that Greene treated it in his story, it certainly
could not have been deemed unpatriotic. At any rate, Greene's slight
story was so swallowed up that there is really less of Greene in this
film than in any other with which his name has been connected.

The same year that Ealing made *Went the Day Well?* (released in
the United States as *Forty-Eight Hours*), Paramount produced *A Gun for
Sale* under the title *This Gun for Hire* (by which title the novel is also
known in America). Greene was not happy with the film since several
changes were introduced to make the story more "relevant" for wartime America: the setting was changed from England in the 1930's to
California in the 1940's where fifth columnists are selling secret
formulas to Japan.

Greene's story is about a hired killer named James Raven who has
a harelip that both physically symbolizes the spiritual deformity of
his personality and helps one to understand the morbid loneliness that
has driven him to become an embittered assassin. Because of his unhappy childhood in a reformatory, Raven is obsessed with the notion

THIS GUN FOR HIRE (Paramount Pictures, 1942). Alan Ladd with Veronica Lake and Laird Cregar. Ladd gained instant fame in the role of the killer, James Raven.

that no one can be trusted, and he is convinced that betrayal lurks at every corner. Even looking at a cheap Nativity scene in a store window reminds him that the little plaster child in its mother's arms is waiting for "the doublecross, the whips, the nails."

Raven is hired by an enemy agent to murder a government minister and thus help to instigate a war. The agent, however, then betrays Raven to the police to get him out of the way once the job has been done. In the course of his fleeing from the police, Raven meets a girl whom he finally brings himself to trust, only to have her turn him over to her fiancé, who has been in charge of the manhunt for Raven all along. After a gun battle Raven dies, so disillusioned with this life that he does not fear to face the next.

"The film got off to a good start," Greene recalls, "but then the heroine was introduced as a female conjurer working for the F.B.I. and that had nothing to do with my story." The film does indeed get off to a good start. Raven (Alan Ladd) keeps a rendezvous with an American scientist who is selling government secrets to Raven's employer, who in turn is peddling them to the Japanese. After Raven takes the secret documents, there is a glint in his eye as he reaches into his briefcase and pulls out—not the money that the scientist expects—but a gun with which he summarily shoots the scientist.

As Raven leaves the building, we momentarily get a glimpse of the more humane side of his personality, which he is always striving to suppress, by seeing him retrieve a crippled child's ball for her. Later he briefly refers to his ugly childhood as an orphan, but that is as close as the film comes to probing Raven's character in the way that Greene does in the novel. Basically the film is a good chase melodrama, but the exciting mood of the film is shattered twice by the curious introduction of two songs that are completely out of keeping with the tone of the film. Ellen Graham (Veronica Lake) sings both of them as part of her magic act and it takes the film some time to recover from both interruptions.

Furthermore the added complication of Ellen's working for the F.B.I. as a lady spy (besides being the girl friend of the detective who is tracking down Raven) makes no contribution to the film—unless it is supposed to back up the patriotic appeal that Ellen makes at one point to Raven about his collusion with fifth columnists: "This war is everybody's business; yours too," she says. There seems to have been a determination on the part of the film makers to sabotage a good film with irrelevancies, but it is a tribute to the movie to say that in spite of its defects it is still a fine suspense story. The film comes to a tense close with the final chase of Raven by the police through a railroad yard and into a chemical plant where he is finally shot.

Despite its departures from Greene's novel, *This Gun for Hire* is a good film in many ways and it prompted Philip Hartung to write in *Commonweal* (May 29, 1942): "The wonderment is that Hollywood hasn't used all of Graham Greene's stories and clamored for more. Not that Paramount's *This Gun for Hire* is unadulterated Greene. But with all the changes in the story, the Greene original still survives. The tense excitement of the novel and the book's cold violence are natural cinema material. What readers of the novel will miss principally are Greene's expertly interwoven asides on the morality of this study of evil." Indeed, one does miss in all of the films of Greene's early entertainments the haunting moral and psychological dimensions that Greene consistently gave to all of these stories. In *This Gun for Hire*, for example, there are few references to Raven's background; nor does Alan Ladd have a harelip as Raven did in the novel. Consequently, in the film Raven becomes a ruthless psychopath. We do not understand his motivation and hence we can hardly pity him.

Nevertheless Alan Ladd did give a fascinating performance as Raven which raised him immediately to stardom. Moreover, the cinematic qualities of the book endure in the film. Thus the opening scenes of both book and movie allow us to watch Raven plying his hideous trade with business-like efficiency. In the novel Greene described Raven's eyes as moving about the room of his victim "like little concealed cameras," photographing the scene: "the single bed, the wooden chair, the dusty chest of drawers . . . ." And the film draws on Raven's (and Greene's) eye for detail throughout.

James Cagney directed a remake of *This Gun for Hire* in 1957 called *Short Cut to Hell*. The turgid title alone has been enough to keep Greene from making any effort to see it. It starred two unknowns, Robert Ivers and Georgann Johnson, in place of Alan Ladd and Veronica Lake. This time Raven was called Kyle, and the girl was a nightclub singer. Philip Hartung, who had some fine things to say about *This Gun for Hire*, is virtually alone in finding the remake comparable to the original film (*Commonweal*, November 15, 1957). Hartung thought *Short Cut* . . . more tense and plausible than the earlier film because Ivers, less handsome than Ladd, had "a convincing touch of hunger in his face" which made him more believable in the key role. But, as Hartung notes, neither film version of the novel dared give Raven-Kyle the harelip or meanness that Greene described so vividly in his novel.

This Gun for Hire, along with *The Ministry of Fear* (1943) and *The Confidential Agent* (1945), form something of a cinematic trilogy of spy thrillers. (In point of fact, the connection between the three stories has been further underlined by Greene's putting them together into a one-volume edition called *Three by Graham Greene*).

The second part of the trio was written while Greene was in

Africa, engaged in secret intelligence work for the British government, during the Second World War. The story moves with what has rightly been called "scenario swiftness" and deals with Arthur Rowe, an unhappy man who has been detained in an asylum ever since he was convicted for killing his invalid wife. Almost immediately after his release from the asylum, he finds himself stalked and pursued by an assortment of menacing individuals. At first he wonders if it is his imagination, but soon discovers that a cake which he won at a charity bazaar on the first day of his release from the institution actually contained a roll of microfilm intended for a Nazi spy who was to smuggle this secret information out of the country.

The sense of pity which had prompted Rowe to kill his wife leads him before the story is over to allow a Nazi spy to commit suicide rather than face capture, and then to declare his love for the dead agent's sister, a refugee named Anna Hilfe, now left alone in an alien land.

Like all of Greene's thrillers *The Ministry of Fear* works on a deeper level than that of melodrama. Rowe at one point says that he feels that the Ministry of Fear is more than just a bureau of Nazi agents; it is also "a ministry as large as life itself to which all who loved belonged. If one loved one feared," for one could never be sure of one's own motives with respect to a loved one. Thus Rowe is nagged by the feeling that he killed his wife more to escape the pain of watching her suffer than to release her from her lingering illness. At the end of the novel he therefore proposes to make this up to his dead wife by taking care of Anna. "Perhaps after all one could atone even to the dead if one suffered for the living enough," Rowe muses. Nevertheless, he fears that if Anna discovers that his feeling for her is more pity than true love she will be deeply hurt. Hence, Rowe wonders if he is again being selfish, by seeking to assuage his feelings of guilt about his wife's death by taking care of Anna.

And so we leave Arthur Rowe at the end of the novel ruefully wondering once more about the integrity of his motives, still very much a member of that larger Ministry of Fear. Thus a remark made earlier in the book by another character takes on new meaning: "Pity is a terrible thing. People talk about the passion of love. Pity is the worst passion of all. We don't outlive it like sex."

This whole probing of Rowe's psyche is missing from the film, but

Greene still has a soft spot for the movie in his heart: "*The Ministry of Fear* was made by dear old Fritz Lang," he says; "and I was delighted that a veteran director of his reputation was involved in the film. But unfortunately the script that he was given to work with cut out the whole middle third of the book in which Rowe goes into a nursing home with amnesia and tries to sort out his life. Without this section the whole point of the novel is missing and the story doesn't exist."

Lang himself had wanted to buy the screen rights to the book when he read it, but Paramount beat him to it, and then hired him to direct the film. "I admired Graham Greene," Lang says. "But when I saw what had been done with the script, I was shocked. Anyway, I had signed a contract and I had to fulfill it." It is easy to understand why Lang was attracted to the novel. The most obvious reason is the anti-Nazi element in the story, which would have appealed to Lang because he had fled Germany in the wake of the Nazi take-over after refusing to make films for the Reich. But there is another reason why Lang wanted to film Greene's novel. As film critics Paul Jensen and Andrew Sarris have pointed out, one often finds in Lang's work, from his early German silents in the 1920's to his last Hollywood films in the late 1950's, a hero surrounded by an unseen enemy whose forces are everywhere. The hero gradually finds that no one can be trusted, for even people who on the surface seem good more often than not turn out to be in league with the enemy.

In *The Ministry of Fear*, then, we have a ready-made Lang situation. The hero (called Stephen Neale in the film) becomes innocently embroiled with a group of enemy spies who are bent on putting him out of the way in order to retrieve the microfilm. Stephen does not know whom to trust, since everyone, even a blind man and a tailor, seems to be in the enemy's employ. Lang builds up a thrilling atmosphere of suspenseful apprehension in the tradition of his best films, and there are Lang touches throughout.

The film opens in a dark room; a door opens, admitting a shaft of light. Ray Milland as Stephen Neale is sitting with his back to the camera and facing the door. A doctor enters and tells him that he is now free to leave the asylum. This scene, which is not in the book, is nevertheless faithful to its spirit, since it conveys that Neale is now attempting to turn his back on his dark past and to walk into the light of the present. Thereupon, he enters an even more uncertain and menacing world than the one which he has just left, for the charity bazaar, which one could usually assume to be a source of innocent fun, turns out to be the source of his later danger.

Stephen wins a cake, and later meets a blind man in a train compartment who seems very interested in Stephen's prize. In the novel the individual is a cripple who comes to Arthur Rowe's room to tell him that there has been some mistake about the contest; but here again the departure from the original story is very much in keeping with the spirit of the book. Making the character a blind man in the movie fits in perfectly with the atmosphere of uneasy anticipation that both the novel and the motion picture are striving to establish at this point. "Preceded by the sound of his tapping cane, he appears through a cloud of steam that gives him almost supernatural overtones," says Jensen in describing the blind man in The Cinema of Fritz Lang.[12] As he talks to Neale there is a close-up of his face which shows his eyes furtively darting around the train compartment, thus indicating to the audience, if not yet to Stephen, that his blindness is assumed for some sinister purpose. While the train is halted during an air raid, the man suddenly grabs the cake and runs off into the night, only to be killed by a falling bomb.

After so perfectly executed a scene, one wonders how the film could have gone wrong—for, as Greene and Lang both agree, it did. The reason is that, just as the deeper dimensions of James Raven's character were not even hinted at in the script of This Gun for Hire, so Arthur Rowe, in being transformed into Stephen Neale in the film of The Ministry of Fear, loses much of the complexity of his character. Consequently, once the source of his peril is revealed, the movie simply settles down to the routine business of rounding up the Nazi spy ring in the manner of a conventional wartime spy melodrama; and the sinister atmosphere that Lang worked so hard to build up earlier in the film is dissipated little by little. This weakness is not to be found in the book, where Arthur Rowe must try to straighten out his psychological problems as well as try to overcome the physical danger that stalks him.

Rowe in the book is a mercy killer who poisons his wife. In the film, however, Stephen tells Carla (the Anna Hilfe of the book) that

[12]Paul Jensen, The Cinema of Fritz Lang. New York: A. S. Barnes & Co., 1969; p. 148.

while he was debating whether or not to give his wife the poison that he had bought, she discovered it and took it herself. This alteration of the original story, unlike the others I have mentioned, violates the intent of the novel, for it eliminates the hero's moral and psychological dilemma by rendering him in no way responsible for his wife's death (although the authorities judge him guilty of euthanasia anyway). The crucial section in the novel in which Rowe goes to a sanatorium to come to grips with his past became irrelevant to the film and was deleted.

The scriptwriter has also freed Stephen from making the decision to allow Carla's brother to take his own life in place of being captured. When Carla and Stephen accuse her brother of being a Nazi spy, he switches off the lights and runs out of the room saying to Carla, "You couldn't kill your own brother." She can and in fact she does. The door slams, a shot is fired in the dark, and we see a pinpoint of light in the door where the bullet pierced it. The door is opened and the light falls across the body of Carla's brother. Thus, with the last member of the spy ring disposed of, Stephen's troubles are over and at the final fadeout he rides off with Carla in his sportscar into the sunlight.

Some film critics have questioned the plausibility of Carla's shooting her brother without hesitation or remorse. While it is safe to assume that Lang would have preferred Greene's handling of the story in this as in other matters, it is also true that Carla's behavior is not inconsistent with that of the typical Lang heroine. In most of his films there is a girl who represents the values of innocence and integrity so sorely lacking in the world that Lang usually depicts. As Andrew Sarris puts it, Lang makes exceptions to his "paranoid" vision of life "in the pure, trustworthy love of beautiful girls, a love capable of destroying the most intricately insidious conspiracies devised by evil minds. Romantic love with its intimations of Christian self-sacrifice flows through both the German and American periods of Lang's career, as strongly in *Spione* (*Spies*) as in *The Ministry of Fear*."[13]

In the third film of our spy trilogy, *The Confidential Agent*, we come to a movie which Greene praises as "one of the few American films of one of my novels that followed the book," although he concedes that "very few other people seem to have liked it." Once one accepts the

[13]Andrew Sarris, "Fritz Lang," in *The American Cinema: Directors and Directions, 1929–68*. New York: E. P. Dutton Co., 1968; p. 65.

THE CONFIDENTIAL AGENT (Warner Brothers, 1945). Charles Boyer in the title role as agent "D". Greene regards this film as one of the most faithful screen adaptions of his work.

fact that handsome Charles Boyer looks no more like Greene's hero, an elderly scholar who has been dragooned into undercover work, than Alan Ladd looked like Raven, one is inclined to agree with him.

Greene composed *The Confidential Agent* in 1938 while he was still engaged in writing *The Power and the Glory*. The latter novel, he feared, would not be a best-seller, and therefore would not provide his wife and two children with sufficient financial support should he be called to serve in the armed forces in the impending war. "So," he says in the introduction to *The Confidential Agent* in the Collected Edition, "I determined to write another entertainment as quickly as possible in the mornings, while I ground on slowly with *The Power and the Glory* in the afternoons."[14]

For the only time in his life Greene fell back on Benzedrine in order to be able to keep up the pace which he had set for himself. "Each day I sat down to work with no idea what turn the plot might take," he remembers; and yet he managed to turn out two thousand words every morning on *The Confidential Agent*. Greene recalls that after a gruelling day of working on two books at once he would return home from his office "with a depression that fell with the regularity of tropical rain." There are no indications in the finished novel of *The Confidential Agent*, however, that it was written in haste and under strain. In fact, Greene himself now finds it "one of the few books of mine which I have cared to reread."

The Confidential Agent is the intriguing study of a reluctant spy. The very reluctance with which the hero, whom we know only as D, carries on his activities is what make him so interesting and sympathetic to the reader. D is pressed into service by what we may take to be the Loyalist government during what appears to be the Civil War in Spain (the circumstances are not specified any further because Greene did not want to localize the conflict). He is to keep the Fascists from making a business deal in England for coal which is badly needed by both sides. Like Raven and Rowe, D finds it difficult to trust anyone in the hostile and violent world in which he moves. He finally asks a servant girl in the shabby London hotel where he is staying to guard his identity papers for him, and she is murdered as the result of her refusal to give them up to the rival agents. D feels that he must avenge

[14]Graham Greene, "Introduction," *The Confidential Agent*, in the Collected Edition. London: The Bodley Head, 1971; p. vii.

the girl's death, because he does *not* believe in God. If one believed in God, he reasons, one could leave vengeance to the Lord. "But he hadn't that particular faith. Unless people received their deserts, the world to him was chaos; he was faced with despair."

D enlists the aid of the daughter of Lord Benditch, the man with whom he is negotiating for the coal, to help him fulfill his mission. At times he seems to be falling in love with her; but that seems to him out of the question since he feels partially responsible for the death of his wife in the Civil War back home and now apparently suffers from psychic impotence. As in Greene's other entertainments, then, there is an attempt on the novelist's part to probe the psyche of the hero, as well as to tell an exciting story; and some of the deeper implications of the novel have found their way into the film.

As Vernon Young has written, "The thriller aspects of *The Confidential Agent* should have engaged the emotions of the general public, while its subtler treatment of moral isolation should have flattered the cirtical minority." As it turned out, the film was too sophisticated for the general public and not sophisticated enough for the critical minority. "Without ballyhooed assurance that it was a daring movie, *The Confidential Agent*, bearing its virtues of candor, excitement, and penetration, was ignored."[15]

This is a pity since the film has some fine things in it, notably the performances of Charles Boyer as the world-weary hero, and of Katina Paxinou, George Zucco, and Peter Lorre as the sinister rival agents. Greene thinks that one of the reasons that the movie was disliked was that "Lauren Bacall was thought to be unconvincing as the daughter of an English aristocrat. But the girl was only second generation *nouveau riche*, and therefore Miss Bacall was right in not giving her any real aristocratic air." Because of the failure of the film, however, its director, Herman Shumlin, best known for his work in the theater, returned to the stage and never made another film.

One of the few critical voices to be raised in favor of the film was that of James Agee in *The Nation* (November 10, 1945). "This is in some ways an exciting and good picture, the best attempt yet, though still inadequate, to make the most of a Greene novel," he wrote. But he too had his reservations about the film: "In spite of some very good

---

[15]Young, *op. cit.*, pp. 125–26.

sets and a number of beautiful shots, Greene's greatest talent—which is, I think, with the look and effluence of places, streets, and things—is not once even approximated. This is odd, because in these respects Greene achieves in print what more naturally belongs in films, and in a sense does not write novels at all, but verbal movies."

The reason that the film does not achieve the authentic atmosphere of the book is simply that, because of wartime conditions, the film could not be shot on location in London and had to be made almost entirely in a Hollywood studio. Hence, even the meeting of D and the girl in the heart of crowded London, except for the insertion of some stock footage of Piccadilly Circus, is patently taking place in the corner of a sound stage. Location shooting would have helped immeasurably to create the proper realistic atmosphere for the film.

Perhaps the strongest affinity that the film has with Greene's novel is that the lines often have the ring of Greene's original dialogue. When the girl asks D at one point if he wants to make love to her, for example, D's reply sums up his whole disillusioned attitude toward life: "I have no such emotions left." Later when a tire explodes on the car in which D and the girl are riding, D instinctively doubles up as if he had been shot. "You see," he explains, "I carry the war with me. I ought to carry a bell like a leper." All of these lines recall dialogue passages from the book and help to lend the film the flavor of Greene's novel.

Only Greene himself has succeeded in writing a film script based on his fiction that is more faithful to his work, and he did in fact adapt the next two of his entertainments to the film medium, *The Fallen Idol* (1948) and *The Third Man* (1949), both of which were highly successful.[16] Then in 1954, Greene provided the story which was the basis of a film called *The Stranger's Hand*, which was directed by Mario Soldati and scripted by two other writers, with Greene acting in what was for him a curious capacity, that of associate producer.

Greene decided to take a hand in the production of this film, because he felt that this might be a way of ensuring that the story would be filmed in the way that he had envisioned it. He did enjoy working with the director and found the Italian crew that worked on the film on location in Venice to be very friendly. But ultimately he

---

[16]I shall consider both of these films in the following chapter.

decided that being a co-producer of a motion picture is no job for a writer. Generalizing on his experience with *The Stranger's Hand* and with *Loser Takes All*, the only other film which he has co-produced, Greene says that the problem of the writer-turned-producer is that "one becomes involved with the producer's monetary troubles; one has to accept actors who are miscast because another man's money is involved." The writer does not have "the blind optimism of the film maker, who tenaciously holds on to the hope that the wrong actors, the wrong technicians, and the wrong color process will somehow come together and produce a lucky accident.[17]

No lucky accident occurred during the shooting of *The Stranger's Hand*. Although in the planning stages it had looked very promising, it turned out to be one of the weakest films ever made from a Greene story. It had two of the stars of *The Third Man*: Trevor Howard (who was also brilliant in the film of Greene's *The Heart of the Matter*), and Alida Valli; and it was about a small boy's entanglements in the world of adult intrigue, a theme which had served as the basis of *The Fallen Idol*. And yet, this time the ingredients did not mix.

The story concerns a small boy who goes to join his father, Major Court (Trevor Howard), in Venice. The latter, an intelligence officer, is kidnapped by Communist agents just before he is to meet his son. The lad is helped by Roberta, a Yugoslav refugee (Alida Valli), and her boy friend, an American sailor (Richard Basehart) to find his father. With the aid of the harbor fire brigade, they do find the major aboard a ship that is to transport him behind the Iron Curtain, and rescue him just in time. It all sounds very exciting, and it should have been; but somehow it is not.

The film gets bogged down in a great deal of dialogue which never seems to clarify either the situation or the motivation of the characters. For example, the personalities of the girl and the sailor are never clearly defined. They seem to quarrel capriciously about whether or not they are going to help the boy, and then, just as capriciously, make up. But the most crucial fault of the film lies in failing to delineate sufficiently a central character, the shabby Italian doctor (Eduardo Cianelli). After being involved in the kidnapping of Major Court, the

[17]Greene, "The Novelist and the Cinema." *loc. cit.*, p. 57. Cf. Jack Edmund Nolan, "Graham Greene's Movies," *Films in Review*, XV (January, 1964), 32.

doctor ironically befriends the lad before he knows who he is, but then continues to show him kindness once he does.

At their first meeting, when the doctor finds the boy wandering the streets, he treats him to some ice cream. Before they part, the doctor makes two rings out of string. He gives one to the boy and puts the other on his own finger. "If you feel lonely," he tells the lad, "remember that you have a friend." In another scene, when Roberta decides to help the boy find his lost father, she tells him to cheer up because "things are not so bad if you have a friend."

The theme which emerges in the film, then, is that everyone needs and responds to companionship. Indeed, the doctor's friendship for the boy is enough to rejuvenate what is left of his sense of integrity, for it prompts him to sacrifice himself for the boy's father and thereby redeem his own squandered life. During the scuffle on board the vessel between the spies and the police, one of the Communist agents attempts to shoot Major Court. The doctor, however, deliberately intervenes between the major and the gunman and is himself killed. Afterward the boy asks his father if anyone died during the gun battle. "Nobody," Major Court replies, "just a stranger." The final shot of the film is a close-up of "the stranger's hand," motionless in death, still wearing the ring of string.

This ending is not as effective as it might have been. To make the doctor's sacrifice more meaningful, we would have had to know him better than we actually do. As it is, the close of the film seems too pat, and one wonders if the doctor rather than the boy should not have been made the focus, for he is the only character in the story who really changes. Even as the film stands, Cianelli's performance as the doctor dominates the movie and is the only memorable thing about it. In any event, it is understandable that after *The Stranger's Hand* Greene decided to avoid accepting any official role in the production end of the film making process.

In 1957 Greene's short story "Across the Bridge" (1938) became the basis of a film starring Rod Steiger. Like *The Stranger's Hand* its theme is the human need for companionship, and like the previous film it was made by John Stafford's independent production company. Greene characterizes the late Mr. Stafford as "a real gentleman in the movie business—which is why he wasn't more successful than he was." Concerning the adaptation of his story for the film, Greene says, "My short story provided only the beginning and the end of the film of *Across the Bridge*; all the rest was invented by the script writers." In fact so much was invented to stretch Greene's spare story into a feature-length film that Greene's original plot is almost submerged completely in the intricacies of the extended story line—though not to the degree that "The Lieutenant Died Last" was engulfed in *Went the Day Well?*.

"Across the Bridge" as Greene wrote it is basically a brief account of the ignominious end of Joseph Calloway, an English financier who flees to Mexico to avoid facing charges of embezzlement and fraud. The story is narrated by a young American, who sees Calloway occasionally when he makes trips across the border into Mexico. With growing fascination, the young man watches the gradual disintegration of the once proud millionaire as he desperately tries to obtain permission to set up permanent residence in Mexico, while representatives of the British police seek to find ways of luring him across the border to the United States where he can be arrested and thereafter extradited. "He looked tired and ill and dusty," the young American says at one point, "and I felt sorry for him to think of the kind of victory he'd been winning, with so much expenditure of cash and care—the prize this dirty and dreary town."

The British finally hit on the idea of stealing Calloway's dog and taking it across the American border. Since the dog is the only friend that Calloway has, he risks capture by crossing the border into Texas to retrieve it. As dog and master head back to Mexico, a police car pursues them across the international bridge. Just as the car is gaining on them, the driver swerves to avoid hitting the dog, and Calloway is hit instead. Down he goes, "in a mess of broken glass and gold rims and silver hair and blood," writes Greene in his vivid cinematic style. Initially, the narrator had thought of Calloway only as an elderly man who had swindled the poor and who deserved everything he got. On seeing that Calloway was prepared to risk everything for his dog, the narrator realizes that after all, Calloway was a human being, having basic human needs, including that for companionship. The original story, therefore, centers not so much around Calloway as around the young narrator, who has himself become more human in witnessing what has happened to Calloway.

This is how "Across the Bridge" appears in Greene's *Twenty-One*

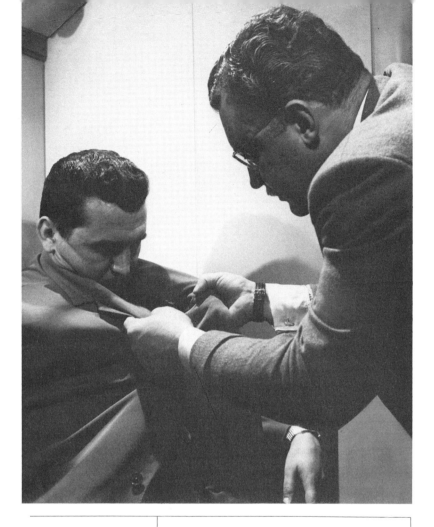

ACROSS THE BRIDGE (J. Arthur Rank Productions, 1957). An international financier on the run from the law (Rod Steiger, right) takes on the identity of another man (Bill Nagy) only to find that he, too, is a fugitive.

Stories. One does not envy the two screen writers who had to lengthen this poignant incident into a feature film. Nonetheless, while admitting that some of the additions and changes which were made are effective, I am bound to say that others are not.

The film rightly opens as one might have expected, with the direct presentation of the financier's decision to flee to Mexico, whereas Greene presents this material in a brief expository section. Calloway becomes, for no immediately discernible reason, a German named Carl

Schaffner who is British by passport but not by birth. Once Schaffner has reached America and boards a train for Mexico, we take leave of Greene's story altogether.

During his train journey Schaffner meets Paul Scarff, who resembles him to some extent. Schaffner gets Scarff drunk and throws him off the train, supposing him dead. Having taken great pains to enhance his physical resemblance to Scarff, Schaffner gets off the train at Scarff's destination with Scarff's passport, baggage—and dog. The plot is further complicated by the revelations that Scarff is not only still alive, but is wanted in Mexico for having committed a political assassination there. Schaffner is forced to reveal his true identity and to help in the capture of Scarff in order to clear himself of the murder charge and remain in Mexico. After Scarff is executed, he becomes a martyr to the people, and because of his hand in Scarff's capture, Schaffner becomes an outcast. No Mexican will speak to him or sell him anything.

The script writers use this situation to explain how Schaffner could become so attached to another man's dog that he would risk everything to get it back. The fugitive's attachment to the dog was less of a problem to explain in the original short story because Calloway had brought the dog with him from England; and besides being his only loyal companion, it also reminded him of the whole way of life of a wealthy country gentlemen that he had left behind. At last we arrive in the film at the climax of the story as Greene devised it. Schaffner is hit by the police car trying to retrieve his dog, and lies dead on the bridge, mourned only by the whimpering animal as the camera pulls away from the scene and the film ends.

I have admitted to a certain admiration for the script writers of *Across the Bridge*, Guy Elmes and Denis Freeman, for their ingenuity in inventing a whole plot line to fill out Greene's short story. Still, it seems to me that they have really done their job not wisely but too well, for the film is too long and top heavy with plot details. Furthermore, the writers have made the serious mistake of enlisting the audience's sympathies on behalf of Schaffner too late in the film. In Greene's story we see Calloway only from the outside, and we are asked only to share the inkling of sympathy that rises in the narrator of the story when he witnesses the circumstances of Calloway's death. For a large part of the film's running time, the viewer feels toward

Schaffner like the narrator of the original story: he is curious about how the fugitive will elude capture, but not really interested in him as a person. Consequently, in the last portion of the film, in the interminable sequence in which Schaffner is driven to despair by the silent hostility of the villagers, it is too late for one to become identified with Schaffner to the point of pitying him as a desolate human being who symbolizes man's alienation and loneliness. Consequently, one begins to weary of the film before it reaches its climax, which is unfortunate, as Steiger's beautifully sustained portrayal of Schaffner deserves our attention throughout.

A much more favorable reaction to the film than has been recorded here has been registered by film critic Martin S. Dworkin. Writing in *The Progressive*, Dworkin finds that director Ken Annakin and editor Alfred Roome "create a rhythm in which the melodramatic climaxes steadily diminish, as the possibilities of action dwindle; and yet the intensity mounts. For another man, all opportunities and strategies are far from exhausted in the situation that is depicted. But it is gradually clear that the fugitive is his own prisoner, in this town on the barest edge of any freedom and belonging—as he can no longer choose even to surrender, although he has long ago given up all that matters. Out of the elements of nothingness," Dworkin concludes, "there is fashioned a film that is considerably more than melodrama, and something of a morality."[18]

One cannot question the serious intent with which the film was made, since the moral and psychological dimensions of the story are clearly brought to the fore as we watch Schaffner change from an apparently heartless criminal into a vulnerable human being. Still it is not unfair to say that *Across the Bridge* would have been a better motion picture had the ending been placed a little closer to the beginning, or had we gotten to know Schaffner as a person sooner than we did.

Looking back on the films that have been adapted from Greene's entertainments by script writers other than himself, it seems that in most cases the scripts have tended to ignore the deeper implications of the stories on which they were based in favor of emphasizing action. I realize that Greene has said that action is the chief interest in

[18]Martin S. Dworkin, "Across the Bridge." *The Canadian Commentator*, IV (November, 1960), 15. Reprinted from the author's article, "Ideas on Screen," *The Progressive*, XXII (January, 1958), 36–37.

his entertainments. Nevertheless, all of the principal characters of Greene's novel-length entertainments have well defined personalities, even if they are not subjected to as much psychological scrutiny as are the leading characters of his serious fiction.

In the trio of spy novels in particular, Greene is at great pains to show that the way in which the hero of each tries to cope with the predicament in which he finds himself is dictated to a large extent by emotional experiences in his past. Raven in *A Gun for Sale* is a calloused killer because of his dreadful childhood. Arthur Rowe in *The Ministry of Fear* and D in *The Confidential Agent* both pursue enemy agents not only to serve their respective countries, but also in the hope that they can somehow make reparation for what they consider to be a guilty past.

When the psychological dimension of a Greene story is diminished, as it has been in most of the films that I have dealt with so far, a portion of the substance of the source story is lost; and therefore the viewer of the film tends to get less involved in the action than the reader of the story does. But all of these motion pictures still remain in one way or another what Greene had intended the original stories to be: entertaining.

Greene's most recent entertainment, *Travels with My Aunt* (1970), was filmed in 1972 by veteran Hollywood director George Cukor. Greene was pleased that one of the co-writers of the film script was Jay Presson Allen, who did an excellent job of retaining the spirit of Muriel Spark's *The Prime of Miss Jean Brodie* in both the stage and screen versions. The lead role of Aunt Augusta, a dotty old lady with a delightfully wicked past, is played by Maggie Smith—who had been Miss Brodie. Aunt Augusta takes it upon herself to initiate her inhibited middle-aged nephew Henry (Alec McCowen) into the more exciting side of life and shepherds him around the world on a trip that turns out to include visits to many of the places where Greene has set his previous novels. They even take a ride on the Orient Express.

"Greene has created some very rich and marvelous characters in his story," Cukor has told me. "The warmth and range of both the elderly aunt and her nephew attracted me to the story. I think it is a rare combination of robust adventure and really funny comedy." Cukor says that he made every effort to do right by Greene's amusing book: "When I acquired the rights to do the film of the novel, I went through it and cross-referenced all of the episodes. Of course we couldn't put everything that is in the book into the film, but every incident of importance in the story has turned up somehow in the picture."

When Cukor summed up his approach to adapting Greene's novel to the screen, it occurred to me that if his outlook had been shared by the other film makers who have turned out motion pictures based on Greene's entertainments, many of the films would have been more faithful to Greene and better movies in the bargain: "When you are dealing with the work of a very talented writer like Greene, your goal should be to preserve the essence and spirit of his work in your film. Otherwise, why base the picture on his story in the first place?"

Why, indeed?

TRAVELS WITH MY AUNT (Metro-Goldwyn-Mayer, 1972). Maggie Smith, as the extraordinary aunt of Greene's comic novel, with director George Cukor. In the role, Miss Smith ranges from an innocent schoolgirl to a worldly septuagenarian, of dubious morals but impeccable eccentricity.

Metro-Goldwyn-Mayer

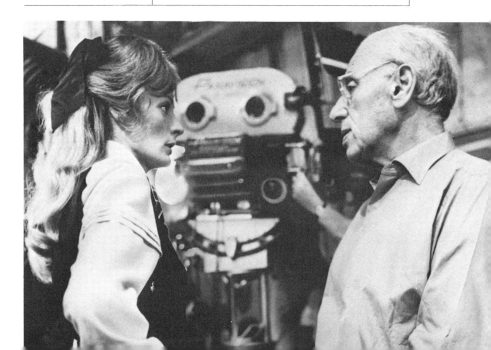

3

OUR MAN IN VIENNA: GREENE'S FILM ADAPTATIONS OF HIS ENTERTAINMENTS

In the course of Greene's *The End of the Affair*, the novelist Maurice Bendrix goes to see a film made from one of his novels. "The film was not a good film," says Bendrix, "and at moments it was actually painful to see situations that had been so real to me twisted into the stock clichés of the screen." Then, unexpectedly, for a few minutes the film came to life. "I forgot that this was my story, and that for once this was my dialogue, and was genuinely moved."

Greene has probably based this description of Bendrix's encounter with a screen version of one of his novels on his own experience with the film medium. If so, it is not surprising that Greene consented to adapt some of his own work to the screen, in the hope that he could multiply those moments which Bendrix described, moments when a work of fiction comes genuinely to life on the screen.

Greene has always approached screenwriting as an exercise of the writer's creative abilities, and in his 1937 essay "Film Lunch" satirized those writers who looked upon it solely as hack work whereby they could augment their income. In the essay Greene pictures a group of writers who are being feted by MGM in order to lure them into "the great chromium studios" to turn out machine-tooled scripts manufactured to company specifications. The writers, "a little stuffed and a little boozed," lean back and dream of the wealth that will be theirs; all that is asked in return is "the dried imagination and the dead pen."[1] Greene wondered if the glittering prizes that the cinema offered to writers might not defeat their own purpose: Can the artist's critical faculty help being a little blunted on £200 (about $500) a week?

Since Greene had expressed these strong misgivings about screenwriting before he had actually written any scripts, I asked him recently if he would care to revise these remarks today in the light of his subsequent experience as a script writer. "In the situation described in 'Film Lunch,'" he said, "I was talking about the Hollywood system in the old days when scripts were worked out at story conferences by a team of writers, and the individual writer was merely a hack hired to help assemble a script. I have been fortunate in my work for the screen. My scripts have not often been altered; I haven't suffered much in that way."

Nevertheless, Greene is very much aware that there are certain drawbacks to filmwriting that do not obtain for other kinds of creative writing. As soon as the script is finished, he points out, its author becomes "a forgotten man. . . . When the lines are at last spoken on the studio floor the scriptwriter is not there to criticize and alter." When he sees the finished film the scriptwriter may discover to his consternation that some of his ideas have been changed and that "extra dialogue has been inserted (for which he bears the critics' blame)."[2]

Still, Greene is a realist, and he has never expected to exercise the kind of control over the production of a film which he has written that he has been able to exert in the case of one of his plays: "Film is not mainly dialogue, as is a stage play. The technique of the stage is relatively simple and the author can exercise some influence over the production of his play through the director. But it is impossible for the screenwriter to have the technical knowledge required to control the filming of his script. This is a fact, not a complaint."

Looking back on his work as a scriptwriter, Greene says in his preface to *Three Plays*, "My own experience of screenwriting has been

[1]Graham Greene, "Film Lunch," *Collected Essays*. Harmondsworth: Penguin Books, 1970; p. 319.
[2]Graham Greene, "Introduction," *Three Plays*. London: Mercury Books, 1962; p. x.

fortunate and happy; and yet with what relief I have gone back afterwards to that one-man business, to the privacy of a room in which I
bear the full responsibility of failure," i.e., to the writing of fiction.

In spite of his initial misgivings about writing for the film medium, Greene wrote his first screen play for the 1939 film *Twenty-One
Days*, based on a John Galsworthy short story, "The First and the
Last." It was a sensational tale of a murderer who hanged himself and
of the innocent man who was subsequently hanged for the original
crime. "If the story had any force at all it lay in its extreme sensa-
tionalism," says Greene in his introduction to the 1970 edition of
Brighton Rock. "But the British Board of Film Censors forbade much of
this material from being dramatized in the film, including the suicide
and the failure of justice. There was little of Galsworthy's plot left
when I had finished. This unfortunate first effort was suffered with
good-humored nonchalance by Laurence Olivier and Vivien Leigh,
who had much to forgive me." In Greene's version of the story, Olivier
kills a man accidentally, and is eventually freed of any suspicion of
having caused the latter's death.

After the Galsworthy debacle, Greene had decided that he would
never again adapt another writer's work for the cinema. He has broken
this rule only once. In 1957 Otto Preminger asked him to write the
screenplay for George Bernard Shaw's *St. Joan*. "Preminger was
insistent that I do the screenplay," Greene explains, "and I did have
six weeks blank, so I acceded. Shaw is not a sacred name to me. I
didn't mind adapting his work." The film was a disaster, largely
because the part of Joan was completely beyond the range of Jean
Seberg, in her first film performance. But Greene defends his script
"for keeping a sense of responsibility to the author while reducing a
play of three-and-a-half hours to a film of less than two hours."

The year after he scripted *Twenty-One Days*, Greene provided the
original story and preliminary screenplay for *The Green Cockatoo* (1940),
a film which starred John Mills and was directed by William Cameron
Menzies. Menzies was an outstanding set designer but was not particularly gifted as a director. But William K. Howard, who is listed as
the producer of the film, *was* an accomplished director, and it is
thought that Howard probably lent a hand in the direction of the film.
That the outcome was a failure is very likely as attributable to direc-

torial problems as to Greene's work on the film. In any event, Greene recalls that the whole experience was, quite simply, "deplorable."

All of the other screenplays that Greene has written have been based on his own fiction. When a writer adapts his own work to the screen he is faced with the temptation to leave his original work fairly intact and not to re-think it in cinematic terms. Specifically, he may well have a tendency to preserve in his script as much of the dialogue in his novel as possible. Asked about his own policy in this regard, Greene replied, "I use dialogue from the novel when it seems to fit. Often in the first version of the script a great deal of the original dialogue is kept. But it is slowly whittled down in order to reduce the dialogue as much as possible. What has the right rhythm in the book because of the surrounding paragraphs may seem unrealistic on the screen and must be modified. Dialogue in fiction must have the flavor of realism, without having to be real, while on the screen the camera emphasizes the realism of the situation. You have to be closer in a film to real-life conversation in order that the dialogue will match the realistic furnishings of the settings, so to speak." In discussing the films which Greene has adapted from his own fiction, I shall note examples of Greene's method of revising dialogue from a story for use in its film version.

Greene himself did the scripts of four of his entertainments, and two of his serious novels. Three of the four entertainments were directed by Carol Reed and are among the best films on which Greene has ever collaborated. The first of these, *The Fallen Idol* (1948), began as a short story called "The Basement Room," which Greene composed in 1935 to relieve the tedium of his voyage back to England from Liberia. The story deals with a theme that Greene has often treated in his fiction, both short and long: the initiation of a youngster into the adult world, i.e., the transformation of innocence by experience, which can sometimes prove cruel and disillusioning, as it does for Raven in *A Gun for Sale* and for Pinkie in *Brighton Rock*.

On the first page of *Another Mexico*, Greene's travel book about Mexico, he writes of his own childhood and how a green baize door in a passage near his father's study separated the world of his family from the world of the school where his father was headmaster. "One was an inhabitant of both countries," Greene recalls; on weekdays of

THE FALLEN IDOL
(London Films Productions, 1948). The lonely boy (Bobby Henrey) misunderstands a quarrel between the butler and his wife (Ralph Richardson and Sonia Dresdel). Below: The jealous wife discovers her husband with his mistress. Moments later, the window swings open, toppling her to her death.

London Films Productions

the alien world on one side of the baize door, on weekends of the familiar world on the other side. "How can life on a border be other than restless?"[3]

In "The Basement Room" the green baize door of Greene's childhood reappears, this time shutting off the world of the nursery, where young Philip Lane spends much of his time, from the basement living room of the butler Baines (to whom Philip feels very close) and his shrewish wife. Philip knows little of the world of the Baines's private domain until his parents go away for a holiday and he is left alone to roam about the house. During that time, he becomes accustomed to going through the baize door and down to the Baines's living

[3]Graham Greene, *Another Mexico* (British title: *The Lawless Roads*). New York: The Viking Press, 1968; p. 2.

room, where he listens to the butler's manufactured stories of his adventures in the Congo. "Baines had seen the world," Philip reflects. Baines had been beyond the railings that Philip must peer through in order to catch a glimpse of the world that passes by outside the huge mansion in which he lives.

Throughout the story, Greene frequently pictures Philip as a largely uncomprehending spectator of the adult world around him. In a crucial example, Philip goes for a walk and espies Baines through the window of a tea shop talking with a pretty young girl. As he peers through the dusty pane, the boy has no idea what is passing between Baines and the girl. When Philip finally joins them, Baines introduces the girl, Emmy, as his niece, although the tenor of their conversation suggests that Baines is involved romantically with the girl and that he is trying to persuade her not to break off their relationship.

On their way back home, Baines asks Philip not to tell his wife what he has witnessed, but Mrs. Baines shrewdly wheedles it out of him. She in turn asks Philip not to tell Baines that she knows. The boy begins to feel more and more uneasy in the strange world of adult secrets and counter-secrets, but things seem to settle down when Mrs. Baines announces that she is going away for a couple of days to visit a relative. Philip and Baines spend the first day that she is gone seeing different sights in the city, and then Baines invites Emmy to the house for the evening.

When Philip goes through the baize door and down into the basement room after supper, he is startled to find Baines kissing Emmy. Philip is being pushed too quickly into the adult world of experience, we are made to fear. This is confirmed when he is awakened during the night by Mrs. Baines, who has returned deliberately to trap Baines with Emmy, and demands to know where they are. Philip is momentarily speechless with terror, so Mrs. Baines leaves him behind to go and search the house herself. Philip then tries to warn Baines by shouting that Mrs. Baines is coming, but he is too late. He sits on the landing of the grand staircase and helplessly watches Baines and his wife struggle on the stairs until she goes over the bannister and falls to her death.

"The whole house had been turned over to the grown-up world," Philip feels. He is afraid that their passions have even flooded the nursery. He decides that he will involve himself no further with the adult world: "Let grown-up people keep to their world and he would keep to his." Accordingly Philip flees into the night.

However, he is soon found by a policeman and brought back home. In the meantime, several other policemen have come to the house to investigate Mrs. Baines's death. Baines looks at Philip imploringly, silently begging him not to tell the police that he has rearranged the body of Mrs. Baines to make her death look like an accident. But Philip will not accept any further responsibility for adult secrets. Without fully realizing the import of his words, he blurts out to the police what he had seen and even supplies them with a motive for Baines's wanting to be rid of his wife by saying, "It was all Emmy's fault."

Philip's premature initiation into the adult world had so great a traumatic effect that he grew up to be an embittered man who subconsciously avoided throughout his life any deep involvements with others. He had loved Baines and as far as he was concerned Baines had drawn him into a world of secrets and fears that he never fully understood. At the end of the story Philip dies a lonely old man who had never again shared the confidences or companionship of others.

The somber note on which Greene ends "The Basement Room" is missing from his script for the film version. Greene regards it as his favorite among the scripts which he has done. "The Fallen Idol is more of a writer's film than a director's film," he says. "The Third Man, though it has proved more popular, is mostly action with only sketched characters. It was fun doing, but there is more of the writer in The Fallen Idol. It was my first real work for the cinema, and I worked closely with Carol Reed during the writing of the screenplay. In general I prefer to work from original material, as I did with The Third Man, or from a short story, as I did with The Fallen Idol, since condensation is always dangerous, while expansion is a form of creation."

At first Greene was surprised that Reed wanted to collaborate with him on a film of "The Basement Room." "It seemed to me that the subject matter was unfilmable—a murder committed by the most sympathetic character and an unhappy ending," which might prove unpopular at the box office. In the ensuing script conferences, however, Greene and Reed gradually developed the original short story into the tale of a boy who believes that his friend has committed a murder which in reality was an accident, and who lies to the police in an effort to shield his friend. Why Greene and Reed retold the story in this fashion will, I think, become clear as I go on.

One of the shrewdest changes in the basic background of the short story was to change Philip into Felipe, the son of a foreign ambassador stationed in London. This not only serves to explain the size of the mansion in which the boy lives, but also underlines the feelings of loneliness and alienation which he feels as a foreigner living in a strange country as well as a child living in an adult world.

"It is always difficult to remember which of us made which change in the original story, except in certain details," says Greene. For example, Reed was responsible for the bit of comic relief provided by the man who comes to wind the old clock. But having the cross-examination of the girl by the police take place next to the bed that she had used with Baines was Greene's idea, as was giving the boy a pet snake ("I have always liked snakes," Greene confides.)[1] The title of the film was chosen by the distributors and Greene has never particularly liked it; although at one point the film was being called *Lost Illusions*, and that would not have been much better.

Once the script conferences with Reed were over, Greene set about writing the screenplay. Since the problem of adapting a short story to the motion picture medium involves expansion rather than compression, as is the case with a novel, it is interesting to see how Greene's original story has been opened out to make a full-length film. The picture begins as the story does, with the parents of Felipe (Bobby Henrey) leaving him in the care of Baines (Ralph Richardson) and his wife (Sonia Dresdel). The first appearance of Mrs. Baines is preceded by a glimpse of her shadow on a wall, as her imperious voice is heard calling for Baines. Her cold, even sinister character is further established by her warning Felipe shortly thereafter about how he is expected to behave while his parents are away.

Although the green baize door is never talked about in the film, visually it serves the same important function as it did in the story; for whenever Felipe goes through it, his hesitant manner projects his awareness that he is entering another world. Reed further underscores Felipe's sense of being an interloper in a world of older people

[1]Graham Greene, "Preface to *The Fallen Idol*," in *The Third Man* and *The Fallen Idol*. New York: The Viking Press, 1950; p. 145. In this edition, the short story, "The Basement Room," on which the film *The Fallen Idol* was based, is published under the title of the film.

by frequently photographing the lad from above to make him look small, or through bannisters to indicate his sense of separation from others. The opening shot of the film, in fact, is a close-up of Felipe on the great staircase, peering through the bars at his departing parents. Consistently, when shooting from Felipe's point of view, Reed uses unusually low camera angles to show how the world looks from Felipe's point of view.

Greene says that he tried to write the script as much as possible from the boy's point of view. To this end, Reed's handling of the camera in the ways just mentioned was decisive in making the viewer feel that he was seeing how the world looked to a small boy. Reed has always been noted for his cinematographic control, and nowhere is this skill more evident than in *The Fallen Idol*. One interchange between Baines and his wife, for example, takes place as they pass each other on the grand staircase, going in opposite directions. They are photographed in an extreme long shot, from Felipe's point of view as he sits at the top of the stairs, and their words are barely audible. In a single shot Reed manages to suggest the cold, divergent quality of their relationship as well as the fact that Felipe is too far removed from their private world to understand what passes between them.

As I mentioned in the preceding chapter, the adapters of Greene's short story "Across the Bridge" stretched it to feature length by piling incident upon incident in a way that did not really help the viewer to get to know the central character any better, and thereby to be able to identify with him. In writing the screenplay for *The Fallen Idol* Greene has not only enlarged the story to the proportions of a feature-length film, but also has brought us closer to Felipe and Baines, and hence to a deeper understanding of their motives for behaving as they do. In the story, when Felipe asks Baines why he left Africa, he replies laconically, "I married Mrs. Baines." In the film Baines's answer awakens sympathy for him in us by implying that he is basically a good-natured, considerate man. He says, "When I came back on leave I married Mrs. Baines. The climate would have got her down. A woman can't stand it like a man can."

Greene foreshadows Felipe's later lies to the police in Baines' behalf by inserting incidents into the film which show the growth of Felipe's conviction that lying is morally good when done to protect a friend. When his wife berates Baines for giving Felipe cake between meals, Felipe leaps to his defense with a lie: "He didn't give it to me, I took it." Not to be put off, Mrs. Baines then accuses Felipe of lying and Baines says in the boy's defense, "Some lies are just kindness." This aphorism is something that Felipe will not forget.

Because in the climactic scene of the film it is important that Felipe watch the death of Mrs. Baines from a certain vantage point, Greene early on establishes the boy's habit of using the fire escape to leave the house in times of tension. Felipe has been sent to his room by Mrs. Baines. From his window Felipe sees Baines going out for what is apparently an afternoon stroll, and he decides to run down the fire escape and catch up with him. Felipe loses sight of Baines for a while, and then notices him talking to a girl in a tea shop. The girl is now named Julie instead of Emmy, presumably because she is played by a French actress, Michele Morgan.

Felipe at first watches the two through the glass of the tea shop window, unable to hear what they are saying to each other. When he goes in and joins them, Baines and the girl discuss the possibility of ending their liason in terms, clear to the audience, that the boy does not understand. Julie says that she is weary of meeting Baines secretly and presses him to ask his wife for a divorce. Finally she says that she will not discuss the matter any further and goes out, slamming the door. The camera pauses for a moment on a sign that is hanging on the back of the door which reads, "CLOSED"—an interesting, almost playful use of a symbol to convey Julie's feeling that she is fed up with the whole affair.

Baines then asks Felipe not to tell his wife of their meeting with Julie, explaining that he is not asking Felipe to tell a lie, but only to keep a secret for a friend. As in the short story, the wily Mrs. Baines extracts the secret from Felipe, and tells him that he must now share their mutual secret that she knows about Julie. At this point, the film takes a dramatic departure from the short story. When Mrs. Baines leaves the house the next day on the pretext of visiting her ailing aunt, we see her sneak back into the house. She is shown eavesdropping on Baines as he phones Julie to persuade her to spend the day with Felipe and him at the zoo and then return to the house for supper.

Just before the end of the zoo sequence, there is an interesting cinematic touch supplied by Reed. As Felipe mentions the name of Mrs. Baines to the others, there is a cut to a closeup of a squawking parrot. This is Reed's way of reinforcing Greene's note in the script that when Felipe mentions the name of Mrs. Baines, it falls over the temporary cheerfulness of the couple like a cloud, reminding them that she must still somehow be dealt with before they can be happy.

In "The Basement Room" there is no hint that Mrs. Baines is actually present in the house while the three are having their picnic supper. Prior to the moment when she awakens Felipe, her presence, so far as the reader knows, is symbolic: "She wasn't really away at all," Greene writes in the story, "she was there in the basement with them, driving them to longer drinks and louder talk. . . ."

In the film, Greene and Reed have wisely decided to make Mrs. Baines's presence in the house known as a fact to the audience, lending a sinister, menacing element to the atmosphere of the whole evening of fun that Baines and Julie and Felipe are having together. We know, as they do not, that observing them all the time is Mrs. Baines, for we saw her return to the house just after she supposedly left it to visit her aunt. Felipe suspects that Mrs. Baines is in the house, for he catches a glimpse of her in a doorway. Baines, however, discounts Felipe's fears as based only in his imagination. "Our game of hide and seek has gone on too long," Baines says sympathetically, and packs Felipe off to bed.

In tipping off the audience to Mrs. Baines's presence in the house in a way that the short story did not, the film adaptation has opted for suspense rather than surprise. Alfred Hitchcock has often said that he prefers suspense to surprise, and he explains why in an interview with Pete Martin. A director can withhold information from the audience so that they will be surprised later on in the film, but the surprise only lasts for a moment, says Hitchcock. He prefers to give the audience all of the facts as early as possible, because that way he can build up an almost unbearable tension. When the viewer knows about a danger that the characters themselves are unaware of, he "wants to scream out to all the other characters in the plot, 'Watch out for so-and-so!' There you have real tenseness and an irresistible desire to know what happens."[5]

When the reader of "The Basement Room" is not let in on the

[5]Pete Martin, "I Call on Alfred Hitchcock," *The Saturday Evening Post*, July 27, 1957; reprinted in Harry M. Geduld, ed., *Film Makers on Film Making*. Bloomington: Indiana University Press, 1967; p. 128.

secret that Mrs. Baines is lurking about the house, he does get the momentary thrill of being surprised when she suddenly appears at Felipe's bedside. But if one is let in on the secret from the outset, as in the film, the momentary surprise is exchanged for a sustained feeling of apprehension such as Hitchcock describes. In the story, Greene was quite right in employing surprise, since the outing of Felipe and Baines followed by the supper with Emmy takes up less than two pages in print. But in the film this material is extended to several minutes of screen time. Hence the suspense engendered in the audience by informing them that Mrs. Baines is in the house all the time persists throughout the zoo and supper sequences. And the sight of Mrs. Baines looming over Felipe's bed is the more startling. Felipe is awakened, as in the story, by a loose hair pin falling on to his pillow from Mrs. Baines's dissheveled hair. "Where are they?" she demands in a hoarse whisper. She has waited all day to catch Baines and Julie together.

We have now arrived at the climactic scene: the death of Mrs. Baines. But since this was unpremeditated murder in the short story and is to be an accident in the film, it is prepared for differently.

When Philip runs to the top of the grand staircase and shouts a warning to Baines, the latter is just about to enter the room where Julie is waiting for him. Mrs. Baines confronts Baines on the stairs and they quarrel, while the frightened Philip runs out on to the fire escape. Inside the house, Baines returns to the room where Julie is, in order to help her get away before she has to face the wrath of his wife. Mrs. Baines is frantic and climbs off the stairway onto a ledge where there is a large hinged window through which she hopes to catch a glimpse of the pair. As she strains to see, she loses her footing and the window swings open, causing her to fall backward onto the staircase. Felipe, who has been watching from the fire escape, cannot see the top of the staircase from his vantage point. Accordingly, he is able to see only Mrs. Baines's body tumbling down the stairs to the floor far below, but not how she came to fall. When Felipe sees Baines coming down the stairs to find out what has happened, he therefore supposes that Baines has pushed his wife to her death (which is exactly what Baines did do in the short story). This whole sequence is brilliantly photographed and edited in a way that allows us to see what actually happened to Mrs. Baines, and also to see the way that it appeared to Philip from the fire escape.

Shocked and grieved at having witnessed what he considers to be a murder committed by his only friend, Felipe runs away from the house and through the shadowy streets. A policeman spies him and tries to coax him to come to the police station. But Felipe sees him only as one more emissary of the adult world, and is reluctant to follow him. Eventually, however, he does.

In the short story it is a policewoman who tries to get Felipe to tell who he is and where he lives. In the film, she has become a frowsy prostitute, and is made to be more successful in getting information out of Felipe than her counterpart in the short story. As played by Dora Bryan, the character provides some comic relief that is welcome after the intensity of the preceding scenes. When asked if she has anything to say in her own behalf just before Felipe arrives at the station, she responds, "Nothing, except that it's not my turn." When she attempts to inveigle Felipe into revealing his identity, she upsets the police officer on duty by asking the boy, "Would you like to come home with me?" She is charming, in her own seedy way, and Felipe is moved to confide in her.

"The Basement Room" ends shortly after the boy returns home from the police station and, because he is confused and upset by the adult world with all its secrets and lies, hysterically blurts out Baines' guilt. In *The Fallen Idol*, however, Felipe's love for Baines (who is shown as a more sympathetic character than he was in the story) overrides his terror and dismay at the situation. Even though Felipe thinks that Baines is guilty of murdering his wife, he still tries to make excuses for his friend. Referring to one of the adventure stories that Baines had concocted for him earlier, Felipe says, "Was it self-defense, like in Africa, Baines?"

Greene extends the story by adding some Hitchcockian twists. As the circumstantial evidence mounts against Baines, Felipe makes matters worse by telling lies in his behalf which, because they are so obvious, incriminate Baines all the more. Another suspense hook which Greene employs in the film is the telegram which Mrs. Baines has sent to Baines announcing that she would be staying away an extra few days. Since Baines has said that Mrs. Baines, and not Julie, was with Felipe and him at the zoo, the telegram would be very damaging to Baines were it to be found. Earlier in the evening Baines and Felipe had playfully made a paper airplane out of the telegram and flown it about the house. Baines now asks Felipe to set about looking for the telegram. Just as Felipe finds it in a flower pot, the family doctor, who has come to examine the body, sees him and takes the paper airplane away from him, saying that he should stop playing games and go to bed. The doctor casually tosses the paper airplane into the air and we see Baines watch it circle the room and fall at the feet of the detective to whom he is talking. The detective picks the thing up and absentmindedly puts it in his pocket without looking at it. The moment of suspense is beautifully underplayed by Ralph Richardson.

It should now be clear why in the film it was dramatically more promising to have Baines innocent of his wife's death. Had he been guilty, he would not have engaged the audience's sympathy as he tries to escape from the growing web of circumstantial evidence. As it is, the viewer, too, holds his breath as the telegram sails about the room and falls before the detective. Greene confirms the sympathetic portrayal of Baines, that he has carefully constructed in the script up to this point, by having him stand for a moment over his wife's body and murmur with a sad wistfulness, "Alice, my dear. What happened to us?" It is the only time in the film that we hear her first name.

In a last, desperate effort to save his friend, Felipe says that he murdered Mrs. Baines. Since he is the first to call her death murder, the police suspect that Felipe has seen more than he says; of course Felipe secretly believes that he *has* seen more than he has admitted. It is fascinating how Greene has been able to spin out a spiral of interconnecting ironies from the fabric of his short story, without giving an impression that he has merely sewed on extra material to make a full-length film. And the ironies continue right up to the end.

The police finally stumble on the real method of Mrs. Baines's death when they find her footprint in some dirt spilled from an overturned flowerpot on the ledge from which she fell. Meanwhile, Julie has begged Felipe not to tell any more lies to the police, since only the truth can now help Baines. Felipe agrees, and resolutely goes to the detective to tell him that it was really he who had broken the flower pot on the ledge. He wants to add that Mrs. Baines had stepped in the dirt the previous day and told him that she was going to leave it there until his mother came home. This fact *could* mean that Mrs. Baines had been on the ledge the day before her death, but not necessarily at the time of her death.

Felipe believes that he witnessed the murder of Mrs. Baines from the fire escape, and what he would reveal now would surely be enough to implicate Baines once more. Felipe is trying to tell the police what he thinks really happened at the moment that they are exonerating Baines, but no one will pay any attention to him. He is left standing alone, puzzled because no one wants to hear the truth now that he has finally decided to tell it. He climbs the stairs to the nursery, having decided to return to his own world after his bewildering experiences among adults, while down below Baines is rightly being freed—but on the basis of evidence that Felipe thinks is worthless.

But the lad in the film has not been permanently wounded by his premature initiation into the complexities of adult life, as was the boy in the story. That this aspect of the original short story has been left out of the film is in keeping with the comparatively lighter tone of the movie, which is basically a thriller. Both the short story and the film, however, have a similar theme, although it comes across in the film somewhat differently than in the story. In the latter the implied theme is that a child's later outlook toward life is more strongly influenced by his childhood experiences than we sometimes realize. In the film the theme seems to be that adults as well as children are affected profoundly by the behavior of others. Speaking of his dead wife, Baines says to Felipe, "We don't have any call to judge her. Perhaps she was what she was because I'm what I am. We've got to be careful, Phil, because we make one another." When Felipe objects that he thought that God made people, Baines answers, "The trouble is, we take a hand in the game." Baines is saying in effect that because of their mutual incompatibility he and Mrs. Baines helped to make each other the bitter and unhappy people they had become.

The acting in *The Fallen Idol* is of a high order. A seasoned actor like Ralph Richardson can respond almost intuitively to a sensitive director like Carol Reed, and therefore Richardson's flawless performance comes as no surprise. Directing a child actor is another matter, however; it is much more difficult to elicit a convincing performance from a youngster. But Reed has succeeded in doing just that with Bobby Henrey. The boy gives no hint that he is conscious that he is acting in a film; rather he seems completely at home in front of the camera. The awkwardness of his gestures, the way that he shambles about the house with his shirt tail hanging out a bit, his hair slightly mussed, all contribute to the naturalness of his performance. Since the story centers around Felipe, the authenticity of young Henrey's portrayal adds to the believability of the entire film.

In summary, *The Fallen Idol* is a good example of how a fine work of fiction can make a superior film if it is adapted in a way that carefully exploits its cinematic potential. Greene at first thought his story an unpromising film subject, as I have already noted. Yet, once he and Reed had worked out the adaptation, Greene's misgivings rightly disappeared. The death of Mrs. Baines, for instance, is no longer a murder committed by a sympathetic character as it was in the original short story, but an accident which looks like murder. This altered situation, as we have seen, provides greater opportunities for creating suspense in the film. Moreover, the decision to make the principal setting of the film an embassy affords the perfect atmosphere for the story. The oversized house not only dwarfs Felipe, thereby serving as an abiding reminder to the viewer that the boy is trying to deal with a world bigger than he can really handle, but also provides the proper shadowy, sinister atmosphere for the death of Mrs. Baines and the events that follow it.

The film seems to gather momentum rather slowly in the early scenes; but once the story begins to move towards its climax one realizes that the script has been very tightly constructed. Minor incidents which at first seem inconsequential, such as Mrs. Baines's knocking over the flower pot and leaving her footprint in the dirt, are later seen to fit perfectly into the total mosaic of events.

Greene attributes to Reed the largest part of the success of *The Fallen Idol* and of the other films on which they collaborated. He praises Reed as a cinema artist who combines "an extraordinary feeling for the right face for the right part" with an exactitude of cutting and, not least important, "the power of sympathizing with an author's worries and an ability to guide him."[6]

Both Greene and Reed wanted to make another film, to follow up the success of *The Fallen Idol*. Sir Alexander Korda, production chief of London Films, conceived the idea of a contemporary story set in postwar Vienna, and asked Greene to go there to devise a screenplay for Reed. As a point of departure for his script, Greene decided to use the opening paragraph of a story which he had begun twenty years earlier

[6]Greene, "Preface to *The Fallen Idol*," *loc. cit.*, p. 146.

and had abandoned. The passage read: "I had paid my last farewell to Harry a week ago, when his coffin was lowered into the frozen February ground, so that it was with incredulity that I saw him pass by, without a sign of recognition, among the host of strangers in the Strand." With this fragment Greene set to work.

"For three weeks," Greene says, "nothing seemed to work. Then I heard about the penicillin racket, and the sewers that ran under the city, and the various elements began to shape up into a story." When he spoke at the National Film Theater in London, Greene recalled that the American backer of the film, David O. Selznick, was not entirely happy with the way that things were progressing. "But Graham, you can't have a film about one guy searching obsessively for another guy," the producer of *Gone with the Wind* and other films objected. "It's not natural. It's the result of your English public schools. And who's going to go to see a film called *The Third Man*? What we want is something in the nature of *Nights in Vienna*."[7] Despite Mr. Selznick's reservations, Greene went ahead.

"My approach to writing an original screenplay is to write a treatment of the story which is then turned into a script," Greene says. I cannot do the kind of treatment that is written in the historical present. I write the treatment like a novel. What today is known as the novel of *The Third Man* is really the treatment which I did before writing the script. That is why I say in the preface to the published story that it was not written to be read but only to be seen." In the preface Greene further explains that since a film depends on characterization and atmosphere as well as on plot, he finds it almost impossible to capture these elements for the first time "in the dull shorthand of a script. . . . One must have the sense of more material than one needs to draw on."[8] *The Third Man*, therefore, had to start as a story which could then serve as the raw material for the script that Greene had been asked to write.

Greene remembers how he and Reed worked together on the revisions of his original story, even acting out scenes, and how the "clear cut-and-thrust of argument" between them helped to sharpen several points. But Greene is the first to point out that these changes

---

[7]John Player Lecture Series, February 15, 1970; *vide supra*, Chapter I, note 6.

[8]Graham Greene, "Preface to *The Third Man*," in *The Third Man* and *The Fallen Idol*. New York: The Viking Press, 1950; p. 8.

were not thrust upon him against his will. As likely as not, he says, they were suggested by himself. "The film, in fact, is better than the story, because it is in this case the finished state of the story," he concludes.

The first difference that one notices between the Greene's treatment and the film which evolved from it is that Colonel Calloway, the British military police officer (Trevor Howard), does not narrate the film as in the original story. The only narration in the film occurs at the very beginning. An unidentified voice (which is really that of Carol Reed) explains the political situation in postwar Vienna while shots of the city appear on the screen as illustrations of his remarks. This short segment was actually added to the film three months after the principal photography had been completed because Korda, the producer, felt that international audiences would not otherwise understand the situation. (The voice of Joseph Cotten, who plays the hero, replaced that of Reed in the American prints of the film). There is no indication of this monologue in the script, but there is material for it in Greene's treatment, including the reference to the contemporary city as differing considerably from the old prewar Vienna "with its Strauss music, its glamour and easy charm." Vienna at the time the story takes place, the film's narrator tells us, is divided into American, Russian, British, and French zones, with the center of the city being policed by an international patrol.

The next alteration that one notices is that the leading protagonist, Rollo Martins, is an Englishman in the treatment but becomes an American in the film—simply because Joseph Cotten was chosen for the part. Since Martins is a naïve individual, his name had to be absurd; but Cotten disliked the name Rollo, so Greene changed it to Holley, a name which occured to him when he remembered "that figure of fun, the American poet Thomas Holley Chivers."[9] It is fascinating to see how one change dictates another. When the hero became an American, the villain had to be American too, since Holley Martins and Harry Lime were boyhood friends. Accordingly, Orson Welles was chosen to play Harry. This was an extraordinarily felicitous bit of casting. Welles appears in only a handful of scenes, but his is the performance that one remembers most. With one American villain in the

⁹*Ibid.*, p. 9.

film, Greene and Reed transformed the nationality of Harry's fellow blackmarketeer, Cooler, from American to Rumanian, and changed his name to Popescu.

Casting also determined another interesting change in the script. For comic relief Greene had created in the treatment a character named Crabbin, who pursues Holley, a writer of cheap Westerns, persuading him to give a lecture on the contemporary novel at his Cultural Re-education Center. When it appeared that the role of Crabbin was to be taken over in the film by two British character actors, Basil Radford and Naunton Wayne, Greene split Crabbin into Captain Carter and Captain Tombs in the script. Alfred Hitchcock had paired Radford and Wayne for the first time in *The Lady Vanishes* (1937) in which he had them sitting together in a European train discussing British cricket scores, blithely unconcerned about the fact that Europe was on the brink of chaos; and Reed had used the pair in a similar fashion in *Night Train* (1940). Since the Crabbin character carries on his cultural program for his little coterie of literati, equally unaware of the turbulent situation in Vienna, it seemed a good idea to have this team play the Crabbin role. Nonetheless, since *The Third Man* already had a large cast, it seemed wiser not to multiply characters any more than necessary, and so Carter and Tombs became a single character once more in the person of Crabbit, who was to be played by Wilfred Hyde-White.

As a last vestige of the fact that Crabbit had at one point been two characters, he is given a female companion in the film. She is a rather plain looking woman of about thirty who has no lines, but she is with Crabbit in every scene in which he appears. He acknowledges her presence only once. The first time he appears in the film, in a hotel lobby, we see him whisper to her with irritation, "I can't very well introduce you to everybody." Presumably she is his mistress, but he wants it to appear that she is his secretary. In any event, her presence is never explained; she is one of those tantalizing bits of detail that Reed sometimes includes in a film just to let the audience make of them what it will.

In addition to reconverting Carter and Tombs once more into a single character, Greene also simplified Crabbit's role in the film. In the treatment, the reason that Crabbin dragoons Martins into giving a lecture for his group is that he has confused Martins's pen name, Buck

Dexter, with that of a prominent British novelist, Benjamin Dexter, whom Greene patterned on E. M. Forster. Greene recalls that Reed rightly objected to what was "a rather far-fetched situation involving a great deal of explanation that increased the length of a film already far too long." Furthermore, since Martins' nationality had been changed, he would hardly have been confused with an English novelist.

Here is a striking example of the interplay between writer and director that takes place in the course of readying a film script for production. Greene realized that as a novelist he was accustomed to creating far more material than could be given adequate treatment within the more circumscribed limits of a film. Hence, he was more than willing to listen to Reed when the latter's cinemactic eye spied out material that would prove too intricate for development in the film.

In its fictional form, *The Third Man* differs from Greene's other novels and stories in that it was composed solely as the preliminary treatment from which a screenplay would be developed and was never intended by Greene to be a finished piece of fiction in its own right. Therefore, I shall not examine it any further as a separate work before going on to a consideration of the film. It will be referred to, however, whenever there is a significant difference between the treatment and the film.

The movie begins with the prologue which I have already described. Martins has come to Vienna because his old friend Harry Lime had promised him a job of some sort. Martins receives a severe shock, therefore, when he goes to Harry's apartment and discovers that his friend has been killed in a traffic accident and is being buried that very day. He hurries to the cemetery, where he meets Colonel Calloway, who invites him to go to a tavern for a drink after the funeral. At the tavern, Martins mourns for "the best friend I ever had." "That sounds like a cheap novelette," Calloway comments, and Martins retorts, "I write cheap novelettes."

In the treatment, Martins reminisces at length about the days when he and Harry were at school together. Harry was the older boy who knew the ropes, and Martins had grown fond of him because Harry had taken him under his wing. This is synthesized in the film in Martins' mention of his first day at school. "Never so damned lonely in my life—and then Harry showed up." But that is enough to establish Martins' long-standing hero-worship of Harry. Calloway attempts to disabuse Martins of his illusions by telling him that Lime was involved in the worst kind of blackmarketeering. But Martins will not hear anything derogatory said about his friend, and departs in a huff.

At his hotel he meets Crabbit, and the latter insists that Martins lecture on the modern novel to the cultural club. Martins accepts the invitation because he is badly in need of money. Kurtz, a friend of Harry's, phones Martins and asks to meet him at the Café Mozart for a drink. In the treatment Martins asks Kurtz to tell him how Harry died, and Kurtz obliges by describing the accident as he says he witnessed it. In the film, Martins says, "Show me how it happened," and there is a cut to the site of the accident outside Harry's apartment building, where Kurtz can thus explain the circumstances of Harry's death more graphically. It seems that Harry was hit by a truck while he was crossing the street to talk to his friend Popescu. Then Kurtz and Popescu had carried Lime's body into a doorway where he died before Dr. Winkel, another friend of Harry's, could arrive.

Martins is suspicious of this account. As he later tells Harry's girl Anna (Alida Valli), everyone present at Harry's death was a friend of Harry's; even the driver of the truck, in whose behalf Kurtz and Popescu testified at the inquest, knew Harry. In the treatment, Martins goes alone to visit the porter of Harry's apartment building (called Koch in the treatment but nameless in the film), in order to check Kurtz's story. The porter had told Martins earlier that he too had seen the accident but had declined to testify at the inquest because he did not wish to get involved in the affair. In the movie, Anna goes with Martins to talk to the porter, and he takes them to Harry's apartment. Once there, the porter makes the crucial remark that, besides Kurtz and Popescu, there was also a third man who carried Harry's body from the street to the doorway. Martins conjectures that it was the unidentified third man who murdered Harry.

At this point there are some significant additions to the scene, which make it more interesting than it was in the treatment. The phone in Harry's apartment rings. Anna answers it, but the party on the other end says nothing. This implies that someone knows that they are in Harry's apartment and wants to warn them not to inquire any further into Harry's death. Then a little boy, Hansl, comes into the room to retrieve his ball, which has rolled in unnoticed by the trio engaged in discussing Harry's death. This incident will become important shortly afterward. Unnerved by the sinister atmosphere that is beginning to surround Harry's death, the porter decides to say nothing further about what he has seen, and asks Anna and Martins to leave.

Martins next visits Dr. Winkel, who corroborates Kurtz's story, as Martins thought he would. So does Popescu, despite Martins's insistence that the porter saw a third man present at the scene of the accident, before Dr. Winkel arrived.

After Martins's interview with Popescu, there are two short scenes in the film which were not in the treatment and which help to add tension and mystery to what is happening. There is a long shot of Kurtz,

Popescu, and Winkel meeting for consultation on a bridge with another man whose back is to the camera. One guesses that this is the
third man of whom the porter spoke, and that they are discussing what
to do about the porter. This scene is followed by one in which the
porter comes to the window and whispers to Martins, as he passes by,
that if he will return later that evening he will be given further information. The porter then slams the window and turns around. There is
a close-up of the porter's face, horrified, accompanied by the sound of
footsteps advancing towards him from the next room, a foreshadowing
of his imminent death.

  The treatment gives no indication that the porter is to be murdered: Anna and Martins return to see him and discover, only on their

London Films Productions

THE THIRD MAN (London Films
Productions, 1949). Joseph Cotten,
trying to find out about the
death of his boyhood friend in
postwar Vienna, thinks he has
just seen him, alive, in a dark
street.

arrival, that the porter is dead. That, in the film, the audience is tipped off that the porter is to be put out of the way is another example of Reed and Greene's opting for suspense over surprise, as they did in *The Fallen Idol*. In the film, we experience the suspense of knowing something sinister is going to happen to the porter, in a way that the reader of the treatment does not.

The film also wrings more suspense from the episode of the boy Hansl than the treatment did. In the treatment he points out Martins in the crowd outside Lime's apartment building, while the porter's body is being carried out of the house by the police. Hansl calls Martins a foreigner. Since many of the neighbors know that a foreigner had recently visited the porter making inquiries, some of them turn their gaze on Martins momentarily; but they do not take Hansl very seriously. In the film, Greene has developed this scene. Hansl not only recognizes Martins as *a* foreigner; but, because he actually saw Martins with the porter when he went to retrieve his ball, he is able to say that Martins is *the* foreigner whom he had seen talking to the porter before the latter was murdered. The faces in the crowd turn one by one towards Martins as Anna whispers to him, "They think you did it." The two begin walking hurriedly down the street, followed by some of the crowd; then they break into a run and finally elude their pursuers by disappearing into a movie theater.

These and other additions in the script which are calculated to increase the element of suspense in the film are very much in keeping with the suspenseful situations which Greene had already created in the treatment. A fine example of suspense that comes directly from the treatment occurs when Martins gets into a car which he thinks is a taxi and it takes him to an undesignated destination. Martins does not know whether he is under arrest on suspicion of the porter's murder, or whether he has been snatched by the racketeers for meddling in Harry's death. It turns out that he has finally been tracked down by Crabbit and hustled off to the Cultural Center for the lecture which he—and we—have completely forgotten about.

There follows a welcome bit of comic relief in which Martins, so preoccupied with more important considerations, gives one incongruous answer after another to the questions put to him by his earnest audience, although his replies seem quite sensible to him. For example, when he is asked to name the literary figure who has influenced him most, Martins causes general consternation by replying that it is Zane Grey, the author of an endless number of cowboy stories.

There is a tense moment injected into this otherwise humorous scene that is only hinted at in the treatment. There, someone asks if Martins is engaged on a new work, and he replies almost absentmindedly that he is writing a story called *The Third Man*. In the film, the question is put to Martins in a menacing tone of voice by Popescu, who has suddenly appeared in the audience. Martins accepts the challenge intended and responds that his new work is a murder story called *The Third Man* which is founded on fact. There is an edge on Popescu's voice that is noticeable to Martins, if not to the others in the auditorium, as he comments that it is dangerous for Martins to mix fiction and fact; he suggests that Martins would be wise to scrap the project. Martins says that he has no intention of doing so, and Popescu shrugs, saying, "A pity."

When Martins leaves the lecture hall Popescu and two of his henchmen are waiting for him, but he eludes them and seeks refuge at the International Police Headquarters. There Calloway takes the occasion to fill Martins in on the precise nature of the blackmarket activities in which Harry Limes was involved. Martins is shocked to learn that Harry was trafficking in penicillin and that he increased his profits by diluting the medicine with infectious elements to the point where those to whom it was given died, went insane, or had to have limbs amputated. Harry's involvement in the whole affair is carefully documented by photos, letters, and other items; and Martins is crushed under the weight of the evidence that his old friend had become a ruthless and inhumane criminal.

We have now reached the pivotal episode from which the original story evolved in Greene's imagination. Martins goes to see Anna to tell her what he has discovered about Harry. As they talk Martins pets the cat that is roaming about Anna's flat. The cat recoils from him and Anna explains, "He only liked Harry." The camera follows the cat over to the window, where it jumps over the sill and climbs down to the street below. Then it goes over to a dark doorway where a man's feet can be seen protruding. The cat licks one of the shoes.

By this time Martins has left Anna's apartment and is walking along the street. He suspects that there is someone in the same doorway and that he is being followed. Martins challenges the man to come out into the open. In a window above him someone draws back a curtain to look out and see what the commotion is about. For only a second a shaft of light falls across the doorway and reveals to Martins what the audience already suspects: it is Harry Lime. Once more the audience has been tipped off to what is going to happen before Martins, and again the resulting suspense has proven a more effective means of escalating the intensity of the scene than surprise would have been.

When Calloway hears what has happened, he exhumes the body buried in Harry Lime's grave. It is that of Joseph Harbin, who had been working as a double agent for Calloway as a member of Lime's gang until he was found out. Lime's fake death, therefore, served not only to make the police think he was out of the way, but also to provide an inconspicuous way of disposing of Harbin.

Martins arranges through Kurtz to meet Harry in an amusement park. The two take a ride on the ferris wheel, which has closed compartments, so that they can talk in private. Martins tries to stir Harry's sense of humanity by asking him if he has any guilt feelings about his victims, and Harry replies by pointing through the window of the car to the crowd below. He asks Martins how much pity he would feel if one of those dots moving about far below stopped moving forever: "If I said you can have £20,000 for every dot that stops, would you really, old man, tell me to keep my money—or would you calculate how many dots you could afford to spare?"

As they part Harry says to Martins, "When you make up your mind, send me a message—I'll meet you any place, any time, and when we do meet, old man, it's you I want to see, not the police. . . . And don't be so gloomy. . . . After all, it's not that awful—you know what the fellow said: In Italy for thirty years under the Borgias they had warfare, terror, murder, bloodshed—and they produced Michelangelo, Leonardo da Vinci, and the Renaissance. In Switzerland they had brotherly love, five hundred years of democracy and peace, and what did that produce? The cuckoo clock. So long, Holley."[10]

"The popular line of dialogue concerning Swiss cuckoo clocks," Greene has said, "was written into the script by Mr. Orson Welles." Because Greene has given Welles credit for that bit, the myth has

---

[10]Graham Greene, *The Third Man*. Modern Film Scripts. New York: Simon and Schuster, 1968; p. 114.

somehow grown up that Welles wrote his whole part; e.g., Peter Cowie
gives the story as fact in *Seventy Years of Cinema* in the course of his
treatment of *The Third Man*. Most of Harry Lime's dialogue, however,
has been taken over directly from the treatment. In point of fact,
Lime's lines in the film are closer to his speeches in the treatment
than those of any other character in the story. The only dialogue for
which Welles is surely responsible is the line for which Greene has
given him credit. That Welles did not write his own part, however,
in no way detracts from the superb way in which he plays it. Welles
radiates a clever charm and sinister fascination that makes us readily
understand how he has been able to manipulate Holley Martins for
his own advantage, from the time that they were at school together.

Calloway has made every effort to get Martins over his immature
illusions about Lime. In order to convince him that he should act as a
decoy for Lime's capture, Calloway takes Martins on a tour of a hospital where he can see the victims of Lime's penicillin racket. Pauline
Kael dislikes the hospital scene (which was not in the treatment) because in her view it underlines more than it should the social message
of the film. "The ghastly hospital scene (which is based on facts) seems
a little unfair," she writes in *Kiss Kiss Bang Bang*. "We've been enjoying
all this decadence and stylish acting and these people living on their
nerves, and then we're forced to take evil seriously."[11]

On the contrary, Greene asks his audience to take evil seriously
throughout the film and not just in the hospital scene. *The Third Man*
is not a spy spoof in which the moral implications of the characters'
behavior can be disregarded. Greene rather develops his story in terms
of a moral dilemma. Holley Martins must decide if a man whom he
has admired since childhood is in reality a criminal who should be
turned over to the authorities. The search into Lime's past in which
Martins engages, then, becomes a moral investigation on Holley's part
to determine whether or not he should assist in Lime's capture.

On the other hand, although the story of the penicillin racket in
which Harry Lime was implicated was based on truth, Greene points
out that he used this reality only as a background for a fictional tale.
In general, he says, he and Reed did not want to make a film that might
in any way be thought to have a propagandist intent: "We had no de-

---

[11]Pauline Kael, *Kiss Kiss Bang Bang*. New York: Bantam Books, 1969; p. 13.

sire to move people's political emotions; we wanted to entertain them, to frighten them a little, to make them laugh." Hence neither the hospital scene nor any other sequence in the film is designed in such a soberingly realistic way that it takes the edge off the film's value as entertainment. For one thing, what Martins sees in the hospital is not depicted with any graphic detail. We see the reaction on Martins's face as he moves from bed to bed, but we never see the victims themselves. For another, the artistic indirection with which the whole scene is handled is evidenced by the final shot in which a nurse peers down on one child's bed, shakes her head mournfully, removes the chart from the end of the bed, and drops the teddy bear that had been on the bedpost into a box of toys on the floor. Here is poetic cinema at its best; for the film not only entertains but also—in Greene's use of the term *poetic cinema*—suggests human values as well.

After what Martins has seen in the hospital, he agrees to lure Harry to a café where Calloway can arrest him. In the treatment, Harry appears in the entrance to the café, but Martins does not point him out to Calloway. Sensing a trap, Lime dashes out of the doorway and runs down the street. If Martins would have called out then, Calloway remarks in the treatment, Lime would have been an easy shot; "but it was not, I suppose, Lime the penicillin racketeer who was escaping down the street; it was Harry."

In the film, this scene is handled differently. Anna comes to the café because Kurtz has told her that Harry is going to meet Martins there. Anna guesses that the rendezvous is a trap. As Harry enters the café it is she who cannot bear to see him captured, and she shouts to him to escape and he disappears. This is the only departure that the film makes from the treatment which I do not consider an improvement. To me, that Martins has not yet gotten his feelings for Harry out of system is a significant and illuminating demonstration of the reluctance with which human beings give up long cherished illusions. The point made in the corresponding scene in the film, that Harry's mistress does not want him caught, is less subtle and less thought-provoking.

The climax of the film is the pursuit of Lime through the sewers of Vienna. It is the perfect setting for the action: sinister shadows thrown by flashlights on the tunnel walls; the rushing waters and the footsteps echoing through the passages. Lime is wounded, but manages to pull himself up an iron stairway in order to try to escape to the street through a manhole. But he is too weak to dislodge the cover, and there is a memorable shot taken from the street level showing Lime's fingers reaching through the sewer grating in his vain attempt to do so.

Martins finds Harry struggling with the grille. Harry, who has lost his gun, stares painfully at Martins who still has one. Calloway and his men hear a shot echo through the darkness, and they turn a searchlight in that direction. Martins emerges into its beam sadly hanging his head. In the end, in spite of all of the reasons that Martins has to despise Harry, he has done him one last favor.

The final scene of the film is Harry's second and definitive funeral. One of the few major disputes which Greene and Reed had during the making of *The Third Man* revolved around this moment. The treatment ends with Martins going off from the cemetery, walking side by side with Anna. Reed wanted the film to end with Anna walking right by Martins and out of the cemetery without even looking at him. Greene argued that an entertainment like *The Third Man* "was too light an affair to carry the weight of an unhappy ending."

Reed held out for the downbeat finale, he has since said, because "a man and a woman don't always get together in life. I don't think you need a happy ending. I don't like to tie up things too neatly. Life isn't like that." Greene had further objected at the time that few people would wait during the girl's long walk from the graveside, "and that they would leave the cinema under the impression that the ending was as conventional as mine and more drawn out." But he now cheerfully admits that Reed was proven right in the end, for the ending, done Reed's way, is perfect. The combination of Valli's gaunt, determined face gazing straight ahead as she walks toward the camera, the bleak autumn landscape of the cemetery, and the mournful sound of the zither music coalesce to make the ending of the film very striking. "I had not given enough consideration to the mastery of Reed's direction," Greene concedes, "and at that stage, of course, we neither of us could have anticipated Reed's brilliant discovery of Mr. Karas, the zither player."[12]

Reed had discovered Karas playing in a café in Vienna which he had chosen for some location work, and decided to use a zither for the

[12]Greene, "Preface to *The Third Man*," *op. cit.*, pp. 9–10.

film's musical accompaniment. Karas's score adds immeasurably to the haunting mood of the film in a way that a full orchestra could never have done. The sound recordist, Barbara Hopkins, remembers that Reed had Karas virtually living in his home in London while the film was being scored. One day during a recording session at the studio, Reed was displeased with a passage that Karas was playing. The director told him that he wanted him to sound the way he had one evening when he had been playing under Reed's kitchen table. "He asked Karas to play under a table. Still not right. So Carol had his kitchen table brought to the studio. That's a man who knows what he wants," concludes Miss Hopkins.[13]

Greene attributes the extraordinary success of *The Third Man* at the box office in some part to the popularity of "The Third Man Theme" which Karas composed for the film. Greene says, "I indicated in the script that there should be a tune associated with Harry Lime," but of course neither Greene nor anyone else could have imagined that the music would become so popular in its own right. For his part, Reed explains the success of the film by saying that it was one of the first British films to be shot almost entirely on location instead of in the insulated atmosphere of a studio. In this way, Reed was able to capture, with the help of Robert Krasker's Academy Award-winning photography, the brooding, corrupt atmosphere of a ruined post-war city. As Pauline Kael puts it in *Kiss Kiss Bang Bang*, the film showed us how war had changed the survivors, made them "tired, ravaged opportunists." The city took on a strong presence of its own in the foreground of the film, and the simple American who stumbled into it was like a tourist in hell, while all the time "the melancholy twang of the zither brought evil seductively close."

To the music and setting, one must surely add Welles's stunning performance as Harry Lime as one of the elements that made *The Third*

[13]Quoted in Robert Emmett Ginna, "*Our Man in Havana,*" *Horizon*, II (November, 1959), p. 38.

THE THIRD MAN (London Films Productions, 1949). Orson Welles during the climactic chase through the sewers of Vienna. This was the most successful screen adaption of a work by Greene.

London Films Productions

Man an outstanding film. Welles, with his suave and evil charm, so dominates the few scenes in which he appears, that one seems to remember him as having had a larger part than he actually did. Brought to life by Welles, Harry Lime walked straight into cinema's mythology, Penelope Houston has written, "on the strength of a line of dialogue about Switzerland and cuckoo clocks and a shot of a hand clutching at a sewer grating."[14]

We must not pass over the uniformly fine playing of Joseph Cotten, Alida Valli, and Trevor Howard. All stand out as individuals, although each has perfectly attuned his respective role to the needs of the film as a whole, so that it becomes part of the total tapestry. All in all, *The Third Man* is a masterpiece: that happy coming together of a fine story and script, realized by a sympathetic director, who has caught the flavor of the story and inspired his cast to generate the kind of dramatic excitement that fascinates an audience.

The Third Man represents the peak of the cinematic careers of both Greene the scriptwriter and Reed the director. Hence, to say that their third collaboration, *Our Man in Havana* (1959) is not as artistically successful is but to recognize that it suffers only by comparison with the standard that Greene and Reed had set for themselves by their previous achievements.

Our Man in Havana first took shape as a novel in Greene's mind shortly after the end of the Second World War, when Alberto Cavalcanti, who had directed *Went the Day Well?*, asked Greene to create a film script for him. Greene got the idea of writing a comedy about the secret service, based on what he had learned while employed by the British Foreign Office in intelligence work in West Africa during the war. In those days, some German agents working in Lisbon came to Greene's attention. They were sending back to Germany "completely erroneous reports based on information received from imaginary agents," Greene records in his introduction to *Our Man in Havana*. "It was a paying game, especially when expenses and bonuses were added to the cypher's salary," and Greene was sometimes tempted to play a similar game with his own superiors in London.[15]

---

[14]Penelope Houston, *Contemporary Cinema*. Baltimore: Penguin Books, 1969; p. 38.

[15]Graham Greene, "Introduction," *Our Man in Havana*, in the Collected Edition. London: The Bodley Head, 1970; p. vii.

"I had learned that nothing pleased the services at home more than the addition of a card to their intelligence files," Greene continues. For example, one agent in the pay of the British government reported to him that a building on a Vichy airfield in French Guinea housed an army tank. Greene sent the report to London with a notation about the unreliability of the agent in question and added that he personally had reason to believe that the building was really a storehouse for old boots. "I was surprised when I earned a rating for his report of 'most valuable,'" Greene concludes. "Somebody in an office in London had been enabled to add a line or two to an otherwise blank card—that was the only explanation."[16]

Greene's wartime sojurn in West Africa was the occasion of his writing *The Ministry of Fear*, which he did in his spare time while he was there, and later provided the setting for *The Heart of the Matter*, which he wrote after the war. But at the time he wrote both of these novels, Greene was still too close to his experiences there to see their humorous aspects. Later, when the plot of *Our Man in Havana* began to take shape in his imagination, Greene began to look back on his experiences in wartime intelligence work with a more satirical eye. In "The Soupsweet Land," which brings his *Collected Essays* to a close, Greene reminisces that on his arrival in Freetown he was taken aside by a British officer and melodramatically told that his "cover" was to be that of an inspector of the D.O.T. (Department of Overseas Trade). But D.O.T. had second thoughts about Greene's masquerading as one of its inspectors while he was working for the Secret Service. Instead, Greene was given a spurious and vague attachment to the local police force, which was difficult for Greene to explain to those people whom he had already told that he was an inspector for D.O.T. "The whole of my life in Freetown had the same unreality," Greene goes on, and he remembers writing to the Colonial Secretary toward the end of his career as an intelligence agent that "in the annals of Freetown my name like Keats's would be writ in water."[17]

Greene was known as agent 59200, the same code number that he was to assign to James Wormold, the hero of *Our Man in Havana*.

[16]*Ibid.*, pp. vii–viii.

[17]Graham Greene, "The Soupsweet Land," *Collected Essays*. Harmondsworth: Penguin Books, 1970; p. 341.

Like Greene, Wormold would also be instructed to communicate with London by means of a book code. As the basis of his code Greene chose a novel of T. F. Powys, "from which I could detach sufficiently lubricious phrases for my own amusement." He began his inauspicious career as an intelligence agent by solemnly locking his code books in his newly acquired safe and then realizing that he did not possess the correct combination with which to reopen the safe. In a maneuver worthy of Wormold's inept resourcefulness, Greene reported to London that the safe had been damaged in transit, and his superiors obligingly sent him another one. In the meantime, Greene extricated his code books from the first safe with a blowtorch.[18] Greene confesses that he has never been astute with mechanical equipment of any kind. For example, when he was in training for his work in West Africa, he says, the commander of the intelligence course "had to abandon the idea that I would ever be able to learn to ride a motorcycle."[19]

With these hilarious real-life episodes behind him, it is no wonder that the spy story that Greene was developing for Cavalcanti was taking on a satirical tone. "The first version was an outline written on a single sheet of paper," says Greene. The story was set in 1938 in Tallinn, the capital of Esthonia. The British agent there was an alcoholic, whose wife led him to cheat in his intelligence reports because of her extravagance. Enemy agents took his spurious reports more and more seriously, however, with the approach of war. Cavalcanti submitted this story outline to the British censor and was told that no certificate of approval could be issued to a film that satirized the Secret Service. "At least that was the story he told me," comments Greene, who suspects that perhaps the plot was not developing in a fashion that the director found promising.[20]

The story remained dormant in Greene's mind for another decade. During this period Greene made several trips to Havana which led him to realize that he had been "planning the wrong situation and placing it in the wrong period." To begin with, "the shadows of the war to come in 1938 were too dark for comedy"; the reader would not

[18]*Ibid.*, pp. 341–42.

[19]Graham Greene, "Introduction," *The Confidential Agent*, in the Collected Edition. London: The Bodley Head, 1971; p. x.

[20]Greene, "Introduction," *Our Man in Havana, op. cit.*, p. viii.

sympathize with a man who was cheating his country in the struggle against Hitler because of an extravagant wife. "But in fantastic Havana, among the absurdities of the Cold War . . . there was a situation allowably comic, all the more if I changed the wife into a daughter."[21]

In the pre-Castro days of the dictator Batista, Havana was a decadent city which no doubt reminded Greene of post-war Vienna. He made every effort to get to know the city and its people, so that he could present his story against the background of the dying days of the Batista regime in an authentic manner. At one point, he even got involved briefly with smuggling, from Havana to a Castro agent in Santiago, clothing badly needed by Castro's guerillas in the mountains. When he met the agent in Santiago, the fear which both of them harbored that the other was really a Batista spy precipitated what Greene calls "a comedy of errors as absurd as anything I described in *Our Man in Havana*."

During this and subsequent stays in Cuba, Greene found the Civil War moving more and more decisively in Castro's favor. Yet, up until the time Castro was preparing to enter Havana, the British Government seemed officially unaware that a Civil War was in progress in Cuba, and continued to support Batista. By the time that Greene finished his novel, therefore, he had no regrets about the satirical tone of his book: "It seemed to me that either the Foreign Office or the Intelligence Services had amply merited ridicule."[22]

Our Man in Havana proved a disappointment to Castro's supporters, however, because they felt that its comic style tended to minimize the terrors of Batista's rule. "I had not wanted too black a background for a light-hearted comedy," Greene explains. Those who suffered under Batista quite understandably failed to realize that the real subject of this entertainment was the satire of the British Secret Service and not the justice of the revolution.

The book is nonetheless firmly rooted in reality, even though it is basically a comedy. Many of the characters were suggested by people that Greene had known in his own spy work in West Africa or had met in Cuba or elsewhere. The character of Hawthorne, the elegant British spy, for example, owes something to an officer who was

[21] *Ibid.*, p. ix.
[22] *Ibid.*, p. xviii.

at one time Greene's immediate superior in West Africa. Hasselbacher, the retired German doctor, is built on a Baron Schacht whom Greene once knew in Capri. Schacht was "a big, sad, gentle man" who had lived there since the end of the First World War, in which he had proudly served the Kaiser.

Even the instruction to Wormold that he use bird droppings when invisible ink is in short supply was suggested by a similar directive which Greene himself had once received. In Freetown, Greene recalls, "vultures were the most common bird—there were usually three or four on my tin roof—but I doubt whether their droppings had been contemplated."[23] This mild flavor of madness permeates most of *Our Man in Havana*. Even the religious element in the novel is lighthearted. Wormold's wife had insisted that their daughter Milly be raised a Roman Catholic, though she had already abandoned the Faith and later abandoned Wormold and the girl. Wormold has no religious creed, but he still continues to respect the Faith that Millie has grown up with; and Millie is not above taking advantage of this fact to get her way. She begs her father for a horse of her own and shrewdly tells him that she has made two novenas for this intention. She fears that she will lose her belief in the efficacy of novenas if she does not get her wish, she says. But since Wormold's vacuum cleaner business is not prospering, he cannot afford the horse.

It is just about this time that Wormold is accosted by Hawthorne with an offer to serve England as a spy. Seeing a way to secure the money for Millie's horse, Wormold agrees and immediately asks for a cash allowance. He also requests that Hawthorne requisition money to enroll him as a member of the local country club—ostensibly in order that he can make valuable contacts, but in reality so that Milly will have a place to keep her new plaything. Hawthorne is delighted to add Wormold's name to the list of his agents, for he can now refer to him in reports as "our man in Havana."

Unfortunately, Wormold has no information to offer in return for the money he withdraws to support his extravagant daughter. His old friend Hasselbacher therefore suggests that Wormold mollify Hawthorne by devising his own secret information. "As long as you lie you do no harm," he says to Wormold. Wormold arbitrarily selects

[23]Greene, "The Soupsweet Land," *loc. cit.*, p. 341.

names from the list of country club members and submits them to his superiors as his informants. Those named include an engineer named Cifuentes and a Professor Luis Sanchez. For good measure, Wormold later adds Raul, an airline pilot, and Teresa, a stripper at the Shanghai Club.

He then begins concocting periodic reports from these agents and dutifully sends them off to London through Hawthorne, using Lamb's *Tales from Shakespeare* as the basis of his book code. Wormold is particularly proud of his idea to transmit to London a touched-up version of the plans of one of the vacuum cleaners which he sells, in the guise of a secret weapon which he purports to have discovered.

The first indication that Wormold gets that someone besides Hawthorne is taking his reports seriously occurs when Hasselbacher's apartment is savagely searched, apparently because he is a friend. The real reason is even more sinister: Hasselbacher is being blackmailed by counterspies who use these tactics as a renewed threat to force him to coöperate with them in putting a stop to Wormold's activities. As Hasselbacher surveys his ruined apartment, he sits down on a chair which gives way beneath his considerable bulk and sends him crashing to the floor. "Someone always leaves a banana skin on the scene of a tragedy," Wormold reflects. Developing this remark, Greene says, "There is a delicate line between tragedy and farce and they go well together; although tragedy and comedy do not. The man who slips and falls on a banana peel—that's farcical. But when he lands it hurts, and he may be close to real tragedy."[24] Hasselbacher, in fact, *is* close to tragedy, for it was he who suggested that Wormold fabricate his reports in the first place, and now is forced to take them seriously.

Wormold's suspicion that Hasselbacher is somehow working against him is aroused by Beatrice Severn, who has been sent from London to be his assistant. In Hasselbacher's apartment, she notices a copy of the same edition of Lamb's *Tales* that Wormold is using for his book code. But Wormold is not really shocked into realizing that the game has gone serious until a Cubana Airlines pilot named Raul is killed in an auto wreck. The "accident" occurred, Wormold realizes, just before Raul was scheduled, according to one of Wormold's fictitious reports, to go on a reconnaissance mission over the site where

[24]"Greene, 'the Funny Writer,' on Comedy," *Life* (January 23, 1970), p. 10.

the secret weapon is supposedly being built. Later, Dr. Cifuentes is likewise ambushed, but escapes with his life.

The introduction of this somber note into an otherwise satirical and light-hearted tale has bothered critics of both the novel and the film. In his book on Greene, David Pryce-Jones defends Greene on this point by arguing that the melodrama is secondary to the farce, "for it is only the most tenuous and indirect thread of imaginative fantasy"[25] that connects Wormold to the violence that he has unwittingly initiated. Greene himself feels that he has not provided too dark a background for his comedy: "It is really a grey comedy, not a black comedy," he said to me. When I insisted that one does feel a bit uneasy about taking the whole story as a lark, once real violence and death enter the picture, he thought for a moment and then replied, "Perhaps in some ways it is a black comedy after all."

I shall return to this point again, but suffice it to say at the moment that Greene did take some pains to keep his comedy from turning too serious. For example, he refashioned the ruthless chief of Batista's secret police, Captain Ventura, into the much less menacing figure of Captain Segura, in order to keep the novel from seeming to be principally an indictment of dictatorship. In other ways too Greene has sought to maintain the atmosphere of a comedy of errors. Very much in this spirit is the uproarious scene in which Wormold and Beatrice visit the notorious Shanghai Theater in an effort to warn Teresa that she is thought to be the Mata Hari of his spy ring, and hence may be in for trouble. Running true to form, Wormold causes a near riot backstage when Teresa misunderstands his intent and thinks he is trying to kidnap her for some unspeakable purpose.

The upshot is that Wormold is arrested and brought to police headquarters for questioning by Segura. Segura, it develops, has had Hasselbacher's telephone tapped, and he plays a tape for Wormold on which Hasselbacher is instructed by a voice with a stutter to inform Wormold of Raul's death. Wormold goes to confront Hasselbacher about this, and finds him dressed in his old officer's uniform, toasting the Kaiser's birthday. Greene owes to Baron Schacht this pathetic picture of a fat old man donning regalia that is too small for him, in order to recall past glories. Greene remembers the baron observing the

[25]David Pryce-Jones, *Graham Greene*. New York: Barnes and Noble, 1967; p. 73.

OUR MAN IN HAVANA
(Columbia Pictures, 1959). Bottles of liquor are the chessmen in this game, and each piece taken must be drunk immediately. Sir Alec Guinness (right) moves to overcome the Chief of Police (Ernie Kovacs) so that he can steal his gun to kill an enemy agent.

Kaiser's birthday in this way every year. When Baron Schacht died, Greene persuaded the police to put his helmet and white golves on his coffin as a small tribute to the old soldier; and Wormold does the same for Hasselbacher, after the latter is murdered for warning Wormold that there is to be an attempt on his life.

The rival agents plan to poison Wormold at a business luncheon to which he has been invited as principal speaker. Greene's masterful handling of suspense is evident in this episode as Wormold tries to avoid taking glasses and plates meant for him. The climax of the scene comes when Carter, a friendly fellow Englishman, offers Wormold a drink from his flask—and stutters while doing so. Wormold deliberately spills the liquor on the floor, where it is lapped up by a dog who promptly limps off yelping, and dies.

The story then takes a chilling turn when Wormold gets Segura drunk and steals his revolver. He then lures Carter out for a night on the town in order to shoot him in some dark street. Greene's earlier, more serious entertainments come to mind as we watch Wormold steel himself against the temptation to feel pity for Carter while he is busy maneuvering him into a defenseless position so that he can kill him. It is at this point, more than at any other, that I think the tint of the comedy darkens from grey to black. By the time Wormold is ready to shoot him, we see Carter as a sad little man, not unlike Wormold himself, who has gotten more deeply involved in an intrigue than perhaps he had bargained for. As they talk Wormold realizes that with every passing second Carter is becoming more human, "a creature like one's self whom one might pity or console, not kill." Carter is becoming more human to the reader too, and therefore one cannot take his death casually, as just another incident in a melodrama, when Wormold finally shoots him.

The farcical mood is soon restored, however, when the scene shifts to the London headquarters of the Secret Service. Wormold's superiors decide to decorate Wormold for his gallant exploits rather than admit that they have been taken in by his schemes. A happy ending is even in the offing since it seems that Wormold and Beatrice have fallen in love and will probably marry. It is not often that Greene's hero and heroine live happily ever after, and it is refreshing to think that Wormold and Beatrice will—in their own unpredicatable way.

Almost immediately after *Our Man in Havana* was published, Greene was commissioned to write the script for the film version. In October, 1958, he and Carol Reed went to Havana to choose locations. "I was worried about how the old regime would react to the nasty suggestions about them in the book," Reed later told Robert Ginna while the film was in production; "but Graham said, 'Don't worry, they'll be all washed up by the time we're ready to come back here for production'"[26] And that is exactly what happened.

Sir Alec Guinness, who has played in *Our Man in Havana* and *The*

[26]Quoted in Ginna, *op. cit.*, p. 31.

Comedians, has told me that he has always admired Graham Greene's understanding of world problems. "Take any of the world's trouble spots from Cuba, the setting of *Our Man in Havana*, to Haiti, the setting of *The Comedians*," he says, "and you will find that Greene has been there two or three years beforehand and accurately dealt with the tensions there through the medium of the novel. I have often said jokingly that when I hear that Graham is going off to visit some part of the globe that I will avoid that place like the plague because that means that a revolution or a war is bound to break out there soon."

After Reed and Greene had decided upon locations for *Our Man in Havana*, they went to Brighton for five weeks, occupying a hotel suite of two bedrooms, with a sitting room between for a secretary. "I would write from 8 a.m. to 7 p.m.," Greene remembers, "and pass my material through the secretary to Carol. Then we would discuss matters at lunch time over beer and sandwiches." Afterward, they went on to Cadiz in Spain, which has something of the atmosphere of Havana, to complete the final version of the script.

Reed believes in totally immersing himself in his film while he is making it. He follows it through every stage of production in order to get the feel of the whole: "After you've been shooting a while and looking at rushes as you go, you begin to see the picture taking shape, establishing a rhythm of its own. That's when you begin to feel the picture's natural pace and you develop it. You can then work with the actors to mold and shape it."[27]

Reed had an exceptionally good cast with which to work in making *Our Man in Havana*, including Maureen O'Hara as Beatrice, Ralph Richardson as "C," the London Secret Service chief, Noel Coward as Hawthorne, and Alec Guinness as Wormold. Reed wanted a strong cast to balance Alec Guinness's portrayal of Wormold: "A star like Guinness is apt to stand out from the people around him by the subtle things he does," Reed said at the time. "Now, in the film, the character he plays is a plain man. It is important that he should not stand out." Alec Guinness recalls that he did not entirely agree with Carol Reed's idea of how he should play Wormold: "I felt that I should have been playing Wormold as a much more clearly defined character, an untidy, defeated sort of man, the kind of person you would see in London with

[27] *Ibid.*

the *New Statesman and Nation* sticking out of his back pocket. But Sir Carol Reed wanted me to play it straight. I did not go along completely with the concept of a central character who was a blank, surrounded by subordinate characters who were more strongly portrayed than he was. At any rate, I don't think that I ever quite caught the character of Wormold in the film." Regardless of differences which Reed and Guinness may have had, however, Guinness's performance is a perfect bringing-to-life of Greene's character.

In general the film stays very close to the novel, for Greene has managed to get most of his original story into the script. Often a kind of cinematic shorthand is employed to get impressions over to the viewer quickly and neatly. For example the oppressive atmosphere of the Batista dictatorship is established in the very beginning of the film by showing a man who has just spit on Segura's passing car, being dragged away by two policemen to be beaten. The eccentric pseudo-sophistication of Hawthorne is telegraphed to the viewer the first time he appears by the grand manner in which he brushes aside a small group of street musicians who follow him in the hope of a tip.

The transitions in the film from one scene to the next are often remarkably cinematic and smooth. When Milly shows Wormold a saddle and harness which she has purchased on credit, he looks rue-fully toward the bathroom and asks, "Where's the horse?" In the novel Milly tells him that it is at the country club, waiting to be bought. In the film, as soon as Wormold asks the question, we hear a horse whinny as we cut immediately to the country club paddock, where Milly and her father are inspecting the horse. (For a split second we think the horse *is* in the bathroom!)

Some of the scenes in the novel work even better on the screen than they did in the book. Hawthorne meets Wormold in a bar and slyly tells him to retire to the men's room where they can discuss the possibility of Wormold's working for British Intelligence. In the midst of their discussion someone enters the rest room and Wormold is forced to hide in a stall until the third party leaves. In the novel the party is no one in particular; in the film it is a police officer. The latter's presence brings an additional element of comedy to the scene, since Wormold fears that the policeman will suspect that a homo-sexual assignation is in progress and will arrest them both. Moreover, Wormold's scrambling in and out of the stall also helps to set the absurd tone that will characterize his career as a spy.

As for the dialogue in the film, Greene has often trimmed down and rearranged lines taken directly from the novel, as well as written new speeches and exchanges. This is not a departure from Greene's view that the dialogue in a novel is not usually suitable for use in a film. Many of the speeches in the novel were too long and intricate to be spoken on the screen; but once Greene honed them down they became quite serviceable as screen dialogue. There are the lines in the novel, for example, in which Wormold expresses his view that life should not be taken too seriously. He reminds Milly of a clown they once saw in a circus, who walked off a ladder every night and fell into the same bucket of whitewash. If everyone was a clown, he says, nothing bad would happen to anyone except a few bruises and a smear of whitewash: "Don't learn for experience, Milly. It ruins our peace and our lives." After all, Wormold concludes, if God learned from experience he would not continue to hope anything from mankind. In three short lines of screen dialogue Greene has preserved the essence of Wormold's speech in the novel and made it a more provocative remark. In the movie, Wormold asks Milly if she remembers the clown at the circus and she responds, "The one who fell off the tightrope into the bucket of whitewash?" "We should all be clowns," he says in return.

The making of a novel into a motion picture demands addition as well as subtraction. The scriptwriter may choose to expand an incident only referred to in a novel, because of its potential dramatic values. Greene has developed one such incident from the novel of *Our Man in Havana* by using it as a point of departure for a couple of delightful short scenes. In the novel Wormold sits down with the names of the country club members and draws up a list of those he will say he has recruited as spies. In the film we actually see Wormold trying to lure the engineer Cifuentes into the men's room of the country club lounge in keeping with the way that Hawthorne enlisted him. But Cifuentes gets the idea that Wormold is making a homosexual advance and storms out of the room. Wormold has once more proved his infinite ineptitude in a very humorous way. This little scene is quite in keeping with Greene's original vision of Wormold in the novel. "The funniness in *Our Man in Havana* always comes from the situation rather than the man," says Greene. "He is a sad man intrinsically. One of the failures whom I like."

Like most men who are failures, his successes usually come in

daydreams. In the novel, Wormold merely records that he has recruited Teresa the stripper. In the film, we see him on one side of the
wide screen typing out his report and hear him say over the sound
track that he has secured the services of a popular actress, while the
rest of the screen is filled with a brief fantasy sequence, in which Wormold pictures himself as a cavalier lover who has captivated Teresa.

One of the key scenes in both the novel and the movie is that in
which Wormold gives a birthday party for his daughter in a nightclub, during the course of which Wormold—and the audience—gets
the first hint that Hasselbacher is working against him. As Greene
wrote it in the script, Wormold makes a reference to Shakespeare and
Milly volunteers the information that her father reads Lamb's *Tales
from Shakespeare* rather than the genuine article. Hasselbacher (Burl
Ives) is visibly startled, as Wormold notices. Robert Ginna, who was
present on the set when this scene was shot, records that at this point
Reed decided that Hasselbacher's reaction should be more obvious so
that the audience would not miss its implication. To this end, Reed
had Hasselbacher rather than Milly identify Wormold's reference, as
an indication that he has lately been boning up on his Shakespeare.[28]

This is a minor addition indeed, but it serves to show that no
matter how carefully a script is worked out in advance, a creative
director can contribute some refinements to the dialogue or action
when the scene is actually before the camera on the studio floor.
Greene in fact says that he counts on the director's intuition, since
the screenwriter cannot foresee everything, and that a script should
always be flexible enough to allow for the inspiration of the moment.

By the same token Reed tried to think of subtle ways of making
the shift of a mood in the story from farce to melodrama as smooth
as possible. "I didn't play Wormold any differently in the latter part
of the film than I did in the earlier part," says Alec Guinness. "It was
Carol Reed who created the sinister atmosphere needed in the last
part of the film." During shooting Reed had said, "Yes, the story
becomes melodrama toward the end. I think we have time to develop
our characters and to bring the audience along, finally giving them
melodrama." Reed went on to say that he was utilizing various cinematic techniques to help create this change in mood: "At the beginning
I feel we should light our sets for comedy. That is, rather brightly

and flatly, catching the beauty of the streets too. Then, as the picture moves toward melodrama, we will shoot with a wide angle lens, getting the effect of the walls closing in. We will use sharp hard lights in the night exteriors, making the streets slick and shiny, getting a brittle black-and-white feeling."[29]

Reed did accomplish this variation of lighting very well. The scene in which Wormold traps and kills Carter is lighted in a murky manner that is quite suitable to the melodramatic action. Greene had already set the tense tone of this sequence by having Carter surreptitiously tip one of his henchmen off to follow him and Wormold in order to try to kill the latter—something which did not happen in the novel. Nevertheless the change from a farcical to a more serious mood still jars the viewer. I disagreed with Pauline Kael when she said that it is unfair to ask the audience to take evil seriously toward the end of *The Third Man*, because that film implicitly asks us to take evil seriously throughout. However, when Miss Kael registers the same complaint about the film of *Our Man in Havana*, she has more of a case.

She writes in *Kiss Kiss Bang Bang* that the film loses its "insanity and exuberance" as it goes on, becoming "too gravely straight-faced" and "low-keyed." This is not to say that there is no room for serious melodramatic elements in a farce, but rather that they should not be allowed to infringe on what Greene himself has called the "fairy tale" quality of his delightfully improbable story. For example the scene in which Wormold shoots Carter would be quite acceptable in a farce, were it not for the fact that Carter is allowed to plead for his life. This is somewhat unsettling for the viewer, whose sympathies should be with Wormold, especially since in the film Carter has arranged to have Wormold killed.

The balance between comedy and melodrama is a difficult one to keep, and if Greene and Reed have failed to maintain it in some individual scenes of *Our Man in Havana*, the over-all effect of the film, as of the novel, is that of an entertaining spy-spoof. It is clear from Greene's latest entertainment, *Travels with My Aunt*, published in 1970, that he has profited by his experience with *Our Man in Havana*, for in *Travels* the comic muse is always in the ascendant although the story also has its share of melodrama.

The lightest story that Greene has ever written is *Loser Takes All*.

[29]*Ibid.*, p. 122.

Written in 1954, it was filmed in 1956 by producer John Stafford, who was to bring "Across the Bridge" to the screen the following year. In its fictional form *Loser Takes All* is, like *The Third Man*, the treatment from which Greene developed his script for the film. Greene calls it a "frivolity," and it is really of slight importance either as a novella or as a motion picture, so I shall not dwell on it long.

Bertram, a middle-aged accountant, tells his boss, Mr. Dreuther, that he is going to be married on his upcoming vacation to Cary, a younger woman. Dreuther, who is called Gom by his employees (for Grand Old Man), suggests that the wedding take place at Monte Carlo. The couple is to precede him there, with the wedding to follow his arrival on his yacht. When Dreuther does not arrive as scheduled, Bertram is forced to spend the interim gambling in order to pay for accomodations for himself and Cary.

In the course of his gambling Bertram puts his background as an accountant to work and develops a system whereby he is able to win huge sums of money at the gaming tables. After only a few days, he is in a position to buy out the company of which he has been an employee for so many years. This upsets Cary, who tells him that he has become obsessed with money and power. She then takes up with Phillippe, a handsome gambler, to spite Bertram. By this time, Dreuther's yacht has glided into port and Bertram confides to him that he is in danger of losing Cary. Dreuther tells Bertram how to go about winning her back.

On Dreuther's instructions, Bertram offers Phillippe some of his winnings so that he can have a chance to prove his own system for breaking the bank at Monte Carlo. Phillippe snaps up the offer, and in so doing discredits himself in Cary's eyes, for he is obviously just as avaricious as Bertram had been. Bertram's stock with Cary rises still higher when he gives up his chance to take over his old company, and Druether responds by making him chief accountant. They all sail off together in the yacht as the story ends.

Attempts have been made by literary critics to uncover serious symbolic significance in this little situation comedy, in the light of Greene's other work; but it seems pointless to pretend that the story is any more than the frivolity that Greene says it is. In my interview with Sir Hugh Greene, the writer's brother, Sir Hugh remarked on this point, "Graham is a magnificent storyteller, and some critics are not satisfied with a good story; they are always trying to read deep allegorical significances into his stories even when they are not there. Graham is more down to earth than some critics will allow." Graham Greene himself seems to be getting his own back at such critics by introducing some specious religious asides into *Loser Takes All*, as when Bertram says that no machine is perfect: "in every join, rivet, screw lies original sin." At another point Bertram says that he and the others who are engaged in working out a system to win at gambling are like "theologians patiently trying to rationalize a mystery." One can hardly take seriously a story that quite rightly treats itself so casually.

J. Arthur Rank Productions, Ltd.

LOSER TAKES ALL (J. Arthur Rank Productions, 1956). Rossano Brazzi (right) was miscast as an accountant who has lost his wife because of his success as a gambler. He discusses getting her back with his employer (Robert Morley), aboard the latter's yacht.

Greene found the film, which, like *The Stranger's Hand*, he co-produced, a total disaster. "We lost the director we wanted and Alec Guinness wasn't available to play Bertram. It was hopelessly miscast, and I wanted to drop the whole project, but the producer had already invested money in it, so we had to go ahead. Instead of a light comedy the film became a rather heavy piece." The casting of Robert Morley as Dreuther and of Glynis Johns as Cary was in keeping with their customary screen images, but Rossano Brazzi could never prove an acceptable substitute for Alec Guinness, and it is probably Brazzi that Greene principally had in mind when he spoke of his disappointment with the casting. Even with his hair powdered to grey and with leather patches at the elbows of his jacket, Brazzi is unconvincing as a middle-aging accountant.

At the time *Loser Takes All* was made, wide-screen films were still something of a novelty, and they often included a "travelogue" sequence intended to take full advantage of the wide-screen format. *Loser Takes All* is no exception to this rule. There is an interlude in which Cary and Bertram spend a day in the country, which seems to have no other function than to show off the French background in wide screen and color. Otherwise, as one critic quipped, the only imaginative use that the director made of the wide screen was "to show Robert Morley stretched full-length on a rococo settee."

Hence *Loser Takes All* simply does not belong in the same class with the three entertainments which Greene adapted for the screen in collaboration with Carol Reed. Taken together, these represent the peak of Greene's achievement in cinema. Greene admits to having been spoiled by their success, both artistic and popular. After writing scripts for Reed, he says, "I began to believe that I was learning the craft, but it was an illusion. No craft had been learnt, there had only been the luck of working with a fine director who could control his actors and production."

Needless to say, Greene is being much too modest in writing off his accomplishments as a screenwriter in this fashion. One has only to compare the screenplays of his serious fiction which he has done himself with those that have been done by other screenwriters, to see that the former, as much as the scripts he wrote from his entertainments, are the work of a craftsman. Let us go on, then, to the films adapted from Greene's serious fiction.

THE COMEDIANS

THE FUGITIVE

Metro-Goldwyn-Mayer

R.K.O. Radio Pictures

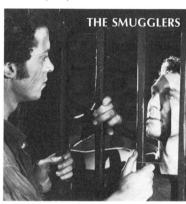

THE SMUGGLERS

THE HEART OF THE MATTER

J. Arthur Rank Productions, Ltd.

London Film Productions

THE END OF THE AFFAIR

BRIGHTON ROCK

Columbia Pictures

Associated British Picture Corporation

THE QUIET AMERICAN

PART TWO:
THE FILMS
OF GREENE'S
SERIOUS FICTION

4

THE MAN WITHIN: ADAPTATIONS OF GREENE'S SERIOUS FICTION BY OTHER SCREENWRITERS

Movie makers must have been wary of tackling Greene's serious fiction. Film versions of his entertainments were being turned out for more than a decade before the first motion picture of one of Greene's serious novels was attempted. Perhaps the studios realized that in filming any of the latter, they would be confronted with the problem of dealing in cinematic terms with the provocative ideas of these stories as well as with the stories themselves.

Although Greene does treat political and religious issues in his entertainments, they admittedly play a secondary role; hence film makers tended to ignore the thematic implications of the entertainments when committing them to film—except, of course, for the instances where Greene himself did the script, as we saw in the previous chapter. But in Greene's serious novels, the social and religious issues around which the plot revolves are so integral to the plot that they can hardly be excluded from the screenplay.

For example, in both *A Gun for Sale* and *Brighton Rock*, Greene makes reference to the religious upbringing of the hero. In *Brighton Rock* the religious attitudes which Pinkie drew from his childhood so dominate his thinking as an adult, that to have omitted this dimension of his character from the screenplay would have undercut the meaning of the whole story. In contrast, Raven's background was in fact left out of *This Gun for Hire*, the film version of *A Gun for Sale*, without doing substantial harm to the movie, although the omission does to some degree oversimplify Raven's character.

The vision that emerges from Greene's serious fiction is basically a religious one, even in the case of those novels, like *The Quiet American*, that Greene considers primarily political in tone. And whenever the films of Greene's serious fiction succeed in embodying Greene's vision, they come close to verifying Greene's concept of poetic cinema as I described it in the first chapter. For, the religious dimension of these novels reminds us of life as it ought to be, while the story itself is showing us life as it is.

Before examining Greene's religious vision as it is reflected in his fiction and in the films made from it, we must first see how that vision developed in the first place. Greene recalls in his essay "The Lost Childhood" that he became dissatisfied with the unreal view of life that he had gained from reading adventure stories by the time he was fourteen, since one could hardly identify with the near-perfect heroes who peopled their pages. Then, one day, he picked up Marjorie Bowen's novel *The Viper of Milan*, and found characters who, because they possessed human weaknesses, were much more true to life. "Goodness had only once found a perfect incarnation in a human body and never will again, but evil can always find a home there," Greene reflected. "Human nature is not black and white but black and grey." He looked around, he says, and saw that it was so.[1]

As he grew older, Greene continued to search for a vision of life that he could live by. At Oxford, he became interested in Roman Catholicism at the time he became engaged to Vivien Dayrell-Browning. "Since I was going to marry a Catholic girl I determined to learn about Catholicism," Greene explains. After Oxford he got a job on a newspaper in Nottingham, and while working there took instructions from Father Trollope, "a fat priest who had once been an actor." They would take tram rides together throughout the city, while they dis-

[1]Graham Greene, "The Lost Childhood," *Collected Essays*. Harmondsworth: Penguin Books, 1970; pp. 16-17.

cussed the beliefs of the Catholic religion, and Greene felt that he was
travelling into a new country: "One began to have a dim conception of
the appalling mysteries of love moving through a ravaged world."
This went on for three months while Greene developed what he calls
"an intellectual if not an emotional belief in Catholic dogma."[2]

Then, in February, 1926, at the age of twenty-two, Greene was
baptized a Roman Catholic "one foggy afternoon about four o'clock"
in Nottingham Cathedral, "a dark place full of inferior statues." Father
Trollope performed the rite, and the only witness to his baptism was a
woman who had been dusting the chairs. "It was all very quickly and
formally done," he recalls. "Then we shook hands and I went off. . . .
I couldn't help feeling all the way to the newspaper office . . . that I
had got somewhere new."[3]

In 1926, Greene became a Catholic; in 1929, with the publication
of *The Man Within*, Greene became a novelist. But he did not then, nor
does he now consider himself to be a Catholic novelist, something that
he has often been called. "I had become a Catholic in 1926, and all
my books, except one lamentable volume of verse at Oxford, had been
written as a Catholic, but no one had noticed the faith to which I belonged before the publication of *Brighton Rock* in 1938," Greene writes.
Even today, some critics still refer specifically to the novels written
after his conversion, distinguishing the earlier books as essentially
different.

"Many times since *Brighton Rock* I have been forced to declare myself not a Catholic writer but a writer who happens to be a Catholic,"
he says. Greene prefers to think of himself as a writer "who in four or
five books took characters with Catholic ideas for his material."[4] But
he insists that the ideas of his Catholic characters, even their Catholic
ideas, are not necessarily identical with his own. For example, in connection with *The Heart of the Matter* Greene has said, "I have small
belief in the doctrine of eternal punishment." In the novel, however,
the hero believes very strongly in hell, and that, for the purpose of the

[2]Graham Greene, *Journey Without Maps*. New York: The Viking Press, 1965; p. 5. *Another Mexico*. New York: The Viking Press, 1968; p. 3.

[3]Greene, *Journey Without Maps, op. cit.*, p. 120; cf. *A Sort of Life*. New York: Simon and Schuster, 1971; pp. 164ff.

[4]Graham Greene, "Introduction," *Brighton Rock*, in the Collected Edition. London: The Bodley Head, 1970; p. vii.

story, is what really matters.[5] Nonetheless, over the years some of his readers have looked upon him as a Catholic first and a writer second, to the extent, he says, that "I found myself hunted by people who wanted help with spiritual problems that I was incapable of giving. Not a few of these were priests themselves."[6]

After writing several books in which religion played a minor role, why did Greene make it the central consideration of several of his novels? He gives two reasons. First, it took him ten years or so to familiarize himself with the Catholic frame of mind, to the point where he could project it convincingly in fiction. Secondly, for a long time he looked upon his religion and his professional life as occupying separate compartments. Catholicism seemed to him more bound up with religious observances than with daily life. It was characterized in his mind as "a ceremony at an altar . . . with the women in my Chelsea congregation wearing their best hats." But the religious persecutions in Mexico and the Civil War in Catholic Spain in the 1930's combined to make Greene examine more closely the effect of faith on action. Catholicism was no longer primarily symbolic; faith was something that affected people's lives and as such the conflicts that it generated were worthy of the novelist's attention.[7]

The late Evelyn Waugh, Greene's colleague both as novelist and Catholic convert, agreed with Greene that "becoming a Catholic opened a whole new field of human experience." But, unlike Greene, Waugh felt that a writer who becomes a Catholic by that fact becomes a Catholic writer, not just a writer who happens to be a Catholic. "If," Waugh has said, "I were a scientific writer, or a historical one, then I could be a writer who happens to be a Catholic. But as a novelist dealing in human experience, the very essence of my work is colored by my beliefs and it would be foolish to claim I was not a Catholic writer."[8]

Greene prefers to avoid the latter term, however, because it could imply that the writer in question is appealing only to readers of his

[5]Graham Greene, "Introduction," *The Heart of the Matter*, in the Collected Edition. London: The Bodley Head, 1971; p. xv.

[6]Graham Greene, "Congo Journal," in *In Search of a Character*. New York: The Viking Press, 1962; pp. 13–14.

[7]Greene, "Introduction," *Brighton Rock, loc. cit.*, p. ix.

[8]Thomas C. Ryan, "A Talk with Evelyn Waugh," *The Sign*, XXXVI (August, 1957), 42.

own religious persuasion, although neither he nor Waugh ever wanted to restrict their public in this way. As Greene puts it, the novelist asks his reader to accept his religious or philosophical premises only imaginatively, i.e., for purposes of entering into his story and identifying with his characters. (Greene has the Catholic novelist Morin say precisely this in his short story "A Visit to Morin" in the collection of stories, *A Sense of Reality*.)

Although a novelist is not a theologian, Green points out, "it is quite possible that a novelist ought to be acquainted with moral theology; I'll concede that he ought to know a decent amount of general theology. But he isn't writing a moral treatise, that isn't his purpose. If it were, he wouldn't write a novel and he wouldn't be a novelist. That is what most of the critics forget."[9] Greene was consequently irritated when a novel like *The Heart of the Matter* was treated by some Catholic critics as if it were a treatise on moral theology. "I seemed to be condemned because Scobie, the hero, had not behaved properly," he said in a BBC-TV interview. "This was a novel—a fiction—an imaginary character."[10]

It was with some trepidation, therefore, that this writer raised the whole question of Greene's Catholic novels and the screen versions of them in our interview, since I thought perhaps that Greene might well be fed up with this topic. Without getting the least bit ruffled, he replied, "I'm not a religious man, though religion interests me. For one period I did write on Catholic subjects, but the majority of my novels do not deal with Catholic themes. One only began with a Catholic subject because one found it a great interest of the moment. My period of Catholic novels was preceded and followed by political novels. *It's a Battlefield* and *England Made Me* were political novels. I was finding my way. Even the early thrillers were political: *The Confidential Agent* deals with the Spanish Civil War. *The Quiet American* and *The Comedians* are political novels. One has come full circle in a way."

In treating the religious aspects of Greene's work, the question of his religious orthodoxy has often arisen, and this question persists in considerations of the screen adaptations of his religious novels.

[9]Robert Ostermann, "Interview with Graham Greene," *The Catholic World*, CLXX (February, 1950), 360.

[10]Christopher Burstall, "Graham Greene Takes the Orient Express," *The Listener*, November 21, 1968; p. 677. This is a transcript of Greene's interview on BBC-TV, November 17, 1968.

Greene is usually charged with Jansenism. One critic, for example, accuses him of damning and exalting characters for "capricious, Jansenist reasons."[11] In a playful vein Greene wrote in "A Visit to Morin" that Morin was "sometimes accused of Jansenism—whatever that might be. . . . The more orthodox critics seemed to sense heresy like a dead rat somewhere under the boards at a spot they could not locate."

Since critics who call Greene a Jansenist do not usually define the term, it would be a good idea to do so before going any further. Theoretically speaking, Jansenism is a doctrine, born in the seventeenth century and almost immediately declared heretical, that minimizes the role played by man's free will in affecting his actions, and exaggerates that played by divine grace, which God arbitrarily grants or withholds, in determining human behavior. Practically speaking, the term refers to the Jansenists' pessimistic, austere view of life, which is preoccupied with the miseries of human existence, and is more conscious of evil than of good in the world.

It is usually the latter meaning that critics have in mind when they call Greene a Jansenist. The charge is based on the fact that he often deals with the wretched side of life and with characters who are lonely, flawed human beings. "Some critics have referred to a strange, violent 'seedy' region of the mind which they call Greeneland," Greene has written, "and I have sometimes wondered whether they go round the world blinkered."[12] Elsewhere he adds, "I mean the Viet Nam War is seedy. The rule of Batista in Cuba belonged to that seedy world—dirt, torture, people half starved. Where do these critics live?"[13]

When I asked him to give me his thoughts on the question of Jansenism in his work, he answered, "People who think they are getting at Jansenism in my novels usually do not know what Jansenism really means. They probably mean Manichaeism, because in the Catholic novels I seem to believe in supernatural evil." The Manichaean heresy is an ancient belief in the duality of Nature based on the eternal conflict of Matter which is evil and Spirit which is good, a conflict in which the evil principle often has the upperhand. "I grew up an Anglican, and a good Anglican accepts supernatural good but not

[11]Simon Raven, "*May We Borrow Your Husband?*: No Laughing Matter," *The Weekend Observer* (London), April 9, 1967; section 2, p. 26.

[12]Greene, "Introduction," *Brighton Rock*, *loc. cit.*, p. x.

[13]Burstall, *op. cit.*, p. 672.

supernatural evil. One gets so tired of people saying that my novels
are about the opposition of Good and Evil. They are not about Good
and Evil, but about human beings. After Hitler and the Viet Nam War,
one would have thought good and evil in people was more understandable. Still, I do not wish to judge any of my characters. I would
hope it was common to most of us to have sympathy for the unfortunate part of the ordinary human character."

I pointed out to Greene the remark that the hero of *The Comedians*
makes to another character: "You believe that evil is necessary? Then
you're a Manichaean like myself." He said that he had forgotten that
passage but that he had meant it playfully, like Morin's remarks about
Jansenism.

In discussing various Roman Catholic artists who have, like
Greene, been accused of Jansenism or Manichaeism, film critic
Raymond Durgnat has nicely laid to rest the specter of these two
"isms" as they appear to hang over the work of a writer like Greene or
a film maker like Robert Bresson. The problem seems to be that these
men often depict characters whose lives are bleak and unpromising,
and who, for all their struggling, never seem to achieve their goals—at
least in this life, writes Durgnat. Possibly the range of experience with
which these artists deal "would be incomplete if advanced as a total
or normative description of Christianity. But if one asks oneself whether
the range of experience within which they are at home lies within
the possibilities of Roman Catholic (or for that matter Protestant)
orthodoxy, surely we have to answer that it does." It seems quite
possible that God would allow people "to endure so much suffering
with so little joy during this lifetime; or what's a heaven for?"[14]

Having looked at Greene's religious vision in general terms, let
us now see how it turns up concretely in his serious fiction and the
films based on it. I shall begin with the movies made from Greene's
serious novels with which he has *not* been associated, before taking up
in more detail in the next chapter those for which Greene himself
wrote the scripts.

I shall not dwell long on Greene's first published novel, *The Man
Within*, since it is rather undistinguished. The title of the film is the
same as the title of the book in England, but was changed to *The Smug-*

[14]Raymond Durgnat, "Bresson's *Diary of a Country Priest*," *Films and Filming*, December, 1966, p. 32.

glers for release in the United States. And it is no compliment to the film to say that the second title fits it better, reflecting the fact that the producers apparently tried to make the novel into an entertainment in Greene's sense of the term, by emphasizing action over character.

Set in the eighteenth century, Greene's novel is about Francis Andrews, a young man who has taken up crime at the insistence of his late father, who was leader of a gang of smugglers. With the death of his father, Francis wants to leave the gang, and he therefore betrays the smugglers to the authorities, even testifying against them in court. Nevertheless, the men are acquitted, and they pursue Andrews for revenge. Andrews goes to the cottage of Elizabeth, a country girl, to hide from his pursuers. In the short time they have been together, Francis has fallen in love with Elizabeth, and even begins, however hazily, to share her belief in an afterlife because this faith seems to have sustained her in her lonely life since the death of her mother and step-father.

Inevitably the smugglers come to the cottage looking for Andrews. At the time, he is drawing water at a nearby well. He hears a commotion in the cottage and, true to his cowardly nature, is afraid to go alone into the house to save Elizabeth. Instead he runs for help to the nearest farmhouse and when he returns she is dead. Carlyon, who had replaced Andrews's father as leader of the smugglers, is waiting for him. Carlyon says that he had remained behind to tell Francis what happened. It seems that Carlyon had arrived too late to save Elizabeth, who died rather than give Francis away. Carlyon is the only friend that Francis ever had among the gang members, and he assures Francis that if he stays out of the gang's way, they will not pursue him any more.

After Carlyon leaves, the police arrive and Andrews gives himself up as the murderer of Elizabeth (for his cowardice had kept him from protecting her). As the police take him away he snatches a knife from one officer and kills himself, in order to be united with her in the afterlife that she taught him to believe in.

Greene does not have a high opinion of the novel and finds it "embarrasingly romantic," but he nevertheless feels that the way the story was altered for the film version involved what he calls "real treachery." Besides not being faithful to the spirit of the novel, he says, "the film made torture a part of the eighteenth-century English legal

THE MAN WITHIN (J. Arthur Rank
Productions, 1947; American release title,
THE SMUGGLERS). Greene himself has
called his first published novel
"embarrassingly romantic," but thinks the
film version, with Richard Attenborough
(left), and Michael Redgrave involved
"real treachery."

system." Indeed the first shot in the film is that of a man holding a hot
poker to the face of Francis (Richard Attenborough), as he is being
questioned by the police about the events that took place in Elizabeth's
cottage on the night the smugglers broke in.

Then, the film embarks on a series of flashbacks, as Andrews tells
his story from the beginning. In general, the scriptwriters have re-
shaped the events of the book to make Andrews a much more sympathetic figure than he was in the novel. For instance, Andrews's
motive in the book for turning in the smugglers is that he is fed up

with belonging to the gang, since all of them, except Carlyon, continually remind him of how inferior he is to his father. Andrews is willing to sacrifice Carlyon in order to get even with the others. In the film, his motivation is made more palatable because he is unjustly convicted of stealing from the gang's common stores, and Carlyon gives him a thrashing in order that the crew will not be able to accuse him of favoritism. In a fit of rage, Andrews then writes the authorities about the gang.

When Andrews is being questioned about what took place in the girl's cabin, we are first shown what he actually remembers as having happened. Andrews comes back to the cabin to find Carlyon (Michael Redgrave) there. The latter tells him that Elizabeth escaped, but that one of the gang was killed in the struggle. Then the police arrive and take both Andrews and Carlyon prisoner. After this flashback, we see Andrews, in a burst of courage, tell the police that he had killed the dead smuggler, and that the man arrested with him (whom he does not name as Carlyon) should be allowed to go free. Carlyon is brought in, and it is obvious that he has been severely tortured. In exchange for Andrews's action in his behalf, Carlyon admits who he is and Andrews is released. Before Francis leaves the prison, Carlyon tells him that he has made a man of himself and that he should go off and find Elizabeth. Carlyon exhorts Francis to forget him and to make something of his new life. In the last shot of the movie, we detect a benign smile on Carlyon's face, disfigured though it is by beating, as he looks through the barred window at Francis going off in the distance, headed toward happiness.

The film does begin with the epigraph of the novel, taken from Sir Thomas Browne, "There's another man within me that's angry with me." But there is little development, in Muriel and Sydney Box's script, of the novel's theme of Francis's search for self-identity, with which the Browne quotation is connected. The film seems to have been designed as a color costume epic rather than a character study. Apparently the film makers were attracted by the period setting of the novel. As Penelope Houston tells us in *Contemporary Cinema*, during and after World War II, British cinema concentrated very much on providing escapist entertainment in the form of historical films and light-minded farces: "One way or another, this was a cinema for a society weary of restrictions and rationbooks; and it seems more than a

coincidence that it barely survived the end of rationing."[15] The film of
The Man Within was a part of this period of British film making and it
is as good a reason as any why the trend did not last.

Greene wryly remembers one anecdote in connection with the
film. He says that after its release he received a letter from someone
congratulating him for being the first novelist to have a story filmed
that dealt with a homosexual relationship. Of course, it is clear both in
the novel and in the film that Andrews's attraction to Carlyon is rooted
in hero worship and the need of a father image, rather than in homosexuality. "At least one person liked the film," says Greene; "and it
turned out to be for the wrong reason."

We come now to the movie versions of three of Greene's religious
novels: *The Fugitive* (1947), based on *The Power and the Glory*; *The Heart
of the Matter* (1953); and *The End of the Affair* (1955). Thematically, they
form a kind of trilogy, since in all three we are confronted with characters who can achieve spiritual redemption only by coping with serious personal failings. The first of these, *The Fugitive*, was based on the
novel which Greene feels has given him more satisfaction than any
other that he has written. Since Greene believes that *The Power and
the Glory* is his best book "by quite a long head," it is understandable
that he would be very sensitive about a film version made from it.[16]

When Greene journeyed to Mexico in 1937, to write a non-fiction
account of the religious persecution which had by then reached its
final stage, he says in his introduction to *The Power and the Glory*,
"nothing was further from my thoughts than a novel." Then, little by
little, the principal characters of an incipient novel began to intrude
upon his consciousness. The character of the fugitive priest began to
take shape in his imagination when he was travelling in Tabasco and
he heard from an inhabitant "of the last priest in the state, who had
baptized his son, giving him a girl's name by accident, for he was so
drunk he could hardly stand." This priest, Greene discovered, had
survived for ten years in the forests and swamps, venturing out only at
night, "and his few letters recorded an awful sense of impotence—to
live in constant danger and yet be able to do so little, it hardly seemed
worth the horror."[17]

[15]Penelope Houston, *Contemporary Cinema*. Baltimore: Penguin Books, 1969; p. 40.

[16]Burstall, *op. cit.*, p. 672.

[17]Graham Greene, "Introduction," *The Power and the Glory*, in the Collected Edition. London: The
Bodley Head, 1971; p. viii. cf. *Another Mexico*, pp. 143–44.

Greene observed the swaggering *pistoleros*, any of whom might have served as the model for his commissioner of police in the novel, except that the idealism which Greene was to give the lieutenant who pursues the fugitive priest in the story "was sadly lacking among these shabby revolutionaries." So he had to invent the lieutenant as a counter to the failed priest. "The idealistic police officer who stifled life from the best possible motives" because he passionately believed that the revolution would help the peasants, was to provide a contrast to "the drunken priest who continued to pass life on" because, despite his personal faults, he was still a priest.[18] "I wanted to show that the man's office doesn't depend upon the man," Greene explained in his BBC-TV interview. "A priest in giving a sacrament believes he is giving the body and blood of Christ, and it doesn't matter whether he himself is an adulterer or a drunkard. It doesn't affect the sacrament."[19]

In presenting the contrast between the priest and the lieutenant, Greene is demonstrating what he once wrote in an essay about Frederick Rolfes: "The greatest saints have been men with more than a normal capacity for evil, and the most vicious men have sometimes narrowly avoided sanctity."[20] Greene emphasizes in the novel how the priest and the lieutenant counter each other by cutting back and forth between them throughout the story in true cinematic fashion. The priest, although he is sacrificing himself for his scattered flock, is a drunkard and the father of an illegitimate child; the lieutenant, although he is ruthless in carrying out his orders to exterminate Catholicism from the province, is a celibate and is dedicated to building an earthly paradise for this people. Both men are aware of their own sense of vocation.

The events leading to the priest's martyrdom closely parallel the Passion of Christ, as Francis Kunkle has indicated in *The Labyrinthine Ways of Graham Greene*: the half-caste beggar who informs on the priest is his Judas; the American gangster, whose dying wish to repent is used as the bait to draw the priest into a trap, is akin to the good thief with whom Christ was crucified; the priest's execution is the culmination of his own Calvary.

But the priest feels that he is nevertheless going to his death

---

[18]*Ibid.*, pp. ix, x.

[19]Burstall, *op. cit.*, p. 672.

[20]Graham Greene, "Frederick Rolfe: Edwardian Inferno," *Collected Essays*. Harmondsworth: Penguin Books, 1970; p. 131.

empty-handed, having accomplished nothing of lasting value. Greene skillfully introduces an incident at the end of the novel, however, to "correct" for the reader the priest's own negative evaluation of himself. The boy Luis, who has detested having to listen to his mother read to him the sentimentalized life of another martyred Mexican priest, is inspired by the death of this priest. Afterward, when the boy meets the lieutenant whom he had previously admired, he spits on his revolver to show his contempt for the man who captured the priest. Later, Luis is the first to welcome to the district the new priest, who will carry on the dead man's work.

The novel was not popular when it was first published, on the eve of the Second World War. Its success in French Catholic circles after the war, however, brought it to the attention of the French bishops, who twice denounced the book to Rome. Finally, in 1955, Greene received a letter from the Holy office of the Vatican condemning *The Power and the Glory* for its "paradoxical" treatment of a priest living "in extraordinary circumstances." Greene recalls that he was treated very gently by Cardinal Griffin, the Archbishop of Westminster, when he politely refused to revise the book, on the grounds that the copyright was in the hands of his publisher: "The affair was allowed to drop into the peaceful oblivion which the Church wisely reserves for unimportant issues."[21]

There is an interesting epilogue to this episode. When Sir Hugh Greene had an audience with Pope Paul VI, in 1964, the pope asked him to convey his good wishes to Graham and to tell his brother that he would very much like to see him. Later, when Graham Greene had an audience with Pope Paul, the latter said that he had read *The Power and the Glory* and some of his other novels. Greene pointed out that the pope had read a book condemned by the Holy Office and Paul replied, "Some parts of all your books will always offend some Catholics. You should not worry about that." This is a counsel which Greene finds easy to take, he says in his autobiography.[22]

No one would have thought of condemning the religious orthodoxy of the film, *The Fugitive*, made from *The Power and the Glory*. Director John Ford gave the story what Greene calls "an Irish-Catholic

[21]Greene, "Introduction," *The Power and the Glory, loc. cit.,* p. xi.
[22]Greene, *A Sort of Life, op. cit.,* p. 79; cf. Burstall, p. 673.

R.K.O. Radio Pictures

THE FUGITIVE (R.K.O. Radio Pictures, 1947). In John Ford's film of Greene's *The Power and the Glory*, Henry Fonda, as the unnamed priest on his way to be executed, looks down at the Judas character who has betrayed him (J. Carroll Naish). Robert Armstrong (extreme left) is the officer commanding the firing squad.

approach." In *The Fugitive*, Greene's drunken priest became a pious and heroic man, and the illegitimate child was made the bastard of the police lieutenant. In short, the film gave all of the integrity to the priest (Henry Fonda), and all of the corruption to the lieutenant (Pedro Armendariz).[23] Greene has never been able to bring himself to see the film. He told me that once while he was travelling, he saw that it was playing in a town where he was breaking his journey. He got almost

[23]Graham Greene, "The Novelist and the Cinema: A Personal Experience," *loc cit.*, p. 55.

as far as the box office when he decided that he would forego what surely promised to be a painful experience, and turned away.

The Fugitive is an example of the kind of film which Greene criticized in one of his *Spectator* columns as being directed toward a public which has been trained to expect a clearly defined hero and villain in every film they see. The producer who wants to reach the widest audience therefore does not think of drama as a conflict of ideas but as a conflict "between the plainest Good and the plainest Evil" (November 19, 1937).

The oversimplification of the characters of the two protagonists in *The Fugitive* was due in part to scriptwriter Dudley Nichols, whom Paul Jensen quotes as saying that he thought a good film should always be "a simple drama of good and evil." Nevertheless Nichols at other times said that he wanted to create subtle and complex characters in his film scripts by injecting them with conflicting urges and motives. Jensen concludes that, regardless of his aspirations for psychological complexity in his characters, *The Fugitive* was "simple drama of good and evil" that Nichols usually turned out: "Nichols never left any doubt as to how we should feel about his people."[24]

The Fugitive was the seventh collaboration of Ford and Nichols (*The Informer, Stagecoach,* etc.), so the director obviously was familiar with the kind of script that Nichols normally wrote. There is, therefore, little doubt that Ford concurred in Nichols's approach to *The Power and the Glory*. In fact, Nichols said afterwards that Ford had viewed the script of *The Fugitive* as "a workmanlike blueprint for action" and made the film very much his own.[25] Ford himself contends that Greene's story was not altered any more than necessary: "You couldn't do the original on film because the priest was living with a woman. Even today you can use four-letter words on the screen, but you can't have a priest living with a woman." Ford gave the interview from which this remark comes in 1968,[26] only a short time before films appeared which did treat explicitly the problem of priests who abandon clerical celibacy, such as *Act of the Heart* (1970) and *Pieces of Dreams* (1971).

The Fugitive is one of Ford's own favorites among his films, a not insignificant opinion for such an eminent director. "It came out the

[24]Paul Jensen, "The Career of Dudley Nichols," *Film Comment*, VI (Winter, 1970), 61.

[25]*Ibid.*, 58.

[26]Peter Bogdanovich, *John Ford*. London: Studio Vista, 1968; p. 85.

way I wanted it to," he explains. "To me, it was perfect, but it wasn't popular. The critics got at it, and evidently it had no appeal to the public, but I was very proud of my work. . . . It had a lot of damn good photography."[27] Ford pared down the dialogue in the script in order to emphasize dramatic photography and there are some fine instances of this in the film. One is the scene in which the peasants bring their babies to be baptized in the long-neglected church. As soon as they enter in a candlelight procession, the soft-focused candleglow transforms the church with an ethereal atmosphere in which the crumbling building becomes once more a place of worship.

Ford and Nichols took full advantage of the melodramatic elements of *The Power and the Glory*, which has been called "a spiritual thriller," by building up the role of the American gangster (Ward Bond). We first see him coming ashore with a forged passport which he presents to the customs official with a handsome bribe enclosed. He later sees a poster which offers a $5,000 reward for his capture and he changes it to read $15,000. Midway through the film, the paths of the priest and the gangster cross for the first time. While the police are closing in on both of them, the gangster engages them in a gunbattle as the priest flees through a cornfield, later escaping himself.

Building on this scene later for dramatic purposes, Nichols injects a bit of Greene's original priest into the Fonda character by having him admit that he has always fled capture, even at times allowing innocent hostages to die for him, while he secretly congratulated himself for being the only priest brave enough to stay on in the country. Nevertheless, at the finale, he is again calmly heroic as he goes to his death, even coolly refusing the lieutenant's offer of a glass of brandy as he goes resolutely to face the firing squad because, as he says, "I want to live my death." How different—and how much more inspiring—is the way that Greene portrays the priest's death in the novel. There, one sees a frightened man overcoming his very human fears in order to fulfill his duty: "He was held up by two policemen, but you could tell that he was doing his best—it was only that his legs were not fully under his control."

The film ends with the peasants mourning the death of the man who was the last priest in the territory. Then there is a knock at the

[27]*Ibid.*, p. 86.

door. When it is opened, the shadow of the new priest who has come to replace the one who has just been executed falls across the threshold. "More than the shadow of the priest should be there," Greene commented when I described this scene for him. "It is important to have the dialogue of the new priest with the child, to show the change of mind in the child toward the dead priest, whom he did not respect until his death; and also to indicate that the Church goes on."

The arrival of the new priest, so important in the novel, was not even hinted at in the American television version of *The Power and the Glory* which was aired on the CBS television network on Sunday evening, October 29, 1961. "Without the appearance of the new priest," says Greene, "the theme of the Church's permanency is entirely missing from the television version." Nevertheless this version was in most respects much more faithful to Greene's novel than was John Ford's film. Many television viewers were shocked at the presentation of a Roman Catholic priest as a drunkard with an illegitimate child, and registered protests with the Columbia Broadcasting System akin to those which prompted Greene's letter from the Holy Office in 1955.

The negative reception that *The Power and the Glory* received from a segment of the American television audience may seem to vindicate John Ford's remark that the original story would have proven offensive to many people had he filmed it as Greene wrote it. However, many people assume that anything aired in the middle of a Sunday evening in prime time must be suitable for family viewing. Hence, had the program been telecast later in the evening, there would have been fewer objections by parents who had allowed their children to watch it. It might even be argued that the story as done on television was too mature for the home screen at the time, in which case it might have been advisable to release it to movie theaters, as in fact was done in England, rather than to televise it. Certainly the TV *Power and the Glory* has a strong cast, headed by Sir Laurence Olivier as the priest, George C. Scott as the lieutenant, and Julie Harris as the priest's mistress; with Cyril Cusack, Martin Gabel, Mildred Natwick, and a uniformly fine supporting cast.

Greene thinks that George Scott gave the stand-out performance in the TV version of the novel and that Olivier was very good, but no match for Paul Scofield's portrayal of the priest in the Denis Cannon-Pierre Bost stage dramatization of the book in 1959. Reflecting on his playing of the role, Paul Scofield has written to me, "My experience in playing the priest in *The Power and the Glory* was a very profound one— it changed my whole attitude to my work as an actor, making me feel (if this is not too large or presumptuous a claim) that there is or should be a spiritual element in the relationship between actor and audience, and that the actor can if he wishes, and is provided with the right material by his author, heighten and bring into focus an awareness of an existence larger than our own. For this I shall always be indebted to Graham."

The Power and the Glory is one of the few works of literature that has been adapted to stage, screen, and television. This is not surprising, since the role of Greene's bedeviled priest is a challenging one, and has tested the talents of some of the best actors of our day: Fonda, Olivier, and Scofield. In addition, the story appeals to different people in different ways because it can be enjoyed as a thriller built around the chase of the priest by the lieutenant, or as a spiritual odyssey of weak human being trying to meet the demands of his high calling, for indeed it is both.

"In the six years that separated the end of *The Power and the Glory* from the start of *The Heart of the Matter* my writing had become rusty with disuse and misuse," Greene writes in his introduction to *The Heart of the Matter* in the Collected Edition. The misuse Greene attributes to his working for the British Foreign Office in Freetown, Sierra Leone, during the Second World War, when he spent a large portion of his time coding and decoding messages to and from London. "I began the book soon after the war in 1946, three years after I had closed my small office and burnt my file and code books."[28]

As Greene began to plan the novel, he initially considered making the central character a priest, as he had done in *The Power and the Glory*. In the course of his stay in Africa, he had met a young missionary from Northern England who interested him, and the character of the young north country priest began to grow in his imagination. Greene eventually abandoned the idea of making him the hero of the novel, however, possibly because he had already done a serious novel about a priest. Instead, his imagination conjured up an image of an Englishman named Wilson, a man of about thirty, sitting on the balcony of the City

[28]Greene, "Introduction," *The Heart of the Matter, loc. cit.*, p. vii.

Hotel in Freetown and watching Scobie, a British Colonial police
officer, pass by on the street below. "Two very different novels began
on the same balcony with the same character, and I had to choose
which to write," Greene recalls. He had to decide whether to make
Wilson the main character of the novel, or a minor character, with
Scobie as the protagonist. If he chose Wilson as the hero, the story
would be an entertainment about an undercover agent pursuing a
criminal in Africa; if he chose Scobie, the novel would become a serious character study.

Because it had been so long since Greene had written a serious
novel, he felt "out of practice and out of confidence," and for months
he could not decide which route the story should take. Finally, he says,
"I left Wilson on the balcony and joined Scobie."[29] But even after he
had started to write the serious novel with Scobie at the center, it was
a long time before he became aware of Scobie's problem: "his corruption by pity."[30]

When we first meet Scobie he is obviously a sympathetic and
compassionate man, whose heart instinctively goes out to the poor
and unfortunate wherever he encounters them. One evening, as he
stops outside the makeshift jungle hospital, he reflects that anyone
who can find it within himself to be happy when he is surrounded by
the misery of others is either evil or ignorant. Scobie looks up at the
stars, which in their remoteness give the impression of being serene
and secure, and he wonders whether, if one knew the facts, "one
would have to feel pity for the planets? if one reached what they called
the heart of the matter?" Scobie's sense of pity, it is clear, is of cosmic
proportions and it is intensified by his feeling that he is one of the
few people who truly recognizes the common responsibility which all
men have to do what they can to alleviate suffering in the world. Thus
pity gives rise to responsibility, and Scobie carries this sense of
responsibility around with him "like a sack of bricks," to use his
phrase. This reminds one of the remark in *The Ministry of Fear* that
"pity is the worst passion of all. We don't outlive it like sex." The
tie-up with *The Ministry of Fear* is an appropriate one, for Greene says

[29]*Ibid.*, p. xiii.
[30]Greene, "Introduction," *The Power and the Glory*, loc. cit., p. ix.

THE HEART OF THE MATTER (London Film Productions, 1953). Trevor Howard interrupts his suicide attempt to which he had felt driven because of the misery he has caused others—a decisive departure from Greene's novel.

that he meant in *The Heart of the Matter* to enlarge on the theme of pity which he had touched upon in the earlier book.

Scobie pities his wife Louise because he has brought her into colonial exile, with a view to achieving the kind of prestige and success that had eluded him in England, only to find that it had likewise eluded him in Africa. We begin to become aware of what Greene has called the corrupting nature of Scobie's pity for others. When Scobie

borrows money from a man suspected of diamond smuggling, in order
to send Louise away on a vacation which he cannot otherwise afford,
he compromises his position on the police force. While she is away
Scobie meets Helen Rolt, a young refugee from a wartime disaster at
sea in which her husband had drowned. Scobie's pity for Helen
gradually leads him into a love affair with her.

When Louise returns from her trip, her suspicions that Scobie is
involved with another woman are furthered by Wilson, another
British colonial, who is secretly in love with her. In order to test Scobie,
she insists that he receive Holy Communion with her at Sunday Mass.
If her husband is living in sin, she reasons, he will either refuse to
receive Communion to avoid committing a sacrilege, or he will go to
Confession beforehand, in which case the priest will not absolve him
of his sins unless he promises to give up the adulterous affair. Louise
is shrewd in predicting that Scobie will agonize over the moral
dilemma with which she has presented him, but she has failed to
reckon fully with Scobie's cosmic pity and his resulting responsibility
syndrome.

Scobie goes to Father Rank, the local priest, for confession. But
the mixture of pity and responsibility and love which he feels for
Helen will not allow him to promise to give her up, and so Father Rank
refuses to give him absolution for his sins. Conversely, the same com-
pound of pity, responsibility, and love which he feels for Louise will
not allow him to hurt her by vindicating her suspicions. The only
alternative which Scobie can find is to receive Holy Communion while
in the state of mortal sin. Scobie's pity even extends to God and he is
sorrowful about offending Him. He prays, "I've preferred to give you
pain rather than give pain to Helen or my wife because I can't observe
your suffering, I can only imagine it. But there are limits to what I can
do to you—or them."

Ulitmately, Scobie decides that his situation has become intolerable, and that he can no longer go on insulting God for the sake of the
two women that he loves. "You'll be better off if you lose me once and
for all," he tells God. Accordingly, obsessed by the thought that Christ
had really committed suicide, Scobie decides to take an overdose of
drugs and thus end his life. If one believes that Christ is God, Scobie
muses, one must believe that he killed himself, hanged himself on the
Cross. God had sometimes broken his own laws, Scobie reasons, "and

was it more impossible for him to put out a hand of forgiveness into the suicidal darkness and chaos than to have woken himself in the tomb, behind the stone?"

Whether or not God does put out a hand of forgiveness to Scobie, as he lapses into final unconsciousness, is the question which the novel poses in its conclusion. We only know that in his last moment of consciousness Scobie says, "Dear God, I love." The ambiguity which surrounds Scobie's death touched off a controversy among both literary critics and readers which helped to make *The Heart of the Matter* Greene's first substantial popular success.

One of the most distinguished commentators on Greene's fiction has always been Greene's fellow novelist and Catholic convert, Evelyn Waugh. His review of *The Heart of the Matter* in *Commonweal* begins by saying that, in the novel, Greene is exploring the relationship of divine justice with divine mercy, and that the ultimate reconciliation of these two divine attributes is a problem whose answer is in the mind of God alone. Nevertheless, since Greene has made this problem the subject of his novel, it is proper for the literary critic to explore how Greene has handled it in fictional terms. Different readers will react to the novel in different ways, Waugh says: "There are loyal Catholics here and in America who think it the function of the Catholic writer to produce only advertising brochures setting out in attractive terms the advantages of Church membership. To them this profoundly reverent book will seem a scandal. For it not only portrays Catholics as unlikeable human beings but shows them tortured by their faith. It will be the object of controversy and perhaps even of condemnation." Waugh continues that non-believers who read it will find the novel engrossing without being aware that it deals with the innermost mysteries of faith. "There is a third class who will understand what the book intends and yet be troubled by doubts of its theological propriety."[31]

A literary critic is usually not concerned with whether or not the central character of a novel has saved his soul, but Waugh maintains that the whole thrust of Greene's novel makes the question an appropriate one. Waugh believes that from the way the story has been executed, Greene wants the reader to infer that Scobie is saved; but Waugh adds that the reader is still entitled to his own opinion.

[31]Evelyn Waugh, "Felix Culpa?" *Commonweal*, XLVIII (July 16, 1948), 322.

Scobie's basic flaw, as Waugh sees it, is that he arrogates to himself the prerogatives of divine providence in trying to play God in other people's lives. His well-meant meddling leads him to interfere in their lives to the point where he assumes responsibilities toward them that he cannot meet without hurting them or others. Scobie winds up believing that, in some obscure way—"at least in a way that is obscure to me," says Waugh—he can set things right by committing suicide, and that he can offer his own damnation as a sacrifice to God for others. "That is the heart of the matter. Is such a sacrifice feasible? . . . To me the idea of willing my own damnation for love of God is either a very loose poetical expression or a mad blasphemy, for the God who accepted that sacrifice could be neither just nor lovable."[32]

On another occasion, Waugh was asked in a shipboard interview, "Mr. Waugh, where's Scobie?" Waugh replied, "In hell, of course."[33] And that does seem to be the logical conclusion that one would draw from his more tactfully worded remarks in his review of the novel. Waugh seems to assume, however, that in order to accept the possibility of Scobie's ultimate salvation, we must also accept the logic that lies behind his motives for killing himself: his wish to hurt neither God nor anyone else any more than he already has. But actually Scobie is in a confused and overwrought state when he carries through his suicide plan. Therefore, in surmising that Scobie is saved we need only recognize that in his anguished frame of mind his motives seem valid to him. As Father Rank reminds Louise—and the reader—at the end of the novel: "The Church knows all the rules. But it doesn't know what goes on in a single human heart. . . . It may seem an odd thing to say—when a man's as wrong as he was—but I think, from what I saw of him, that he really loved God."

When Greene was questioned about the ending of the novel at the time it was published, he said, "I wrote a book about a man who goes to hell—*Brighton Rock*; another about a man who goes to heaven—*The Power and the Glory*. Now I've simply written one about a man who goes to purgatory. I don't know what all the fuss is about."[34] When I reminded Greene of this statement, he replied, "It is really an oversimplification to say that Pinky in *Brighton Rock* went to hell, the priest

[32]*Ibid.*, 324–25.
[33]"Shocker," *Time*, October 29, 1951, p. 103.
[34]*Ibid.*

went to heaven, and Scobie went to purgatory. What I really meant was that, for example, *Brighton Rock* is written in such a way that people could plausibly imagine that Pinky went to hell, and then I cast doubt upon it in the ending. The real theme of the three novels, and of *The End of the Affair* which followed them, is embodied in the priest's phrase at the end of *Brighton Rock*: 'You can't conceive, my child, nor can anyone, the appalling strangeness of the mercy of God.' In any case, as far as *The Heart of the Matter* is concerned, I don't like the book and have never cared to reread it."

Greene expands on his dislike for the novel in the introduction which he wrote for it in the Collected Edition: "The scales to me seem too heavily weighted, the plot overloaded, the religious scruples of Scobie too extreme." Greene says that he intended to show "the disastrous effect on human beings of pity as distinct from compassion." Pity, as Greene sees it, is bound up with pride, while compassion is not: "When you pity you treat the person as an inferior, while with compassion you're treating the person as an equal." The character of Scobie, therefore, was intended to show how pity can be the expression of pride: "Suicide was Scobie's inevitable end; the particular motive of his suicide, to save even God from himself, was the final twist of the screw of his inordinate pride."[35]

Scobie, as Greene conceived him, is a self-deluded man who thinks that he can manage other people's lives. Consequently, Greene would be the last to endorse the motives which Scobie advanced for taking his own life. Nonetheless, Greene still leaves open the question as to whether God intervened in the end to save Scobie from himself. For, as Greene has reiterated on various occasions, the overriding theme of *The Heart of the Matter* and of the other three novels with which it is associated is "the appalling strangeness of the mercy of God."

The novel's popularity made it almost inevitable that it would be filmed, and so it was in 1953. Waugh had said that Greene's narrative style in *The Heart of the Matter* was so cinematic that it seemed that in writing the novel Greene had assembled the scenes by clipping them from an endless length of film; in each scene Greene's camera eye was

---

[35]Greene, "Introduction," *The Heart of the Matter, loc. cit.,* pp. xiii–xiv, xv; cf. Burstall, *op. cit.,* p. 674.

constantly moving about picking out significant detail. But Waugh expressed the fear that a film maker who lacked Greene's talent as a story teller could turn the novel into "the dreariest kind of film."

While the film of *The Heart of the Matter* is not an entirely felicitous rendering of the novel, it is certainly not the dreary film that Waugh had anticipated. Waugh had noted in his review of the novel that Greene had caught the atmosphere of the African setting very vividly: "the sweat and infection, the ill-built town which is only beautiful for a few minutes at sundown."[36] This seedy atmosphere has been marvelously preserved in the film in scenes shot on location in Africa. One does not forget, for example, the shot early in the movie of Louise (Elizabeth Allen) asleep under a mosquito net, her hair matted with perspiration, her head lying on a rumpled pillow.

Carrying this image in his mind, Scobie (Trevor Howard) tells Father Rank (Peter Finch) that he "feels responsible for Louise, for what she has become," as he remembers this image of her. Developing the theme of pity and responsibility just as it is found in the novel, Scobie later tells Helen that she should not feel guilty because she has so quickly forgotten her dead husband. He confesses (in lines taken directly from the novel) that he felt relieved when his young daughter had died after suffering a long illness, because "when they are dead our responsibility ends."

Helen is played by Maria Schell, an excellent German actress. Miss Schell's accent is explained in the script by making her an Austrian girl who had married an Englishman; but there is no way to get around the fact that Helen is supposed to be nineteen in the novel and in the film, and Miss Schell is obviously older. The moviegoer fails to understand, therefore, that Scobie is initially attracted to Helen because he sees her as a surrogate for his own dead daughter and feels very protective toward her. It is consequently easy to miss the point that it is Scobie's excessive sense of pity, and not his sexual desire, which, at the outset at least, is drawing him to Helen.

For his part, screenwriter Ian Dalrymple has done everything he can in his script to bring Scobie's psychological conflicts into relief. He often employs actual lines from the novel, usually in a condensed form, in the film's dialogue. For example, Father Rank complains that

---

*Waugh, "Felix Culpa?" *loc. cit.*, 324.

people send for him only when they are dying, and that he seems to be of no use to the living: "If people are in trouble they'd go to you, Scobie. And if you were in trouble where would you go?" The irony of this speech works perfectly both in the novel and in the film, for, by this point in the story, Scobie is in deep trouble and really does feel that neither God nor man can help him.

The film carefully charts from the beginning the build-up of Scobie's spiritual conflict. Scobie's religious scruples become evident when he tells Helen that he cannot divorce his wife and marry her, because he is a Roman Catholic. Helen taunts him by saying, "It doesn't stop you from making love to me—it only stops you from marrying me." Scobie replies, "It would take too long to explain. One would have to begin with the arguments for God." At another point Louise asks him why he doesn't arrange his schedule to be able to accompany her to Sunday Mass, and he answers that she has enough faith for both of them. The following Sunday, however, while he is sitting in his car waiting for a traffic light to change, he winces when he hears the bells of the nearby church ring. This is an effective visual way of showing that Scobie has a tender religious conscience. Therefore, when he is confronted with the possibility of making a sacrilegious Communion, it is clear that his decision will not be an easy one for him to make. He tries to explain to Helen, who is a nonbeliever, that adultery endangers his own security, but going to Communion in a state of mortal sin is profoundly evil. Besides damnation for him it means "striking God when he's down." Although Greene feels that this interchange in the film is something of an oversimplification of the corresponding scene in the book, it does explain Scobie's Catholic point of view fairly sensibly, in a manner that the many non-Catholic members of the audience would be able to understand.

Asked why non-Catholics do not seem to find his using peculiarly Catholic concepts, such as the sacrilegious reception of Communion, an obstacle to appreciating his stories, Greene replied, "Any author writing strictly for a Catholic audience would not reach a large public. It goes back to what I said in my essay in *Footnotes to the Film*: if you excite your audience first, you can put over what you will of horror, suffering, truth. This is still true and applies to a novel as well as to a film. By exciting an audience I mean, let me repeat, getting them involved in the story. Once they are involved they will accept what you present them."

"I am not a Roman Catholic myself," Sir Hugh Greene noted in our interview, "and yet I find that Graham allows us to see far enough into the Catholic mind in a story like *The Heart of the Matter* to see Scobie's point of view as fully believable. One grants a willing suspension of disbelief and accepts that this is the way that a man like Scobie would behave. Graham knows how to make Catholicism accessible to his public; he makes it a part of the world in which he and others live."

Scobie's suicide is foreshadowed in the film as in the book by the suicide of a young British army officer named Pendleton. Unaccountably, the Catholic priest from Northern England with whom Scobie discusses Pendleton's death in the novel becomes an African Protestant minister in the film, although the conversation is basically the same. The minister reminds Scobie that suicide is the unforgivable sin, but Scobie says firmly, "Even the Church can't teach me that God doesn't pity the young. If I did it, it would be unforgivable, since I know. But he didn't know a thing." Therefore, when Scobie considers taking his own life it is just as clear in the film as it was in the novel that he knows what is at stake.

The film follows the spirit of the novel with remarkable fidelity up to the end, but then presents a manufactured conclusion that is disappointingly different from the one in the book. As the film would have it, Scobie loads his gun and looks at a statue on his desk of the Blessed Virgin holding the Christ Child. He prays to God, "Don't you see it's you I have to hurt, not Helen or Louise." He goes out to sit in his car where he plans to shoot himself, repeating, "I want to stop hurting people." Before Scobie can carry out his decision, however, he hears a cry for help and goes to assist someone being beaten up in a street fight and is himself killed in the line of duty. His faithful servant finds him just before he dies and hears his last words, "Tell Mrs. Scobie that God made it alright—for her." This change in the ending can only be interpreted, says Moira Walsh in *America* (December 4, 1954), "as a divine intervention to give Scobie time to repent of his original intention to kill himself and die with a clear claim to salvation."

Father John Burke, the religious technical adviser on the film, has told me that Scobie's suicide was handled in this curious manner in the film against his advice, because the producers thought that Catholics would object to a Catholic taking his own life. Greene himself adds, "I tried to persuade the company to leave the suicide in. Trevor Howard, who is an intelligent actor, said he would do a re-take of the ending without a fee. I even figured out a way of doing it without Trevor Howard: I wanted to show Scobie's hand writing a suicide note with the gun at hand, thus making it clear that he had definitely made up his mind to take his own life. At that moment he would be called away to the police action and be killed, apparently with the intention of suicide in his mind all the while. I disclaim the ending of the film as it is."

Apart from the ending (no small consideration), *The Heart of the Matter* stands as one of the better attempts at bringing one of Greene's serious novels to the screen. The theme of both the novel and of the motion picture illustrates what Greene has said about the characters of serious fiction: "These characters are not my creation but God's. They have an eternal destiny. . . . They are souls whom Christ died to save." Evelyn Waugh comments that this statement of Greene's explains his preoccupation with flawed human beings: "The children of Adam are not a race of noble savages who need only a divine spark to perfect them," Waugh writes. "They are aboriginally corrupt. Their tiny relative advantages of intelligence and taste and good looks and good manners are quite insignificant. The compassion and condescension of the Word becoming flesh are glorified in the depths."[37] Sarah Miles, the heroine of *The End of the Affair*, is just such a person. She has all of the advantages which Waugh describes above, and yet she has serious emotional and religious problems, beside which these qualities seem even to her to be insignificant.

There is one technical element in *The End of the Affair* which is noteworthy, both with regard to the novel itself and the film that was made from it. For the first time in his serious fiction Greene employs a narrator, from whose particular point of view we see the events of the story unfold. It is true that the police officer Calloway narrates the fictional version of *The Third Man*, but he is a professionally detached observer who relays to the reader the events of the story as they happened. The subjective first person narrator, through whose outlook

[37]*Ibid.*, 323.

the events of the story are filtered, was used for the first time by Greene in an extended piece of fiction in *The End of the Affair*.

Greene chose to tell this story in the first person because he felt the need to break away from his accustomed manner of narration. While reading *Great Expectations*, he observed how Dickens seems to use the first person technique with ease, and decided to try it himself. But Greene soon found that this method of story telling did not come as easily to him as it seemed to have come to Dickens. "Many a time I regretted its use and contemplated beginning the whole book again . . . in the third person," he says. He thought that he should lighten the heavy tone that Bendrix, his narrator, set on the first page of the novel when Bendrix announced that his story was to be more of a record of hate than love. "I dreaded to see the whole book smoked like a fish with his hatred," Greene recalls, so he introduced the amiable private detective, Mr. Parkis, into the story to provide a bit of humor.[38]

The narrator, Maurice Bendrix, is writing a novel about a civil servant and gets acquainted with Sarah Miles in order to learn something of her husband's habits in pursuing that line of work. He becomes more and more interested in Sarah and finally becomes involved in a love affair with her. Bendrix constantly mars their meager happiness by his nagging fears that either Henry Miles will discover what is going on, or that Sarah will find someone else. (Since one of Bendrix's legs is shorter than the other, he is chronically insecure about his loveableness).

Then one night Bendrix is knocked unconscious during an air raid, when the house in which he and Sarah are staying is partially destroyed. The next day Sarah ends the affair without explanation, and Bendrix assumes that his fears have been realized. They see no more of each other for almost three years, until Bendrix and Henry Miles meet quite by accident on the street, and Henry invites Bendrix home to discuss a personal problem. In a supremely ironic scene Henry, who never suspected Sarah's affair with Bendrix, now confides to Bendrix that he suspects that his wife has taken a lover. Bendrix is secretly more jealous than Henry, and it is Bendrix who engages a detective to gather evidence against Sarah. The detective manages to

[38]Graham Greene, "Introduction to *The End of the Affair*," *Introductions to Three Novels*. Stockholm: Norstedt, 1962; p. 47

snatch her personal diary (which, rather surprisingly, she never seems to miss), and from it Bendrix learns what has been going on.

Through the device of the diary, Greene is able to switch narrators and fill in the spiritual dimension that has been missing from Bendrix's account of what has been happening. When Bendrix was felled under the debris during the air raid, Sarah had thought that he was dead. She hysterically promised the God in whom she had heretofore professed no belief that she would give Bendrix up if he was allowed to live. Apparently God took her up on her offer, for Bendrix did regain consciousness, and Sarah resolutely decided to keep her side of the bargain.

I asked Greene whether he intended that we should believe that God actually accepts offers of this sort, or whether God spared Bendrix's life quite apart from Sarah's renunciation of him. Greene responded that he always believes that God answers such prayers to a point, "as a kind of test of a person's sincerity, to see whether in fact the offer was merely based on emotion." God therefore uses such occasions to test the person's faith.

Sarah's offer was clearly based on more than emotion, for she is faithful to her resolve right up to the time of her untimely death from fever. Indeed, her diary implies that her renunciation of Bendrix has led her to sanctity. At one point, when she first began to perceive that the love of God was beginning to displace all of her earthly loves, Sarah went to visit a self-styled atheist named Smythe in order to reconfirm her waning unbelief. But Smythe's arguments were no match for the religious transformation that was then taking place within her. Besides, she had a well-founded suspicion that Smythe's hatred of God stemmed less from rational arguments, than from the bitterness which he felt because his face was partially disfigured by a strawberry birth mark.

Sarah records that she is beginning to comprehend that God has been leading her through human love to divine love: "Did I ever love Maurice as much before I loved You? Or was it really You I loved all the time? Did I touch You when I touched him? Could I have touched You if I hadn't touched him first, touched him as I never touched Henry, anybody?" She realizes too that God can even use jealousy and bitterness as tools of his grace, for Bendrix was on God's side all the time without knowing it, working, with his anger and jealousy, for their separation, in spite of himself, just as God was working for it. Indeed, Sarah feels that in the very intensity of their love, she and Bendrix were building toward their inevitable separation: "For he gave me so much love and I gave him so much love that soon there wasn't anything left when we'd finished but You." Later Sarah says in her last letter to Bendrix: "I've caught belief like a disease. I've fallen into belief like I fell in love. . . . I've fought belief for longer than I fought love, but I haven't any fight left."

In attempting to chronicle Sarah Miles's pilgrim's progress from adultery to sanctity, Greene has met the challenge of trying to make her spiritual experience plausible to readers. He is not asking us to believe as Sarah ultimately does, but only to believe that what has happened to Sarah has a great deal of meaning for her. Greene is satisfied with his portrait of Sarah, and feels that he has drawn her better than any other woman he has created in his fiction.

After the death of Sarah, one wonders where the novel can go for the last fifty pages. But there is much more to the story. Sarah, who prayed constantly in her last days for those whom she loved, now seems to be interceding for them from the other side of the grave. For example, the strawberry birth mark disappears from Smythe's face, shaking him considerably in his stance of unbelief. This intrusion of the miraculous into the narrative is a brave invention on Greene's part, Waugh contends in his review of the novel: "His voice is listened to in many dark places and his defiant assertion of the supernatural is entirely admirable." On the other hand, Waugh does question whether Greene in places has not allowed the novel to become too emphatically sectarian: ".It transpires, for instance, after the heroine's death that she was baptized by a Catholic priest while still a child. There is some speculation as to whether 'it took'; whether it was an infection caught

THE END OF THE AFFAIR (Columbia Pictures, 1955). Deborah Kerr plays a woman undergoing a religious conversion both her lover and her husband fail to understand.

in infancy, and so on. But Mr. Greene knows very well that she would
have been as surely baptized by the local vicar. It would be a pity if
he gave the impression of the Catholic Church as a secret society. . . .
Clearly that is not his intention nor can it be justly read into his words,
but in the dark places where his apostolate lies, I can imagine some
passages carrying a whiff of occultism."[39]

Other critics found the events following Sarah's death difficult to
accept, and the critic for the *New Statesman and Nation* went so far as to
say that *The End of the Affair* might be the last book by Graham Greene
that a non-specialist in moral theology would be able to review.[40]

In assessing the last section of the novel, we must ascertain the
function that Greene intended it to fulfill in the overall scheme of the
story. The key to understanding these events in their proper context
is to be found in the recognition that, while Sarah is an important figure in the novel, Greene is equally interested in the influence that she
has on Bendrix. That is why Bendrix narrates most of the story. If the
story had been told in a conventional impersonal narrative style instead of through Bendrix, it would have merely been a pious and
pedestrian tale of a mistress who repents and becomes a saint. As
Bendrix narrates, however, we begin to catch glimpses of the profound
effect that the actual telling of the story is having on him. In trying to
fit the facts together in a coherent way that will make sense, Bendrix
seems to be understanding them himself for the first time.

"When I began to write our story down, I thought I was writing
a record of hate, but somehow the hate has got mislaid," he says, adding that he is coming to love and believe in Sarah as he re-experiences
their life together in the re-telling. If his hatred of Sarah is gone, he
fears that he will likewise cease to hate the God who took her away
from him. For if God exists and Sarah could change as she did, Bendrix
reasons, then anyone could be a saint by making the leap of faith that
she made. But he is determined *not* to make that leap. "I hate you,
God," he says, "I hate You as though You existed. . . . I'm too tired
and old to learn to love. Leave me alone forever." Nonetheless, Bendrix
had written at the beginning of his account that "hatred seems to

[39]Evelyn Waugh, "The Heart's Own Reasons," *Commonweal*, LIV (August 17, 1951), 458–59.

[40]"Shocker," p. 99, gives a survey of the critical reaction to *The End of the Affair* at the time of its
publication.

operate the same glands as love." Hence, we strongly suspect that Sarah's love will heal his hatred for God and turn it to love. The title of the book is ironic, therefore, since for Bendrix the search for love is by no means over.

Since the completion of the novel, Greene, too, has become dissatisfied with the last section: "I realize now that I was cheating. The incident of the strawberry mark had no place in this book; every so-called miracle should have a natural explanation, and the coincidences ought to have continued over the years, battering at the mind of Bendrix, forcing on him a reluctant doubt."[41] In other words, if the apparent miracles all admitted of natural explanations as well as supernatural ones, it would better appear that God is tempting Bendrix to believe and not forcing him.

Yet Bendrix's inner battle with belief does come through to the reader as genuine and not contrived, precisely because Greene does not present Bendrix as a believer looking back on his days of unbelief as he narrates his story. Greene rather portrays Bendrix as a man who is struggling with his doubt, even while he is actually engaged in setting down the experiences that are tempting him toward faith. This struggle is still going on when the novel ends, and it is what makes the novel so fascinating.

If it was difficult to portray Scobie's religious experience in the film of *The Heart of the Matter*, the task of presenting the spiritual dimension of *The End of the Affair* on the screen was no easier. Deborah Kerr, who played Sarah in the film, has said to me, "I loved the film and believed in it, even though it was not a great success. It was almost impossible to bring across on the screen the changes in Sarah that were taking place, as Mr. Greene was able to do in the novel. I believe that a woman could change and be willing to sacrifice her lover for a higher motive, and I played it that way. But this was difficult to convey in the film." It was equally difficult to convey the changes in Bendrix in the movie, not only because the role was beyond the range of Van Johnson, but because the story in the film is told for the most part in direct narrative, and we do not often get Bendrix's reflections on how he is being affected by what is happening.

On this point, Edward Dmytryk, who directed the film, informed

[41]Greene, "Introduction to *The End of the Affair*," loc. cit., p. 47.

me that it "originally was shot in the flashback fashion in which the novel was written, with more of Bendrix's comments on the sound-track. But Columbia was worried that a story that was told out of chronological sequence would confuse the mass audience. So they requested that we rearrange the scenes in strict chronological order. Graham Greene saw the picture in its original, pre-release form and liked it very much. He was disappointed when the film was re-edited, and I personally prefer the picture in its original form myself."

It is a trifle unfair to concentrate on the film's flaws, however, since *The End of the Affair* is Greene's most delicately nuanced novel and therefore very difficult to translate to the cinema screen. In fact I am pleasantly surprised that the film works as well as it does. The snatches of commentary that still remain on the soundtrack do help to set the tone of the story. For example, as he gets to know Sarah better, Bendrix reflects, "Sarah was made for peace and lasting love. I only hoped that it would be me in whom she would find them." Because he has never before been loved the way Sarah loves him, he says, "I began to think that I was in a strange country without maps." These two remarks taken together help to foreshadow the religious dimension which the story shortly takes on, for Bendrix is entering a strange country, where he is to be led through and beyond human love to divine love.

Just as some of Greene's original dialogue was adapted for the film of *The Heart of the Matter*, as a way of preserving the religious implications of the original novel, so Lenore Coffee has incorporated some of the lines from *The End of the Affair* into her script for the film. Thus the script wisely uses the words of Sarah's diary as the novel does, to add a spiritual perspective to the events which we have already seen portrayed from Bendrix's uncomprehending point of view. For example, the air raid scene in which Bendrix is pinned under the rubble is repeated, the second time with Sarah's commentary from the diary spoken over the soundtrack. The film furthermore preserves the ambiguity of the novel concerning whether or not Sarah's prayer recalled Bendrix to life or whether he had been temporarily unconscious. This is accomplished by having Bendrix say when he awakens, "When I came to I had a terrific sense of space and distance." Sarah comments in her diary, "When he spoke of his strange sensations, I thought he was trying to remember what it was like to be dead. . . . Now I wish he were safely back dead again under the door. Now the agony of being without him starts."

The film is able to distill the novel's treatment of Sarah's spiritual conflicts, which fill several pages of her diary in the novel into two conversations which she has with a priest (Stephen Murray). His advice is simple and straightforward: "If you've made a vow to someone you don't believe in, you don't have to keep it." "If there is a God," Sarah responds, "He put the thought of that prayer in my mind and I hate him for it." During a later visit Sarah tells the priest that she has kept her promise but there has been no virtue in doing so; she would rather be a cheerful sinner. Reassuring her, the priest says, "You have taken the first step. It would be more painful to go back than to go on."

Sarah's conversations with the priest serve to balance her encounters with the atheist Smythe ((Michael Goodliffe). It is as if she were in dialogue with two sides of her personality, one pulling her to faith, the other to disbelief; and this proves to be a very effective way of dramatizing her inner conflicts on the screen. After the dialogue, with both the priest and with Smythe, Sarah finally is able to resolve her conflict. The last time she goes to see Smythe she tells him, "You have taught me to believe in God by your hate. You can't hate something that isn't there. Your belief is far deeper than mine." Having opted for faith, Sarah eventually dies happy.

Bendrix meets Sarah's mother at the time of Sarah's death, as he does in the novel. She tells him that she had been a Catholic once. Sarah's father was not, however; and she had had Sarah baptized as a child to spite him, after their estrangement. The script has Bendrix's reply to Sarah's mother in words that neatly summarize his reflections on the incident in the book: "You can't mark a child for life by a splash of water and a few murmured words."

Since the whole episode of Sarah's secret baptism is retained in the film, it is surprising to find that the miracles which follow Sarah's death in the book have been left out. Even to a Catholic novelist and literary critic like Evelyn Waugh the baptism incident seemed sectarian in a way that the miracles did not. Yet, according to Dmytryk, "We didn't want the real miracles that occur after Sarah's death in the novel to be included in the film. It's one thing to write about miracles in a novel and quite another to present them in a film. When you show them on the screen you seem to be insisting that the audience believe that they really happened. The miracle that we were interested in preserving in the film was the one that occurred in Sarah's mind. She believed that her prayer brought Bendrix back to life and that belief changed her whole life. That is what is important to the story."

But the absence of the miracles from the film means that much more weight has to be put on Sarah's last letter to Bendrix in the film than in the novel in order to provide reason for Bendrix's reluctant turning in the direction of faith at the end of the movie. What we hear Sarah read over the soundtrack really combines material from the letter as it appears in the book with passages from Sarah's diary. The section added to the letter from the diary is the one in which Sarah says that she and Bendrix were really unwitting accomplices with God in the breakup of their love affair; and the portion from the original letter used in the film at this point is that in which Sarah says that she has caught belief like a disease. (Both of these passages have been cited earlier). Bendrix's response in the movie is addressed to the dead Sarah: "Have it your way. I believe that God exists. But I'm tired. Give me a little time."

Without the miracles that preceded this final scene in the book, the film makes Bendrix's last murmured prayer seem less than adequately motivated. I grant that Greene himself was not satisfied with the inclusion of miracles in the book, but he has said that he would have handled them differently, not dropped them altogether. Still, the film is not without merits, even in its edited version. Edward Dmytryk's direction is adept and the supporting cast is exceptional. Peter Cushing gives dignity and sympathy to his portrayal of Henry Miles; John Mills completely inhabits the role of Parkis, the eccentric detective whom Bendrix hires to trail Sarah; and Michael Goodliffe brings authority to his interpretation of the part of the atheist Smythe.

Although Greene was ultimately disappointed with his first serious attempt to use first person narration in *The End of the Affair*, the experience he gained in writing that novel led him to employ the first person again in *The Quiet American*, "which imperatively demanded its use," and which, he thinks, "is a more successful book."[42] *The Quiet American* is one of the novels which Greene would say has a political rather than a religious theme, although there is a religious

[42]*Ibid.*, pp. 47–48.

aspect to the story. Greene turned to a political theme after *The End of the Affair*, his brother Sir Hugh Greene feels, because he thought he had gone as far as he could with religious themes, and wanted to take a fresh approach to his fiction writing. Besides, he was becoming at the time increasingly interested in the Indo-China war.

Greene made four trips to Indo-China while he was preparing the novel, serving as *The New Republic's* correspondent for the war that was raging there between the French and the Communists in the early 1950's. There is an unmistakable air of authenticity about the novel because, as Greene says, "I had seen so much of the country and got to know the issues over a period of years." He has even included actual incidents in the novel. The two bomb explosions that he brings into the story, for example, were based on incidents that actually took place in Saigon in 1953.[43]

Greene says that his ill feelings toward America were nurtured by his visits to Viet Nam while he was gaining background for the novel. Since these feelings are relevant to *The Quiet American*, let me briefly sketch how they developed. So far as I can ascertain, Greene's first major expression of these feelings was in 1952, and had to do with the then frenzied operations of the House Committee on Un-American Activities, and its investigations of individuals who were alleged to have Communist sympathies. Charlie Chaplin had been asked to appear before the group, and when he indicated his willingness to do so, he received a letter informing him that he would not be required to testify. After Chaplin set sail for Europe to supervise the premiere of his film *Limelight* there, however, he was informed in mid-ocean that he could not return to the United States unless he agreed to answer charges centering on his personal character and political beliefs. Chaplin decided not to return to America (although he has done so since, in 1972, to accept a special Academy Award in Hollywood).

At the time, Greene addressed to him an open letter in which he demolished the suspicions of Chaplin's loyalty to the United States. Then Greene went on to remind Chaplin that when he had visited him a few days earlier he had suggested that Chaplin do a film about his recent brush with anti-Communist witch-hunting. In Greene's

---

[43]Graham Greene, "Dedicatory Note," *The Quiet American*. New York: Bantam Books, 1968; p. i.

proposed film, Chaplin's Tramp character would be summoned from obscurity to answer for his past before the Un-American Activities Committee. Greene records that Chaplin had laughed the suggestion away; but in point of fact, Chaplin's next film, *A King in New York* (1957) was in some ways similar to Greene's original suggestion. Chaplin plays the deposed king Shahdov of Estrovia whose appearance before the committee is, as one might have predicted, hilarious, and he succeeds in reducing the hearing to a shambles with the aid of a fire hose.

As far as Greene himself is concerned, the whole Chaplin affair served to augment his disaffection for America. He ended his open letter to Chaplin with these words: "In attacking you the witch-hunters have emphasized that this is no national matter. Intolerance in any country wounds freedom throughout the world."[44]

Prior to the Chaplin affair, in February, 1952, Greene had applied for an eight-week visa to come to the United States to receive the Catholic Literary Award for *The End of the Affair*. He was temporarily denied a visa under the McCarran Act, which barred anyone who was or had been a Communist from entering the United States. At the age of eighteen Greene had joined the Party at Oxford as a prank, but had dropped out shortly thereafter, he says in his autobiography, when he learned that membership did not automatically entitle him to a free trip to Moscow and Leningrad.

This former membership in the Communist Party was now an impediment to his visiting the United States; but after three days he was "cleared" and allowed an entry permit. Subsequently, however, following publication of the Chaplin letter, the red tape involved in his coming to the U.S. was considerably increased. Late in 1952, after a month of negotiations for permission to make another business trip to America, Greene was again granted a visa. By then, however, he was fed up, and he refused it. Because of the case of Greene and others like it at the time, a group of American educators headed by Lawrence A. Kimpton, Chancellor of the University of Chicago, protested to the Secretary of State, Dean Acheson, that the enforcement of the McCarran Act had deprived the United States of the knowledge and

[44]Graham Greene, "Dear Mr. Chaplin," *The New Republic*, CXXVI (October 13, 1952), 5.

experience of prominent men of letters, and "seriously damaged the reputation of our country."[45]

But it was Greene's observation of American foreign policy in the Far East, while he was a war correspondent in Viet Nam in the early 1950's, that really provided the concrete basis for his criticism of the U.S. in *The Quiet American*. In one report in *The New Republic*, Greene wrote that it was difficult for the Vietnamese peasants to feel gratitude for American aid "when a gift is permanently stamped with the name of the donor" who tacitly demands in return cooperation in the Cold War. This irritated them more than the maladroitness of some of the American gifts: "The razors for hairless chins can be sold again perhaps (though to whom?) . . . . and the white powder (that nobody tells them is milk and a few wily people may tell them is poison for their babies) can be spilt in the cracks of the ground and the tins scoured and used. . . ."[46] Greene gave his negative feelings toward the U.S. fictional focus in *The Quiet American*, but in a reasoned and not excessively hostile way, as I think will be evident from an analysis of the novel.

As in *The End of the Affair*, the narrator of *The Quiet American* at first seems quite dispassionate in the way he relates the story of someone who has recently died. As he continues, however, our suspicions that he is unfolding a story in which he was personally and deeply involved are confirmed. The narrator in this instance is Thomas Fowler, a cynical British war correspondent who prefers to be called a reporter rather than a journalist, since he merely reports on what he witnesses and has no personal interests or commitments in the world which he observes, as a serious journalist does. "I'm not involved," is the first article of his personal creed; it is also the second, third, and fourth articles as well. He professes himself not to believe in any religious creed (Thomas is an appropriate name for him), although he does at times address himself to the God in whom he insists that he does not believe, as did Bendrix in *The End of the Affair*.

In direct contrast to him is Alden Pyle, the American of the title. Pyle is an idealist who believes that American intervention and aid in Indo-China can solve all the political problems there. Fowler

[45]"Greene not Red," *Newsweek*, February 11, 1952, p. 28.

[46]Graham Greene, "Last Act in Indo-China," *The New Republic*, CXXXII (May 9, 1955), 11.

criticizes Pyle because idealism, when it is naïve and inexperienced, is dangerous. Fowler's attitude is vindicated when Pyle's meddling proves disastrous later in the story. But this turn of events should not be dismissed as merely an expression of Greene's anti-American bias. In the larger context of Greene's total vision, Pyle's innocence proves inadequate in attempting to cope with a world corrupted by the presence of evil of which Pyle seems blissfully unaware. Because Pyle is unprepared to cope with a fallen world that does not respond to his idealistic views, he unwittingly becomes the pawn of others who cynically manipulate him in their bid for political power. Greene has been criticized for making Pyle an unreal, one-dimensional character, who serves as a foil to Greene's own anti-American views. "The character of the young American is so close to caricature that nothing but disaster can be expected from his ingenuous zeal," one critic has said of Pyle.

The reports which Greene sent from Viet Nam during the Indo-China war in the early 1950's make it clear that he was personally convinced that the American policy at the time was just about as Pyle elucidates it in the novel; i.e., that good will and economic aid could secure peace in Indo-China. This approach, Greene believed, was well intentioned but ill advised from the start. Moreover, as far as the character of Pyle is concerned, perhaps Greene is not as hard on him as we might first think. For, we must remember that we see the American from Fowler's jaundiced point of view, that of a man seeking to live an uncommitted life in the midst of a world that is on the edge of chaos. If Greene criticizes Pyle, he also criticizes Fowler.

Like Bendrix in *The End of the Affair*, Fowler insists throughout the novel that his basic longing is for peace, and that his only wish is to be left alone. Yet, in spite of himself, he does feel compassion for those in pain. For all his staunchly maintained stance of uninvolvement, he has to admit, "I cannot be at ease (and to be at ease is my chief wish) if someone else is in pain." Fowler's peace of mind is so contingent on the peace of others that when he is wounded in a skirmish, he begs the rescue team to turn their attention first to another man, a soldier whose moans had caused Fowler personal anguish all the while they were waiting for relief.

Another time Fowler sees the body of a dead child lying in a ditch and says to himself, "I hate war." Greene says that when critics call

THE QUIET AMERICAN (United Artists, 1957). Politics and jealousy over a girl become mixed in an argument between the quiet American (Audie Murphy) and a cynical Englishman (Michael Redgrave) in a French military bar. The criticism of American foreign policy in Greene's novel all but disappeared from the film version.

a scene such as this the mere product of the strange, violent, seedy region of the mind that they call Greeneland, he wants to exclaim, "This is Indo-China . . . carefully and accurately described. I have been a newspaper correspondent as well as a novelist. I assure you the dead child lay in the ditch in just that attitude."[47] The image of that child stays with Fowler throughout the novel, as does that of a dead infant in the arms of its mother after an explosion in the city square of Saigon.

[47]Greene, "Introduction," *Brighton Rock, loc. cit.*, p. x.

Fowler learns from the Communist Heng that Pyle, "impregnably armored by his good intentions and his ignorance," has gotten involved with the renegade General Thé, who is trying to establish some sort of Third Force, which seeks to rival both the Communists and the French imperialists for power. It is this group that has twice set off bombs in public places where innocent people have been hurt or killed, in a calculated effort to foment hysteria, so that Thé can seize power. "Sooner or later one has to take sides—if one is to remain human," Heng advises Fowler, in attempting to enlist the Englishman's aid against Thé's group. Fowler, obsessed with the thought that Pyle in his own misguided innocence may yet do harm to more innocent people, offers to lure the American into the hands of Heng and his band. But first, he wants to assure himself that his own motives are genuine and not rooted in his jealousy of Pyle, for having taken the Vietnamese girl Phuong away from him.

Accordingly, Fowler invites Pyle to his apartment for a drink, in one last effort to dissuade him from having anything further to do with General Thé and his terrorists. If Fowler fails, he will deliver Pyle into the hands of the Communists. During their conversation Pyle stubbornly maintains that if America helps Thé come to power, he will be friendly toward the United States. In exasperation Fowler says, "How many people have to die before you realize that there's no such thing as gratitude in politics." Fowler then goes to the window and flips through the pages of the book which he has been holding. This is the signal to the Communist agent below that he is arranging a meeting for later that night, on the way to which the Communists will intercept Pyle.

At this point a religious factor begins to assert itself more and more in the story. As Pyle is about to leave Fowler's flat, the latter tells him that if for some reason he cannot meet him for dinner at the club, he should come back to the apartment to continue their discussion. "I handed back the decision to that somebody in whom I didn't believe," Fowler muses; "you can intervene if you want to—a telegram on his desk; a message from the Minister. You cannot exist unless you have the power to alter the future."

But Providence does not intervene in Pyle's behalf. He proceeds to the club to meet Fowler for dinner as planned, and is murdered on the way. "They killed him because he was too innocent to live," says Fowler when he hears of it. "He was young and ignorant and silly and he got involved." Fowler also has the nagging feeling that his own involvement in the Pyle affair has come too late, and, like the American's meddling in politics, it has brought only death.

At the end of the book Fowler feels the need to confess to someone what he has done. Earlier, he had scoffed at the idea of Confession, asserting that man had invented God because he needed to believe in a being capable of understanding him, and that he personally found the idea of Confession morbid and unmanly. In the end, however, Fowler admits the need to confess that he has profited by Pyle's death: with Pyle out of the way and the agreement of his estranged wife to a divorce, he is now free to marry Phuong. He tells the detective Vigot, who is investigating Pyle's death, that the Frenchman would have made a good priest, since it would be so easy to confess to him; but, unfortunately, a policeman does not keep the secrets of the confessional to himself as a priest is bound to do. So the novel closes with Fowler's thinking, "How I wished there existed someone to whom I could say that I was sorry." And one suspects that, like Bendrix, Fowler will perhaps turn, reluctantly, to God. Possibly Fowler will remember, as the reader does, Pyle's reply when Fowler had said that he had no reason to believe in God. "Nobody can go on living without some belief." It is beginning to look as if this statement will finally prove true of Fowler too.

The screen version of *The Quite American* was adapted, produced, and directed by Joseph L. Manckiewicz in 1957. "That film was a real piece of political dishonesty," Greene says. "The film makes the American very wise and the Englishman completely the fool of the Communists." This reversal of the situation as it was developed in the novel recalls the realignment of the characters of the priest and the lieutenant in *The Fugitive*.

"And the casting was appalling," Greene goes on. "The Vietnamese girl Phuong was played by an Italian" (Georgia Moll). The late Audie Murphy's limited acting ability looked even more inadequate than usual in the company of such seasoned performers as Sir Michael Redgrave in the role of Fowler and the French actor Claude Dauphin as Vigot. "I'm working with a handicap," Murphy had once confided to a film director. "I have no talent." This disarming candor did not improve his acting, however, and his portrayal of the important role of Pyle weakened the whole film.

The Quiet American begins with some location shots of the celebra-

tion of the Chinese New Year in Saigon. Over this is superimposed a
printed preface which tells the audience that the year is 1952, and that
three hundred miles north of Saigon the Emperor, who ruled by permission of the French, is fighting a war against the Communist army.
The preface continues in a sardonic tone: "But at war or at peace Chinese New Year was a time to forgive one's enemies, square one's accounts with one's God and creditors and to rejoice in a world that for
two days might be considered a happy one."

The camera than follows a gigantic paper dragon's head as it floats
away from the festivities that are in progress along the river, and comes
to rest near the body of Alden Pyle, face down in a ditch. After this excellent cinematic beginning, the film cuts to Fowler as he talks to Vigot.
Fowler describes Pyle as "one of those Americans who hold out helping hands around the world, not one of those noisy, bellowing Americans at the Continental Bar—a quiet American." Here and throughout
the film Mankiewicz neatly paraphrases or condenses speeches from
the book, as almost all of the dialogue citations which I shall make
from the film will exemplify.

Fowler is asked to identify Pyle's body in the morgue. As he gazes
down at the corpse, the film shifts into the long flashback which con-
stitutes the bulk of the movie. As in the book, then, we are seeing the
action from Fowler's point of view, although we are not often reminded of this. "He was determined to do good—to peoples, conti-
nents, worlds," says Fowler's voice over the sound track, as he begins
to narrate the events leading up to Pyle's death. "Well, he was in his
element now, with the whole universe to improve."

Fowler's own cynical attitude is established when he introduces
Phuong to Pyle and comments, "Phuong means phoenix; that is a fabulous bird which rises from the ashes—except that nothing nowadays
is fabulous and nothing rises from its ashes." By the same token, Pyle's
idealistic attitude is established by his retort, "Is that an opinion or a
fact, Mr. Fowler?" They then proceed to argue about the war that is
in progress.

Sometimes Mankiewicz over-emphasizes Fowler's patronizing
hostility to Pyle in the film, as when Fowler asks him for a cigarette
and Pyle tells him to keep the pack. "I asked for one cigarette," says
Fowler tartly, "not economic aid." Incidents of this kind tend to slant
the viewer's sympathies in favor of Pyle more than Greene intends in

the book, and serve to foreshadow the film's reversal of the ending. Still, Fowler is allowed some thought-provoking lines in the film, as when he says that it is useless for Pyle to speak to Phuong of his plans for the future: "The future means nothing to her. The future is a foreign tense; people who live from day to day have very little use for it."

Fowler and Pyle both get a taste of what it means to live from day to day when Pyle's car mysteriously runs out of gas one night on a deserted road. They take refuge in a nearby watchtower in which two guards are on duty. As in the novel they pass the night discussing religion and politics, and the heart of this conversation is in the film. When Pyle asks Fowler what he believes in, the reply is characteristically pragmatic: "I believe my back's against this wall, and that the guards' guns are loaded." But when Fowler again criticizes America's interference in Indo-Chinese affairs, Mankiewicz does not allow him to have the last word as Greene does in the novel. Pyle responds to Fowler in the film with a speech in which he defends American foreign policy with this patriotic peroration: "America is a young country that is expected to supply answers to the problems that the world hasn't solved in fifty centuries."

Before the debate can go further, the Communists attack the tower. Fowler injures his leg in the skirmish and Pyle carries him to safety just as the watchtower explodes in the background. But the film does not include at this point the brief scene from the book in which Fowler shows himself endowed with a sense of compassion by manifesting more concern for the injured soldier than for himself. Mankiewicz does establish Fowler's humanity, however, in a later scene in which Fowler is appalled at seeing the dead victims of one of the explosions engineered by General The's Third Force. Fowler confronts Pyle about his coöperation in this catastrophe but Pyle denies any complicity in this or any other bombing. Disregarding this, Fowler snaps, "I assume your motives are good; they always are. I wish sometimes you had a few bad motives. You might understand a little more about human beings." In the novel there is another line in the speech which is not in the film: "And that applies to your country too, Pyle." This sentence and many others like it were probably cut in an effort to soften the book's criticism of United States foreign policy.

After the Communists have convinced Fowler of the American's involvement in the bombing plots, he agrees to act as decoy in their plan to get rid of Pyle. In the scene in which Fowler urges Pyle for the last time to give up his association with General Thé, the film emphasizes that Fowler's decision to go ahead with the plot is based as much if not more on his selfish determination to get Phuong back than on his determination to keep Pyle from doing any more harm. This is evident in the film, for it is only after Pyle says that he is taking Phuong with him when he leaves Saigon that Fowler goes to the window and gives the fatal signal. He even reads a passage about jealousy from *Othello* while he stands at the window, whereas in the novel he is holding a volume of Victorian poetry and makes no reference to jealousy at all. Although Fowler still pretends to leave the final decision of Pyle's fate to God, as he did in the novel, the point that he is consciously motivated by jealousy as well as by humanitarian reasons is made abundantly clear by his voice saying over the action, "I wanted Phuong and I wanted the world to be like it was before *he* came." Fowler's motivation is much more ambiguous in the novel, where he says, "I wanted him to go away quickly and die. Then I could start life again—at the point before he came in."

This ambiguity in the book was Greene's intention, since he wanted the reader to realize that Fowler was to some extent subconsciously prejudiced against Pyle because of their mutual involvement with the same girl. Because of this very ambiguity Fowler will never be able to feel self-righteous about Pyle's death, for he will never know to what degree jealousy influenced his decision to collaborate with the Communists against Pyle. And Fowler's resulting uneasiness on this point is further increased by his re-possession of Phuong in the end, a possession which he feels somehow ill-gotten.

I have noted that there are indications throughout the screenplay that Mankiewicz has distributed the audience's sympathy more toward Pyle than toward Fowler, which is a departure from Greene's intent in the novel. In the film's climax Mankiewicz reveals what he has been leading up to all along. The extended flashback concludes with Fowler once more standing over Pyle's body in the morgue. Then Vigot tells Fowler that even though he has no evidence that will implicate Fowler officially in Pyle's death, he thinks that Fowler should know, just for the record, that Pyle was telling the truth when he contended that he was innocent of any involvement in the bombing disasters. It was easy for the Communists to incriminate Pyle in Fowler's eyes, Vigot points out, because they were able to nurture Fowler's jealous prejudice against Pyle. Fowler says in a stunned voice, "What do you want?" "For you to see yourself plainly for once," Vigot answers. He then goes on to tell Fowler that he has been used by the Communists, and has played right into their hands.

In making it appear in the film that jealousy deluded Fowler into betraying an innocent Pyle to the Communists, Fowler's behavior becomes much more heinous than Greene had portrayed it in the book. Mankiewicz seems to have felt that Fowler must be punished in a more obvious manner than by living with his doubts, as he is condemned to do in the novel.

Accordingly, when Fowler goes to tell Phuong in the film that his wife has finally agreed to a divorce, and that he can marry her, she tells Fowler that she hates him for destroying Pyle and that she prefers working as a paid escort in a nightclub to marrying him. "He gave himself to me; you never did," she says to Fowler. "Now it is too late for you, you who never worried about the future." Shaken by this rejection, Fowler wanders out onto the street. He says, as he does in the book, "I wish there existed someone to whom I could say I was sorry." But the line is not said with the hopeful implications it has in the book. For in the film Fowler has just discovered that he had Pyle killed for nothing. Vigot, still acting something of the "priestly role" which Greene gave him, says to Fowler, "I drive past the cathedral . . ." Fowler, in utter despair, grimly and firmly shakes his head, and forlornly wanders away from the camera, a profoundly diminished man, and he is finally lost in the crowd.

Mankiewicz totally exonerates Greene's quiet American by overloading the Englishman with the self-deception that both Pyle and Fowler shared in the book. Consequently, Greene's negative feelings toward the film are quite understandable. "One could almost believe that the film was made deliberately to attack the book and its author," he says. "But the book was based on a closer knowledge of the Indo-China war than the American director possessed and I am vain enough to believe that the book will survive a few years longer than Mr. Mankiewicz's incoherent picture."[48]

Pauline Kael wrote in *Kiss Kiss Bang Bang* that "there are so many

---

[48]Greene, "The Novelist and the Cinema." *loc. cit.*, p. 55.

fine things in the film (especially Redgrave's portrait of a man whose cold exterior is just a thin skin over his passionate desperation) that perhaps you can simply put aside the offending compromises of the last reel. But for anyone familiar with the novel, that is nearly impossible."[49]

While not exactly allowing Mr. Mankiewicz "equal time," I think it only fair to give his reflections on adapting fiction to the film medium. He is, after all, a first-rate screenwriter-director who has won Academy Awards for both his sophisticated writing and direction of *A Letter to Three Wives* and *All About Eve*. In the days when Mankiewicz was a producer at Metro-Goldwyn-Mayer, he quarrelled with F. Scott Fitzgerald over changes which he had made in Fitzgerald's script for *Three Comrades* (1933). Andrew Turnbull's edition of Fitzgerald's letters preserves two long protests which Fitzgerald sent to Mankiewicz asking him to reconsider these alterations and reminding the producer that he was dealing with a successful novelist who knew how to handle dialogue. "Oh, Joe, can't producers ever be wrong?" Fitzgerald pleaded. "I'm a good writer, honest."[50]

Reminded of this episode recently, Mankiewicz told interviewer Andrew Sarris, "Writing dialogue for a novel and writing dialogue for the stage or screen are two different crafts. Margaret Sullavan couldn't read most of Scott's lines, and I rewrote them." Mankiewicz continued, "The novelist has an entirely different relationship with his reader than the screenwriter has with his audience. With a book, the relationship is between the printed page and the reader's intellect. The response is cerebral. On the screen the dialogue is heard, there is not time for cerebration—the response is to the rhythm and sound of the speech almost as much as to its content."[51]

Yet Mankiewicz used a great deal of Greene's original dialogue in the film; often condensed or paraphrased, it is true, but sometimes verbatim. Indeed, the changes which Mankiewicz did make were often dictated more by the alterations which he had made in the characters of Fowler and Pyle than by any other consideration. For example, the conversation in which Fowler tells Vigot that the latter would have

---

[49]Pauline Kael, *Kiss Kiss Bang Bang*. New York: Bantam Books, 1969; p. 422.

[50]F. Scott Fitzgerald, *The Letters of F. Scott Fitzgerald*, ed. Andrew Turnbull. New York: Dell, 1966; p. 587.

[51]Andrew Sarris, "Mankiewicz of the Movies," *Show*, March, 1970, p. 29.

made a good priest proceeds along much the same lines as does the corresponding conversation in the novel, except that tacked onto it is Mankiewicz's radical departure from the spirit of Greene's novel: Vigot's revelation that Pyle was not guilty of doing the things for which Fowler had had him killed.

Greene himself, we learned in the previous chapter, has tended to revise much of his own dialogue when he adapts one of his novels to the screen. I asked British director Ken Russell, who once contemplated filming Greene's *A Burnt-Out Case*, if he feels that dialogue written to be read often does not sound dramatically right when it is heard from the screen. Russell answered that in his screen version of D. H. Lawrence's *Women in Love* (1970), the dialogue was almost all taken verbatim from the book. "If one adapts one's own novel to another medium," Russell explained, "he feels that he's done it this way once; in the interim it has grown in his mind, since one's ideas about any subject change and grow over a period of time. But if I adapt something written by someone else to the screen, I am approaching it fresh and want to leave the thing the way it is as much as possible."

A Burnt-Out Case is one of the few novels by Greene that has yet to be filmed. "Plans to film it earlier were abandoned when we could not get the kind of director and the cast that we wanted at the time," says Greene. Since Russell's *Women in Love* has been much admired as a good example of how a novel can become a film, his handling of *A Burnt-Out Case* would have made a promising screen project.

Greene looks upon the book as one of his religious novels. "In *A Burnt-Out Case* I wanted to show the various grades of belief and unbelief," he said in my interview with him. "The hero's faith was lost temporarily and then came back. In the novel there is a fanatical believer; a good believer—the superior of the mission who is too busy to concern himself with doubt; and the doctor, who has a real belief in his atheism." Greene's reflections on faith and doubt would prove an interesting addition to the films made from his religious novels.

Looking back on the film adaptations of Greene's serious fiction by scriptwriters other than himself, I find that all of them have their moments of what Greene has termed poetic cinema, and I have pointed out some of these earlier. But all of them in some way fall short of expectation. For example, John Ford and Joseph Mankiewicz, two of Hollywood's foremost directors, tried to reshape Greene's material to their own specifications, and all of their considerable technical and artistic skill was spent in turning out rather ordinary films that might have been great. When I asked Ken Russell what his approach would be to filming a serious novel by Greene, he echoed the sentiments that George Cukor expressed with respect to filming Greene's *Travels with My Aunt*: "I do not subscribe to the old idea that unless you change something beyond recognition when you adapt it to the screen that you are not being creative. This attitude is a terrible affront to the original author of the novel, especially if the author in question happens to be a writer of the calibre of D. H. Lawrence—or Graham Greene."

5

BROWN IS NOT GREENE: GREENE'S FILM ADAPTATIONS OF HIS SERIOUS FICTION

Although only Greene's lighter fiction had been filmed prior to 1947, in that year films were made of no less than three of his serious novels: *The Man Within*, *The Power and the Glory* (under the title *The Fugitive*), and *Brighton Rock*. The producers of *The Man Within*, Muriel and Sydney Box, did their own screenplay; John Ford, the director of *The Fugitive*, had one of his favorite scriptwriters, Dudley Nichols, adapt *The Power and the Glory*; and director Anthony Asquith asked playwright Terrence Rattigan, with whom he had worked before, to adapt *Brighton Rock*. But Asquith and Rattigan, along with their producer, Anatole de Grunewald, were not able to get the film into production. When John and Roy Boulting discovered this, they acquired the rights to the novel and asked Greene himself to do the screenplay. "John and I have an enormous admiration for Graham Greene as a writer," said Roy Boulting of himself and his twin brother during their conversation with me, "and we decided to ask Graham, who is an innately cinematic writer, to do the screenplay himself."

Brighton Rock would cause any screenwriter difficulties since it is a melodramatic gangster story with a theme that is deeply religious, and this combination is a difficult one to make work in a film. Greene

had originally planned the novel as a detective story, but the first fifty
pages are all that remain of that idea, he says in his introduction to
Brighton Rock, because the novel began to take on more and more of a
religious dimension as he wrote it.

Brighton had appealed to Greene as the setting for the novel from
the start. Indeed, he has always been fascinated by the place, one of
England's most popular summer seaside resorts. "No city before the
war, not London, Paris, or Oxford, had such a hold on my affections,"
he says.[1] Greene first went there as a child of six and was entranced by
it, and has often gone there since to work out a difficult point in a book
or a screenplay. He followed with interest the gang wars that centered
around the confidence racket at the Brighton racetrack before the
Second World War. Colleoni, the gang leader in *Brighton Rock* (whom
Greene probably named for the fifteenth-century Italian soldier of
fortune), had a real-life prototype in one of the mob bosses of the time.
Greene gave further authenticity to the underworld characters in the
novel by spending several hours learning gangster slang from one of
their number.

Greene had intended to write a suspense yarn about the Brighton
that he knew, but he ended up creating a Brighton that was as somber
as the tormented souls who inhabit his novel. When Greene asks himself why he excluded from his imaginary Brighton so much of the
pleasant Brighton of his own experience, he can only answer, "It was
as though my characters had taken the Brighton I knew into their own
consciousness and transformed the whole picture (I have never again
felt so much the victim of my own inventions)."[2]

Fred Hale, the first character to appear in the novel, is described
as someone who does not belong "to the early summer sun, the cool
Whitsun wind off the sea, the holiday crowd"; and he shares that
quality with many of the other characters in the novel. Since it is from
their point of view that we see Brighton, we rarely get a hint of the
freshly painted piers, the cream houses, or the flower gardens. We
see Brighton as they do, as the landscape against which their inner
turmoils and external conflicts are played out.

Hale knows from the beginning of the story that Pinkie Brown

---

[1]Graham Greene, "Introduction," *Brighton Rock*, in the Collected Edition. London: The Bodley
Head, 1970; pp. x, xi.

[2]*Ibid.*, p. xii.

and his mob are seeking to kill him for throwing in his lot with Colleoni's rival gang. Hale had betrayed Kite, the leader of Pinkie's gang, to Colleoni, and Pinkie is seeking revenge for Kite's murder in order to prove himself a worthy successor although he is only seventeen. It was, in fact, Raven, the central figure of *A Gun for Sale*, published two years before *Brighton Rock* in 1936, who had killed Kite. Therefore the initial conflict in *Brighton Rock* grows right out of *A Gun for Sale*, another indication that the former began as an entertainment.

Raven and Pinkie Brown are much alike, especially since both of them had a grim childhood which prepared them for a life of crime. Indeed, Raven seems almost to be an early sketch for the more fully drawn Pinkie, who believes that the only way to survive in this earthly hell is to inflict pain on others before they get the chance to inflict it on you.

Greene's own childhood was less than happy, and he has described it for us in more than one of his non-fiction works. In *Another Mexico* he writes that Berkhamsted School, which he attended while his father was headmaster there, was a kind of hell for him. It was "a land of stone stairs and cracked bells ringing early," of dormitories where everyone was never quiet at the same time, and of lavatories which had no locks on the assumption that privacy could only be misused; "one began to believe in heaven because one believed in hell; but for a long while it was only hell that one could picture with a certain intimacy."[3]

Greene sums up the condition of the students of Berkhamsted School by paraphrasing the line from Wordsworth in which the poet says that heaven surrounds children in their infancy. Greene says instead, "Hell lay bout them in their infancy," a remark which he also uses to characterize Pinkie Brown's youth in *Brighton Rock*. The young Greene found being the son of the headmaster a real liability, for it put him in what he calls the "hopeless position of divided loyalties."[4] Sir Hugh Greene comments on this remark of his elder brother's: "My father being the headmaster led to one's being treated with caution by the other boys, and this bothered Graham with his greater sensitivity more than it bothered me. Graham had the constant feeling of living

---

[3]Graham Greene, *Another Mexico* (British title: *The Lawless Roads*). New York, 1968; pp. 2, ff.; cf. *A Sort of Life*. New York: Simon and Schuster, 1971; pp. 73, ff.

[4]Christopher Burstall, "Graham Greene Takes the Orient Express," *loc. cit.*, p. 674.

on a frontier—the school on one side of the green baize door and our home on the other. Pinkie Brown has the feeling of living on a frontier—his criminal background on one side and his religious background on the other. It is this sense of living on a border which is the basis of the affinity between Graham's boyhood and Pinkie's, although the border in each case is quite different."

Graham Greene tried unsuccessfully to run away from home when he was sixteen, and was sent to live with a psychoanalyst in London. He found the experience helpful, but emerged from it "wrung dry." Greene recalls how at the age of seventeen he found a revolver in the bedroom which he shared with an elder brother who had been in the war, and decided to have a go at Russian roulette, as a way of assuaging the boredom and loneliness which were the constant presences of his youth. "I did it six times," he says. "It was very exciting at first. I did it at long intervals—perhaps a month would go by before I'd do it again. But finally it had lost its kick, so I finished off with two shots on the same afternoon. It was no more exciting than taking aspirin for a headache."[5]

Greene shows sympathy for Pinkie Brown's unhappy youth, but this is not only because Greene himself had an unpleasant childhood. Greene maintains that the novelist should manifest compassion for all of his characters, the guilty as well as the innocent. Any character for whom the writer fails in sympathy has not to that extent been truly re-created, since the novelist's task, as Greene sees it, "is to draw his own likeness to any human being, the guilty as much as the innocent. Isn't our attitude to all our characters more or less—There, and may God forgive me, goes myself?"[6]

This attitude of Greene's is borne out in *Brighton Rock*, for there is no character in the novel from whom he would want the reader to withhold his sympathy. For example, one of the most likeable people in the book is Ida Arnold, the overweight and over-aged prostitute who befriends Fred Hale just before he is murdered. Ida has no religion except that of enjoying life and helping others to enjoy it too. "She was of the people, she cried in cinemas at *David Copperfield*, when she was drunk all the old ballads her mother had known came easily to

[5]*Ibid.*, 672–73; of Greene, *A Sort of Life, loc. cit.*, pp. 128, ff.
[6]Graham Greene, et al., *Why Do I Write?*. London: Percival Marshall, 1948; p. 48.

her lips, her homely heart was touched by the word tragedy." Therefore, when Fred disappears in the course of their evening together,
and his body is later found in the river, Ida's heart goes out to him.
Like D, the hero of *The Confidential Agent*, Ida operates on the principle
of "an eye for an eye" precisely because she does not believe in God.
If one believes in God, one can leave vengeance to him. But if there
is no God, vengeance belongs to the individual, in this case to Ida.
"I'm a stickler where right is concerned," she says.

Hale had come to Brighton as part of a publicity stunt for the
newspaper for which he worked. He was to circulate among the holiday crowds at Brighton and leave calling cards along his route. Anyone
finding one of these cards would be eligible for a prize from the newspaper. In the course of his day at Brighton, however, Hale came to be
cornered by Pinkie's men, and died of a heart attack before he could
be strangled to death.

With Hale dead, Pinkie sends Spicer, one of his henchmen,
around the amusement park to distribute the rest of the newspaper
calling cards, in order to confuse the police about the precise time
and place of Hale's death. One of the cards is left in Snow's Diner,
where it is picked up by a waitress named Rose. Pinkie discovers that
Rose saw Spicer leave the card at one of the tables, and fears that when
she sees Hale's picture in the newspaper she will tell the police that it
was not Hale who left the card, but someone else. This would lead the
police immediately to suspect that Hale did not commit suicide or die
of natural causes, but possibly was murdered. Accordingly Pinkie
finds it necessary to become friendly with Rose in order to discover
what she knows. That they were both raised as Catholics in the same
slum, Nelson Place, gives them something in common, but Pinkie is
nevertheless secretly revolted by the girl, as he is by all women.

Pinkie's attitude toward women is rooted in his loathing for sex,
which in turn goes back to his childhood when he shared the same
room with his parents and had often witnessed what Pinkie thought
of as their Saturday night sexual *encounters*. Ever since, he has thought
of sex as a furtive act of darkness, and at one point in his youth even
considered becoming a priest in order to avoid marriage. Pinkie tries
to keep a tight rein on his emotions, and the only thing that can really
stir them is music, although he tries to resist its effect on him. While
dancing with the pathetically ensnared Rose, to the strains of . . .

Music talks, talks of our love,
   Gracie Fields funning,
The gangsters gunning,
   Talk of our love . . .

Pinkie is moved romantically in spite of himself. Any music can affect him for it speaks to him of things that he does not understand. Even the Latin hymns that he had sung as a choir boy return to his consciousness over and over again, bringing with them "the smell of incense and laundered surplices." One infers that as long as Pinkie is capable of responding in some way to true human emotions, he is still capable of being redeemed by love, both human and divine.

Pinkie recalls a Latin hymn while he is dancing with Rose and this leads them to a discussion of their common religious background. He says that although he no longer practices the Faith, he still believes in it: "These atheists, they don't know nothing. Of course there's hell. Flames and damnation." "And heaven too," Rose adds. "Oh, maybe," Pinkie agrees with some reluctance. Here Greene is making a direct reference to recollections of his own childhood when he and his companions at school found it so much more easy to believe in hell than in heaven, for heaven seemed as remote and unreal as the deplorable statuary in the school chapel. "Hell lay about him in his infancy," Greene writes, employing the same phrase to describe Pinkie's childhood which he had used to describe his own. "Heaven was a word; hell was something he could trust. A brain was capable only of what it could conceive, and it couldn't conceive what it had never experienced." The cells of Pinkie's brain were formed of the school's cement playground, the room he shared with his parents as a child, the dying Kite in a railway station waiting room. That is why he is moved to ponder the remark made by the crooked lawyer Prewitt, who quotes for him Mephistopheles's answer to Faustus in Marlowe's *Doctor Faustus*, "This is hell, nor are we out of it."

Pinkie resents that he has not had a chance to catch a glimpse of heaven, when hell is so familiar to him. He does not want to admit that he is offered such a glimpse in the person of the noble and innocent Rose who has become devoted to him. Pinkie tries to resist responding both to her love for him or to her religious convictions. It is Rose who supplies for him the missing word in the aphorism that he cannot quite recall. Pinkie says, "Between the stirrup and the ground, he something sought and something found." The operative "something" which is beyond the reach of Pinkie's memory is mercy. Pinkie admits that one could be saved "between the stirrup and the ground," but only if one repents. And he does not think that he will repent of his past sins at the moment of his death, even if he has time to do so: "You couldn't break in a moment the habit of thought: habit held you closely while you died." He feels that the ribs of his body are like steel bands, holding him down to eternal unrepentence. It doesn't matter anyway, he concludes, since he was never made for peace and does not believe in it.

Rose cannot fully comprehend Pinkie's religious notions, but she understands Ida's point of view even less than Pinkie's. Ida keeps pestering both of them about Hale's death, insisting that justice must be done. Rose says in a rare burst of temper, "What does she know about us. She doesn't know what mortal sin is. . . . She couldn't burn if she tried. . . . I'd rather burn with you than be like her. . . . She's ignorant." Rose's expression of feeling brings Pinkie closer to her than he has ever been before. "What was most evil in him needed her: it couldn't get along without goodness."

Ida does not speak their language; she talks of justice, of right and wrong, but never of sin and repentance, of good and evil, concepts that might strike a chord in Rose if not in Pinkie. When Rose says to Ida that she is not going to leave Pinkie, because she has not given up hope that he may repent of his past, Ida answers that people do not change: "Look at me. I've never changed. It's like those sticks of rock: bite it all the way down, you'll still read Brighton. That's human nature." (Ida is referring to "Brighton rock," a kind of stick candy that has the word *Brighton* imprinted on it in such a way that the word appears on the ends of the stick at whatever point one breaks it off.)

Although Ida is inspired by purely human motives in trying to convict Pinkie of Hale's death, and to save Rose from being corrupted by him, there is a kind of virtue in Ida that one cannot but admire. "One can respect an atheist more than an agnostic," Greene has written elsewhere. "Once accept a God and reason should carry you further, but to accept nothing at all—that requires some stubbornness, some courage."[7] Ida is nothing if she is not stubborn and courageous.

[7]Greene, *Another Mexico, loc. cit.*, p. 32.

She has the courage to confront Pinkie and tell him that she is trying to gather evidence against him, and the stubbornness to keep trying to get the police to reopen the case, despite the fact that the coroner has reported that Hale died of a heart attack.

Ida senses, correctly, that Hale had a heart attack while he was being strangled. Her suspicions are confirmed when Cubitt, one of Pinkie's mob, drunkenly tells her that Spicer, another member of the gang, has been murdered. Ida reasons, again correctly, that Pinkie has put Spicer out of the way because Spicer was the one who planted Hale's cards around Brighton after his death, and Pinkie was afraid that Ida might pressure Spicer into talking. Pinkie is aware that his situation is becoming more and more precarious, and decides to marry Rose because it is inadmissible for a wife to testify against her husband.

Rose, of course, take's Pinkie's proposal as the utmost demonstration of his love for her. Pinkie's experience on his wedding night, however, is a traumatic one, for he is obsessed with the idea that he is somehow surrendering part of his manhood by submitting to sexual intercourse. This is how women judged you, he muses, "not by whether you had the guts to kill a man, to run a mob, to conquer Colleoni." He feels that "the game of life" has got him at last, as it had gotten his parents. Rose, blithely unaware of Pinkie's brooding thoughts, asks him to make a record for her in the amusement park, as a memory of their wedding. Instead of speaking the message of love which Rose expects, he records, "God damn you, you little bitch, why can't you go back home forever and let me be?" He gives her the record and she looks forward to having a chance to play it.

Pinkie finds Rose's continued devotion stifling, and because he has never trusted any woman, he fears that some day she will turn on him and betray him to the police. Accordingly he decides to capitalize on her present love for him by making a suicide pact with her which he has no intention of keeping. He persuades her to go with him to a deserted place by the seaside where they can end their lives together. Rose is willing to join Pinkie in damnation; she will not let him go into eternal darkness alone.

Pinkie gives her his gun and asks her to be first. In the most suspenseful moment in the entire novel, the reader waits to see if Rose will go through with what she believes to be the supreme proof of her love for Pinkie. As she lifts the revolver to her head, all of the old religious teachings of her childhood come crowding into her mind, tempting her to virtue, as if to sin. Just as she is about to shoot, Ida appears with a policeman and stops her. This is no *deus ex machina*. Greene has foreshadowed Ida's eleventh hour appearance by letting the reader know earlier that she had finally collected enough evidence to have Pinkie arrested. She had found out from a member of Pinkie's gang, who wanted no part in any more deaths, where Pinkie and Rose had gone and caught up with them in time to save Rose.

Pinkie raises a bottle of vitriol to hurl at his pursuers, but before he can throw it the policeman smashes it in the gangster's face with his baton. "It was as if the flames had literally got him and he shrank—shrank into a schoolboy flying in panic and pain." Pinkie hysterically throws himself over the fence that lines the cliff edge and hurtles into the darkness of the sea below. "It was as if he had been withdrawn suddenly by a hand out of any existence—past or present, whipped away into zero-nothing."

Rose is disconsolate because she fears that she has lost Pinkie forever, that they will miss each other in the world to come, "mercy operating somehow for one and not for the other." The sniffling old priest to whom she makes her Confession thinks otherwise. "You can't conceive, my child," he tells her, "the appalling strangeness of the mercy of God." He advises her that in the event that she has a child that she should raise him to pray for his father. After all, if Pinkie truly loved her, that shows that there was some good in him. Comforted by his words, Rose replies that she has proof of Pinkie's love for her in the record that he made for her, and she goes home to play it for the first time.

The closing scene of the novel seems, at first glance, to confirm the fact that Pinkie has been damned. The priest says that if Rose's love for Pinkie had prompted in him a return of love for her, however meager, it might have proved redemptive for him, helping him to rise from human love to divine love. We know, however, that the record contains not a protestation of love, but of hatred. Hence, one might conclude that Pinkie has unequivocally demonstrated himself incapable of responding to human love, and that there is no hope that he could have expressed even a minimal love of God that would have enabled him to save his soul.

This is the way many critics have read the ending of the novel. Evelyn Waugh, for example, said that Greene had challenged "the modern mood" that tends to turn away from the concept of hell "by creating a completely damnable youth. Pinkie of *Brighton Rock* is the ideal examinee for entry into hell"[8]. With all due respect to Mr. Waugh—and a great deal is due him both as novelist and critic—I find an explanation of the novel that maintains that Pinkie is certainly damned a trifle too facile. Throughout the novel Greene illustrates his theme of divine mercy by indicating how Pinkie is continually tempted to good by God.

Greene uses Pinkie's susceptibility to the emotional impact of music as an indication of the fact that Pinkie is not as impervious an individual as he would like to believe. Romantic love songs tend to blend in his imagination with religious music, and the latter often leads him to unwanted thoughts of his religious upbringing. At one point, when he is tempted to succumb to the amorous blandishments of a woman, he is conscious of the music issuing from a nearby dance hall beating on his resistence. Greene draws a parallel with this scene later when Pinkie is driving Rose to the place where he intends her to die. Pinkie feels an enormous emotion welling in him as the words of a Latin hymn from the Mass recur in his mind; but he tries to resist, as he had tried to resist the dance music, with all of the bitter force of his hatred for his unhappy youth. Still, he cannot help wondering if at some later time he will repent of what he is about to do. More than once in the novel Pinkie sensed "a faint nostalgia for the tiny dark confessional box," and the peace that it offers. That nostalgic feeling returns to him as he drives, and he tells himself, "Even if death came suddenly, driving home tonight, the smash of the lamp post—there was still 'Between the stirrup and the ground.'"

I think that Greene has endeavored to leave the question of Pinkie's ultimate salvation open. It is true that I have quoted him as saying that *The Heart of the Matter* was about a man who went to purgatory, *The Power and the Glory* about a man who went to heaven, and *Brighton Rock* about a man who went to hell. In commenting on this statement, however, Greene said, "What I really meant was that, for example, *Brighton Rock* is written in such a way that people could plau-

---

[8] Evelyn Waugh, "Felix Culpa?" *loc. cit.,* p. 322.

sibly imagine that Pinkie went to hell, but then I cast doubt on it in the ending. The real theme of the three novels, and of *The End of the Affair* which followed them, is embodied in the priest's phrase at the end of *Brighton Rock*: 'You can't conceive, my child, . . . the appalling strangeness of the mercy of God.' I wanted to introduce a doubt of Pinkie's future in the words of the priest, a doubt whether even a man like that could possibly merit eternal punishment. It is appalling, the strangeness. Because the mercy of God obviously is operating in some inexplicable fashion even with the gas ovens of Auschwitz. In fact I wanted to throw doubt on hell altogether. I'm a great believer in Purgatory. Purgatory to me makes sense, while hell doesn't."[9]

The specific doubt that Greene casts on Pinkie's damnation is based on the possibility that divine love, by way of Rose's human love for him, may have at last gotten through to him despite the remarks he made to her in anger on the recording. Although Greene throughout the novel frequently takes us into Pinkie's consciousness to share his thoughts, Greene deliberately describes Pinkie's death from Rose's point of view so that, like Rose, we are ignorant of what his dying thoughts were. In point of fact, the last time we are allowed to read Pinkie's mind in the novel, the unbidden thought that is running through his unconsciousness is a phrase from the Mass: "He was in the world and the world was made by him and the world knew him not."

Today Greene feels that his discussion of divine mercy in *Brighton Rock* was "far too obvious and open for a novel."[10] Yet because it was so integral to the novel, it would have to form a part of the screenplay. One of the elements of the book that made Greene's task of adapting it for the film medium somewhat easier is the cinematic flavor of the narrative style, which provided several scenes which would prove visually exciting on the screen. For example, in the scene where Pinkie is "carved" by some of Colleoni's men at the racetrack, Greene describes in the book in a visual image how Pinkie shields his face from an assailant's knife with his hand and is slashed on the knuckles. Greene then adds an auditory image to the visual image in true cinematic fashion: Pinkie "began to weep, as the four-thrity went by in a drumbeat of hoofs beyond the rail."

---

[9]Burstall, *loc. cit.*, pp. 676–77.

[10]Greene, "Introduction," *Brighton Rock, loc. cit.*, p. x.

"The script of *Brighton Rock* I am ready to defend," says Greene. "There were good scenes, but the Boulting Brothers were too generous in giving an apprentice his rope." John and Roy Boulting work together on all of their films, with one producing and the other directing. In the case of *Brighton Rock*, Roy acted as producer and John directed. John Boulting remembers that he and his brother had moments of anxiety about whether or not film audiences would accept the religious elements of *Brighton Rock* on the screen: "But religion is a built-in part of Graham's work; it is the ingredient that makes his fiction special and unique. So in the end we decided that it would be a challenge to present this complex novel on the screen the way that Graham had envisioned it."

The first real problem that they encountered was with the film censor. In England the British Board of Censors rates films according to their suitability for general patronage; for children accompanied by a parent or adult guardian; or for adults only. Theater owners throughout England are bound by law to adhere to the ratings given to films by the Board, which can also ban a film entirely if it is deemed unfit for theatrical exhibition. As a result, most film producers submit the script of a picture which they are about to make to the Board in order to deal with any objections that the Censors might raise prior to production.

In due course, Greene submitted the script for *Brighton Rock* to the chairman of the Board of Censors, Brook Wilkinson, who made objections that Greene considered absurd. "The script was slashed to pieces," says Greene. "The whole film was weakened by the censor's well-meaning agnostic care for the beliefs of others." The censor refused to let Pinkie quote any parts of the Mass, for instance, because he was a murderer, and it was thought that this would offend Roman Catholics.

A preface was added to the beginning of the film which states that the story is set between the wars, when there were gangsters at Brighton, but that this Brighton is happily no more. When I inquired if this preface was the censor's idea, Roy Boulting replied that he and his brother wanted to shoot the film on location—something that was not common in the British film industry at the time. "This required a great deal of coöperation from the local authorities in Brighton and they feared that unless it was indicated in the film that the days of the

racetrack gangs were over, some people might come to Brighton looking for trouble. Brighton before the Second World War was the center
of the warfare among the racetrack gangs, and this provided Graham
with the milieu for his story. As a kind of technical adviser on the
film we had a man who had carried a razor for Sabini, the gangster
chief on whom Graham based the character of Colleoni."

John Boulting adds, "There have always been two Brightons;
Brighton has always been a strange mixture of holiday crowds plus a
seamy subworld which is really an overspill of people from the slums
of the east end of London. But it is true that the postwar Brighton is
not like it was in the days of the race gangs, so we didn't mind affixing
the preface to the film in exchange for being able to do the film on location."

After the preface the film opens with a shot of a man napping on
the beach at Brighton with a newspaper shielding his face from the
sun. The newspaper carries an announcement of Fred Hale's appearance at Brighton that day. Then the film shifts to the boarding house
where Pinkie's gang hangs out and a scene in which Greene gets across
a great deal of exposition in a short time, in the course of a conversation between the members of the gang before Pinkie himself appears.
Cubitt notices Fred Hale's picture in the newspaper and discovers
that he is to be in Brighton that very day in connection with the newspaper contest. Dallow then explains Pinkie's reason for wanting Hale
killed: "Pinkie loved Kite, and Kite trusted Fred, and if Fred hadn't
written that paragraph about the slot machines, Kite'd be alive today."

We are now prepared for the first glimpse of Pinkie (played by
Richard Attenborough, who played Andrews in *The Man Within* the
same year). He is lying on the bed in his shabby room endlessly tying
knots in a piece of string. Dallow enters the room and shows him the
newspaper, and Pinkie stares at Hale's photograph. Pinkie and his
henchmen go immediately to the Brighton amusement park where
Pinkie confronts Hale and threatens him. After Pinkie disappears into
the crowd, the film communicates Hale's anxiety by the same device
used in the novel. A hawker asks Hale if he wants to buy shoe laces or
razor blades. At the words, "razor blades" Hale grimaces, remember-
ing that it was with a blade that Kite was killed.

Hale begs one stray girl after another to accompany him around
the park, reasoning that Pinkie will try to kill him only when he is

alone. Finally Ida Arnold (Hermione Baddeley) consents to go along with him "for a bit of fun." In the novel Greene does not describe the death of Hale. Ida leaves him momentarily for a trip to the ladies' room and when she comes back he has disappeared. Greene shrewdly has wrung much more suspense out of Hale's death in the movie by depicting it directly. As Ida goes away to retrieve a lost handkerchief, the camera stays with Hale. He stiffens to see Dallow and Cubitt looking for him, and ducks into "Dante's Inferno," a fun house where customers are conducted on a tour of the "underworld" in a small train. Hale sits down in the little train and is relieved to see that he has eluded Dallow and Cubitt. As the train moves into a dark tunnel the camera pulls back to reveal that the passenger sitting next to Hale is Pinkie. The train sweeps into the darkness amid the happy screams of the passengers, who are unaware that something genuinely horrible is happening while they are occupied with the artificial terrors of the fun house.

The sea runs along the side of the train track and in the darkness of the tunnel we are still able to see Pinkie push the terrified Hale out of the car to his death in the waters below. When the train comes to a stop at the platform Ida can be seen looking for Hale as Pinkie leaves.

When next we see Pinkie he has won a prize at the shooting gallery. It is a doll which he swings by the hair as he walks along. In the novel the prize is a likeness of the Blessed Virgin. Greene uses it in the book to indicate Pinkie's surface disdain for religion, as he describes Pinkie walking along "holding the Mother of God by the hair." In the film, Pinkie's treatment of the doll serves to show his aversion for the female of the species. While he is talking to someone in the following scene, Pinkie is shown pulling out the hairs of the doll's head one by one, before finally letting it fall to the floor to smash into pieces. This prepares us for the next scene in which he tries ever so awkwardly to ingratiate himself with the fragile Rose, for he is unaccustomed to manifest tenderness.

Greene has taken the pains to work even the most subtle thematic implications of the novel into the film, something that perhaps only the original author of the book would have been able to do. There are several occasions in the film, as in the book, in which Pinkie shows himself susceptible to music, implying that he is not as calloused as he fancies himself. As he and Rose listen to the sounds coming from the

BRIGHTON ROCK (Associated British Picture Corporation, 1947). Richard Attenborough as Pinkie, one of the "razor-slashing racecourt gangsters in Brighton between the wars," as one critic described them. Greene, after initial doubts, came to consider Attenborough as ideally cast in the central part.

dance pavilion he remarks on the romantic quality of the music and boasts that he knows all about love. Then the secular music reminds him of religious music, and when he sees that Rose carries a rosary their conversation turns to their mutual Roman Catholic background. Drawing on the dialogue of the novel, Greene has Pinkie affirm his belief in the Faith that he no longer practices: "Of course it's true. These atheists, they don't know nothing. Of course there's hell. Flames, damnation, and torments." "And heaven too?" asks Rose. "Oh, maybe," he replies.

The religious aspects of the story do not keep the film from being a thriller, however, any more than they kept the book from being one. For example, the film builds up tension, as Pinkie prepares to murder Spicer, in a manner that is in some ways more gripping than it was in the novel. At the gang hideout, when Pinkie reaches the top of the hall stairs he overhears Spicer expressing his apprehension to the others that they all will be implicated in the murder of Fred Hale. As he listens, Pinkie puts one hand on the shaky bannister. Then he enters the room where the others are talking and announces that he is going to visit one of the racetrack bookies who has become remiss in paying for the gang's protection. Pinkie picks up a razor and abruptly turns on Spicer and threatens him with it, telling him that he had best not turn yellow. This scene makes clear to the audience in a very economical way why Pinkie plans to liquidate Spicer, and also how he intends to use the faulty bannister to make it look like an accident.

Greene further sharpens the dramatic action of the novel for the film by portraying the death of Spicer. In the book, Pinkie enters Spicer's room and the action then switches to another location. When it returns to the boarding house, Pinkie is standing over Spicer's body at the foot of the stairs. In the motion picture, Pinkie goes into Spicer's room, forces him out onto the landing, and drives him through the weakened bannister to his death. In the film, then, the viewer's sense of dread at what is to happen is not allowed to subside during a cutaway to another scene, as in the book.

Throughout the picture Greene has sought to take as many cinematic shortcuts as possible, in order to keep the pace of the story from flagging. For example, there is the scene in which Ida first suspects that someone other than the man himself went around distributing the calling cards to give the impression that Hale was still alive. As Rose tells Ida that she had served Hale a bottle of beer while he was in the diner, over the sound track Ida immediately hears Hale's earlier words, "I can't drink bottled beer. It doesn't agree."

For the sake of simplicity Greene has amalgamated the characters of Phil Corkery, one of Ida's beaux, and Jim Tate, a bookmaker, from whom Pinkie's gang extorts money. With the Tate character now a boyfriend, Ida is enabled to find out more easily about the rivalry of Pinkie's and Colleoni's mobs and how they are tied in with Hale's murder.

Since the movie has followed the spirit of the novel so closely all along, the filmgoer is just as psychologically prepared for Pinkie's death at the end as is the reader of the novel, and the gangster's disappearance over the cliff into the void is breathtaking. But the final scene of the film is a departure from the novel which is quite unexpected in the light of the fidelity to the book up to this point.

It is a nun, rather than a priest, who speaks to Rose of "the appalling strangeness of the mercy of God," and suggests that if Pinkie loved her, then there is some hope for him. Rose then proudly produces the record which Pinkie had made for her and puts it on the phonograph. The message that Pinkie had recorded earlier was, "You want me to say I love you. Here's the truth. I hate you, you little slut." Now as the camera moves in on the phonograph turntable we hear Pinkie say, "You want me to say I love you," and at that moment the phonograph needle sticks, and the phrase "I love you, I love you . . ." is repeated over and over. The camera pans up to a crucifix on the wall and the film ends.

I was surprised to learn from Greene that he had altered the original ending of the story himself. "I liked the ending of the film," he told me, "and I am completely responsible for it. I have complete justification for the needle sticking on the gramophone record. I knew the censor and the distributors would not accept the ghastly ending of the book. I also knew that thinking people would realize that one day Rose would play the record and move the needle beyond the crack and thus get the shock with which the book ends. The inevitable outcome was only delayed. It was the director's idea to pan up to the crucifix on the wall, however. This gave the impression that the needle stuck miraculously. Earlier in the film Pinkie had tried to destroy the record, but was interrupted by Rose. This explains the crack in the record; there is nothing miraculous about it."

"In general," says Roy Boulting, "the ending of the film emerged out of the refusal of the censor to accept the ending of the novel. Brook Wilkinson, the censor at the time, was an elderly gentleman, who had an Edwardian, not to say Victorian, attitude toward life and morality. Graham and I had a conference with Mr. Wilkinson about the screenplay after John had already begun shooting the picture, and Graham worked out an ending for the film which was basically a compromise that would preserve the essence of the novel's close. The idea of the camera's panning up to the crucifix as the final image of the film was decided on the studio floor while the scene was being shot. I liked this image because to me it implied that the needle sticking on the record was an example of the 'appalling strangeness of the mercy of God' working in behalf of the girl, shielding her from the knowledge of the kind of man Pinkie really was until she was better prepared to accept it."

John Boulting, however, thought of the ending in a slightly different way: "The additional shot of the camera panning up to the crucifix for me added an ironic touch. The audience knew what Pinkie had really said on the record and the final image of the crucifix for me was an ironic comment on Rose's religious faith, which was much too naïve." In any event, the ending of the film is thought provoking, as witnessed by the varying interpretations of it given by the three creative artists who were involved in fashioning it.

Greene was unhappy with the casting of a pretty young woman as the nun in the final scene: "I wanted an old nun with a cold in the head, and the setting to be a dingy room with a faded holy picture on the wall. Instead the director had a beautiful young lady as the nun in a white room that looked like a hospital." Greene had wanted to have an elderly person in this part, someone who obviously had suffered through life but could still offer compassion and hope to others.

"Perhaps the nun had too much of The Bells of St. Mary's about her," John Boulting concedes. "But Roy and I had the view that since the film had told a pretty grim story it would be better to end on a more pleasant image. In those days audiences didn't easily accept a film that had an unhappy ending in the way that they do now. Hence we wanted to soften the ending a bit, without taking any of its upbeat quality away."

Greene also had reservations about the casting of Hermione Baddeley as Ida Arnold: "Her style of acting did not belong to the same level of reality as the other performances in the film. She played the part rather as a music hall turn." It is true that Ida *was* a music hall performer, and Hermione Baddeley rightly portrayed this side of Ida in the scenes in which Ida was in the spotlight, as it were. But Greene still feels that she carried a bit of this over into the dramatic scenes, in which Ida should have been shown to be more sensible and serious.

John Boulting's feeling about Hermione Baddeley's performance is that "she got the surface of the character right, but she missed the depth of the character—that might have been the fault of my direction." Roy Boulting, on the other hand, says that "the depth of Ida's character would be difficult for most people to comprehend. She embodies all of the lower-middle class virtues; yet Graham seems to imply in the story that Pinkie has a better chance for salvation than Ida because he is operating in the realm of grace, whereas Ida, who is an atheist, is outside that realm. I think Ida as Graham created her is only explicable in these terms, but it was very difficult to convey the depth of her character in the film as a result."

Greene had initially expressed misgivings about the casting of Richard Attenborough as Pinkie, saying that he thought the young actor, who had played Pinkie in a stage version of the novel, was not physically right for the part. In the end, however, after he saw the film, he wrote a note to the Boultings saying that Attenborough was as close to Pinkie as he had conceived him as any actor could be. By and large Greene is happy with the way the film of *Brighton Rock* turned out, and it does rank in the upper echelon of Greene screen adaptations.

After all of the negotiations in which Greene and the Boulting Brothers engaged with the British Board of Censors over the script for *Brighton Rock*, it is ironic that Reg Whitley, the reviewer of the London *Daily Mirror*, criticized the Board for being too easy on the film. The following day the *Mirror* published an answer to Whitley's review by Graham Greene, in which Greene rejected Whitley's praise of the novel at the expense of the screenplay because he was the author of both, and had tried to preserve in the film the religious theme of the book. "Any modifications of that theme are the responsibility of the British Film Censor," he continued, "who objected to various passages in the dialogue of a specifically religious nature. Apparently one is allowed a certain latitude in using the name of God as an expletive, but any serious quotation from the Bible is not permissible on the English screen. But in spite of this handicap, I should have said that what your critic describes almost too kindly as the 'subtle religious theme' was as present in the film as in the book." Greene concluded that the *Mirror* critic's disgust with the film was "an indication that one purpose of the film—the presentation of a character possessed by evil—has been successfully achieved."[11]

The other serious novel of Greene's brought to the screen in his own adaptation is *The Comedians*, which MGM asked him to prepare for filming in 1967. The Comedians has a primarily political rather than religious theme, although it does have a religious dimension. "*The Comedians* is not a Catholic novel," says Greene. "The hero Brown happens to be a Catholic; it was this formation that made him the type of person he was; and Brown, as I said in the preface to the novel, is not Greene, even though Greene is a Catholic and the story is told in the first person. *The Comedians* is essentially a political novel." Greene points out in the dedicatory note that the fact that Brown is a Catholic does not automatically make the book a Catholic novel: "It is often forgotten that, even in the case of a novel laid in England, the story when it contains more than ten characters would lack verisimilitude if at least one of them were not a Catholic. The ignoring of this fact of social statistics sometimes gives the English novel a provincial air."

If any novel laid in England should have a Catholic character or two, then a novel set in Haiti should have several, since Haiti is Roman Catholic by tradition. All of the natives have a Catholic background, although in many cases it is mixed with a large helping of voodooism. Greene has always made it a practice to make an extended visit to a locale where he intends to set a novel, in order to give an air of authenticity to his story. Many of the characters in this novel are based on people whom he knew while he was in Haiti, but the physical traits and habits of speech that he borrowed from them were "boiled up in the kitchen of the unconscious" and emerged "unrecognizable even to the cook in most cases."[12] But Greene's picture of Haiti under the rule of the late Papa Doc Duvalier is in no way invented. While visiting Haiti he found the country "the most monstrous place imaginable" and Papa Doc himself "a ghastly person."[13]

Although Greene has not darkened his picture of tyranny in Haiti

[11]Both Reg Whitley's review of *Brighton Rock* and Greene's answer appeared in the program notes for a screening of the film at the National Film Theater in London in 1960.

[12]Graham Greene, "Dedicatory Note," *The Comedians*. London: The Bodley Head, 1966; p. 5.

[13]"A New Honor and a New Novel," *Life*, February 4, 1966, p. 44.

for dramatic effect, neither has he lightened it for comic effect as he did his portrayal of the Batista regime in Cuba in *Our Man in Havana*. The title of *The Comedians* does not refer to the notion of a clown. Greene is rather using the word *comedian* mainly in the larger sense in which it is used by the *Comédie Francaise* in Paris. A comedian is an actor, who plays either comedy or tragedy. In extending the use of the word to Brown and the other principal characters in the novel, Greene means to imply that they are either playing parts thrust on them by circumstance, or enacting a rôle which is meant to cover up their true selves.

In this sense of the term, the most obvious comedian in the novel is Jones, the charming con man who has worn many disguises throughout his life in order to swindle people. Greene says that the quotation from Thomas Hardy on the title page of the novel refers to Jones: "Aspects are within us, and who seems most kingly is the king." "Jones seems to be kingly even though he is a trickster," Greene explains. "He is good company, and one almost does not mind being tricked by him because he makes people laugh."

The novel begins with Brown reflecting on Jones' death, and how he died the hero he had always pretended to be, in effect by calling his own bluff for once. As in *The End of the Affair* and *The Quiet American*, Greene gives us a narrator who himself takes part in the story that he is telling. Brown begins the story at the point of his return trip from New York to Port-au-Prince, the capital of Haiti, after an unsuccessful attempt to sell the hotel which he owns there. On board the ship he gets acquainted with Jones and with an American couple, Mr. and Mrs. Smith. The Smiths hope to encourage the Haitians to become vegetarians like themselves, as part of a program for social betterment which they plan for the country. As a gesture, Mr. Smith had run against Harry Truman in the 1948 presidential election, and he is still referred to as "the presidential candidate." "Smith, Jones, and Brown—the situation was improbable," Brown comments; their three names are interchangeable, "like comic masks in a farce."

Brown often thinks of life as a comedy, and not at all the tragedy for which he was prepared at school by the Jesuit Fathers who taught him. He contends that it is only his sense of humor that enables him to believe in God at all. God is "the authoritative practical joker" who drives us on throughout our lives "towards the extreme point of comedy." This view of life provides Brown with an attitude of detachment toward whatever befalls him, an attitude one might almost admire, were it not for the fact that it has developed into a cynicism that is approaching despair. Brown believes that one must choose the role that one wishes to play in life and change it as circumstances demand. He traces this attitude back to his mother, whom he remembers as "an accomplished comedian." Her motto had been, "As long as we pretend, we escape."

She had managed to convince the Jesuits of the College of the Visitation in Monte Carlo of her moral rectitude and solvency, and entrusted them with the education of her son. She then left for parts unknown and never paid his tuition. Years later, Brown was summoned to her bedside as she was dying, in the Hotel Trianon in Port-au-Prince, of which she had become the owner. Before she died (during the act of love with her black paramour) she bequeathed the hotel to her son. Her last words to him were, "You really are a son of mine. What part are you playing now?" At the time, Brown did not know what she meant; but since then, he admits, he has often found himself playing various rôles to achieve personal ends in matters of love and of business. He now realizes that his mother had judged him correctly as a true son of hers, in spite of the years of training that he received from the Jesuits aimed at his growing up to be a man of integrity.

For a while the Jesuits thought that young Brown might have a vocation to join their order. But the question of Brown's religious vocation was solved once and for all by his first bit of rôle playing. Made up as an older man for a college play, Brown took advantage of his appearance to gain entrance to the casino at Monte Carlo. There he both won some money and lost his virginity to a woman whom he had met at the gaming tables. His adventure was discovered when he inadvertently dropped a gambling chip instead of a coin into the collection basket at Sunday services. Although Brown was summarily expelled from school, in the intervening years he was never able to erase the Jesuit influence of his boyhood. The Jesuits seem to symbolize in the novel the ideals of Western Christian culture to which Brown no longer subscribes. Brown says that he left all such absolutes behind him in the school chapel.

Nevertheless, at times he asks himself what the good fathers would think of what he has become: an aimless, somewhat seedy hotel keeper who is carrying on an adulterous affair with Martha Piñeda, the wife of a Latin American ambassador. Because Brown has faith in neither God nor man, he is never able to convince himself that Martha Piñeda, his mistress, is any truer to him than she is to her husband. Martha tries to explain to him that he invents the people around him, and that he does not listen to anything they say which is out of keeping with the part that he has written for them to play in his own life: "My dear, try to believe that we exist when you aren't there. . . . None of us is like you fancy we are. Perhaps it wouldn't matter much if your thoughts were not so dark."

Although Brown's outlook is basically nihilistic, he nevertheless nurtures an admiration for Dr. Magiot, who is a Communist, because Magiot has something to believe in. Brown reflects at one point that he and other rootless individuals like him have resisted "the temptation of sharing the security of a religious creed or a political faith," but they admire the dedicated, the Dr. Magiots and Mr. Smiths of the world, "for their courage and their integrity, for their fidelity to a cause." This idea of commitment is intimately related to the theme of the novel, which springs from the title. For, the comedians of the story can never be committed to the roles they play in life in the way those who have a creed, political or religious, are committed to living out that creed. We shall see these two interlocking themes develop as the story goes on.

Once Greene has made us familiar with Brown's past, the novel moves forward in the present. Upon reaching his hotel, Brown finds the dead body of Dr. Philipot, one of Papa Doc's ministers who has fallen out of favor, lying in the empty hotel swimming pool. The doctor had sought asylum at the hotel while Brown was away, and had cut his own throat when he thought he heard the approach of Papa Doc's secret police, the *Tontons Macoute* (a term meaning "bogeymen" in Haitian patois). Greene's description of the situation affords us a perfect example of the cinematic element in his writing technique, which enables the reader to visualize the whole scene: Dr. Philipot lay on the floor of the empty pool; "above the head was the dark circle of the pipe. We had only to turn on the water to wash the blood away; he had been as considerate as possible."

Brown summons Dr. Magiot to help him remove the body from

the hotel grounds. As Magiot peers down at the corpse, he muses that Dr. Philipot could hardly be said to have been guilty of theological despair. "In this despair there was nothing theological," he says. "In his case the sense of survival did not put forward a commandment of God as an excuse for inaction." Commenting to me on this passage, Greene said, "Since most people in Haiti are Catholics, presumably Dr. Philipot is too. Magiot is a precise and clear man. Many Catholics think suicide amounts to theological despair, which is a mortal sin. But Magiot doesn't believe that Dr. Philipot thought of his suicide in these terms. He was escaping from an intolerable situation and that was uppermost in his mind when he ended his life."

Brown often discusses religion with Magiot (who, like himself, has abandoned Roman Catholicism) as a way of reaffirming his own disbelief. Magiot chides him for this: "I retain faith, even if it's only the truth of certain economic laws, but you've lost yours." "Have I?" Brown says in return. "Perhaps I never had one. Anyway, it's a limitation to believe, isn't it?" I asked Greene to expand on this passage and he responded: "When I have Brown say that it is a limitation to believe I do not mean that faith makes one less of a person. I mean rather that if, for example, one believes in the resurrection, all kinds of other contrary beliefs, such as annihilation at death, are out of the question. At any rate, Brown is really using his remark as a debating point."

In thinking about his conversation with Dr. Magiot later on, Brown tries to defend his continued lack of commitment to any goal or ideal, by maintaining that since he has not limited himself to believing in anything, he is open to everything, "to the whole world of evil and of good, to the wise and to the foolish, to the indifferent and to the mistaken." He has chosen "nothing except to go on living." "This argument interested me," he says upon reflection. "I daresay it eased the never quiet conscience which had been injected into me without my consent" by the Jesuit Fathers of the College of the Visitation.

For Greene, the key to the passage is contained in the reason that Brown gives as to why this line of argument interests him: "Brown is indulging in a bit of intellectual trickery. He is trying to justify himself against the Magiots of the world." It bothers Brown that Magiot still holds on to his belief in Communism instead of believing in nothing like Brown himself; yet he respects Magiot for being the way he is.

Brown learns to respect the Smiths too, although he initially thought them hopeless American idealists (resembling Pyle in *The Quiet American*). When the *Tontons* disrupt the funeral procession of Dr. Philipot, Mr. and Mrs. Smith stand by Madame Philipot and her child to shield them from being harmed or insulted by Captain Concasseur (whose name means "steamroller" in French) and his men. While Brown and the others look on in amazed inaction, Concasseur strikes Mrs. Smith in anger for interfering, and she stays her husband from retaliating by reminding him that they were treated worse by the police in Nashville, Tennessee. The Smiths had participated in a pro-Negro demonstration there and had been roughed up more than once by the police. This reference to Nashville is Greene's way of reminding the reader that inhumanity is by no means confined to Haiti or indigenous to it. "Haiti was not an exception in a sane world," says Brown; "it was a small slice of everyday taken at random."

In an insane world, Jones, the con man, functions very well, of course. Having been imprisoned immediately on arriving at Port-au-Prince, because he carried an introduction to a government official who had fallen from power, Jones has managed to wangle his way into the government's confidence to the extent of making a deal to supply Haiti with American arms. Jones is a comedian in every sense of the word. He not only assumes various guises throughout the story but he also is a source of comic relief. His ability to fill the latter rôle reaches a peak in one particular scene. After the government officials learn that Jones is out to swindle them, he obtains asylum in Piñeda's embassy by slipping past the police conspicuously but effectively disguised as a Negro matron.

Once he has taken up residence there, he regales everyone with his tales of his heroics in World War II. Young Philipot, the nephew of the deceased government minister, is especially impressed, and hopes to enlist Jones as the leader of his little band of ill-trained guerrillas who hope to duplicate in Haiti Castro's successful takeover in Cuba. Brown encourages Jones to take on the challenge that is being offered him because he suspects that Martha Piñeda has been having an affair with Jones during his sojourn in the embassy. Brown is wrong about this, but he is right in sensing that Jones would like to have the chance to do something generous and noble, for once, after a lifetime spent in being an opportunist and fraud. Jones in essence calls his own bluff and agrees to go through with the foolhardy mission. Brown agrees to drive Jones to his rendezvous with the guerillas in the wilderness, and the novel takes on an air of suspense similar to that of Greene's entertainments.

En route, Jones gradually realizes that "the game's turned serious" and feels the need to confess. "If I had a dog here tonight instead of you, I'd confess to the dog," he says. He admits that any boasts he has made about having slept with Martha were lies: "She's only one of the fifty women I've never had the courage to touch." Jones further admits that, far from being a war hero, he was in fact rejected for military service because of flat feet.

When Brown and Jones reach their destination, they are confronted by Captain Concasseur who has found out about the rendezvous. But Concasseur is shot by Philipot, who then takes Jones off with him into the interior. All too soon the mission fails. The guerrillas are routed in a skirmish with the government soldiers, and those that are not killed take refuge in the neighboring Dominican Republic, in an old lunatic asylum. Jones, it seems, fell behind in the retreat because of his flat feet, and has been shot by the enemy. "He was a wonderful man," Philipot tells Brown. "The men loved him. He made them laugh." That tribute would probably serve as well as any for Jones's epitaph.

A Mass is held for Jones and the others who died in the skirmish. A Haitian refugee-priest gives an impressive homily on St. Thomas the Apostle's words: "Let us go up to Jerusalem and die with him": "The Church condemns violence, but it condemns indifference more harshly. Violence can be the expression of love, indifference never. . . . In the days of fear, doubt, and confusion, the simplicity and loyalty of one apostle advocated a political solution." The priest almost seems to be speaking directly to Brown when he concludes, "He was wrong, but I would rather be wrong with St. Thomas than right with the cold and the craven. Let us go up to Jerusalem and die with him."

In this way, Greene brings to the surface the underlying theme of commitment that permeates the novel. Greene has portrayed various kinds of commitment, and we see Brown's reaction to each. There are Mr. and Mrs. Smith with their conviction that their vegetarian views can help the Haitian people. Brown finds them naïve, but he is forced to admit that at least they are sincere and want to help. Although he has rejected Catholicism, he is repelled when he sees many Haitians forsaking it for voodooism, even though they are but seeking wherever they can for some relief from their desperately unhappy lives. Nor will he turn to Communism, as his friend Dr. Magiot has done. After the latter is apprehended by the *Tontons* and executed, Brown receives a letter which Magiot had written to him shortly before his death.

In it Magiot reminds Brown that Catholicism and Communism have one thing in common: "They have not stood aside, like an established society, and been indifferent. I would rather have blood on my hands than water like Pilate. . . . If you have abandoned one faith, do not abandon all faith. There is always an alternative to the faith we lose. Or is it the same faith under another mask?" The question which the novel poses through Magiot is, Can a man remain aloof from his fellow men and uncommitted to any goals or beliefs in a world that is crumbling around him? Brown, like Fowler in *The Quiet American*, contends that it is possible, and maintains that he left involvement behind with the Jesuits. Once, he might have taken a different direction, he says; but it is too late now.

Brown cannot even feel much regret over losing Martha, whose husband has been posted to an embassy in another country. "Neither of us would ever die for love," he says. "We would grieve and separate and find another. We belonged to the world of comedy and not of tragedy." As the novel ends, Brown has taken a job as an undertaker's assistant in Santa Domingo. He has merely taken on a new rôle, and has a new mask to wear.

"The fact that Brown seems to end in continued disbelief does not mean that I am taking back anything from my Catholic novels," Greene pointed out in our conversation. "One wants to touch all kinds of characters in one's fiction, those who have faith, those who have lost it, and those who have never had it. If one lived in a Communist State he would want to write about a capitalist, I suppose." Hence Greene the believer is interested at times in writing about the unbeliever. Besides, it is clear that Greene is not suggesting that his hero's total lack of convictions, either religious or political, is the right attitude with which to cope with life. Greene has shown in the various characters in *The Comedians* man's need to believe in some set of values if he is to avoid capitulating to despair, as Brown seems to have done. And, significantly enough, it is Magiot whom Greene allows to have the last word in the novel, in the form of his posthumous plea that Brown not continue to stagnate in his state of uninvolvement; and these sentiments are underscored in the refugee-priest's homily. The reader is left with the suggestion that their words may eventually make inroads into Brown's present nihilistic outlook and restore some of the ideals that he once accepted.

As I mentioned earlier, many of the characters and events in *The Comedians* are drawn from life. Greene notes in the preface, "The *Tontons Macoute* are full of men more evil than Concasseur; the interrupted funeral is drawn from fact, . . . and though I have never met the young Philipot, I have met guerrillas as courageous and ill-trained in that former lunatic asylum near Santo Domingo."[14] The director of the film version of *The Comedians* wanted to match the authentic air of the novel by filming it on location, but of course Haiti was out of the question. Papa Doc Duvalier tried to dissuade any other government from allowing the film to be made, the late Haven Falconer, an executive at MGM at the time, has told me. Finally, permission was secured to make the film in Dahomey, Africa, where the people and the terrain resemble Haiti very much. [*Editor's note*: The Haitian government had formally protested the publication of the novel in 1966, and the theatrical release of the film in 1967. On its first television showing in the United States in October 1971 on the Columbia Broadcasting System network, the Haitian Embassy in Washington issued a denunciation: "The author claims the plot of the story is based in Haiti. Such is not the case. Haiti is a land of smiling, singing, dancing, happy people with a joy of living. It is not a country of crime, of witchcraft or of diabolic excesses of any kind. . . . The Haitian government is convinced that this television program is propaganda intended to adversely affect tourism and its efforts to improve its economy and the lives of its people. . . . It is an affront to the dignity of the Haitian people, to all black communities and to all the Third World."—Ref.: *The New York Times*, CXXI (October 30, 1971) 41,552; p. 63.]

---

[14]Greene, "Dedicatory Note," *The Comedians, loc. cit.*, p. 6.

Greene told me that when he was asked to do the screenplay, he was tempted to decline: "The rights were bought before the novel was published. I had just finished writing the novel and I was too close to it, but I went ahead. One of the problems that I encountered was what to do about the flashbacks in the novel covering Brown's past life. I realized that I would have to leave out Brown's past life for all practical purposes since there wasn't time to develop it in the film. His mother, his days at the Jesuit College, etc., all had to be virtually passed over. But, beginning in the present without the past, Brown would not have any character. So, bit by bit, I brought out different sides of his character and developed them in the dialogue in order to make up for the missing flashbacks. For example, I brought out Brown's boyhood background in the references that Brown makes to his childhood and school days in the dialogue."

"My biggest problem when adapting one of my novels for the screen," Greene continued, "is that one cannot tell a story from the single point of view of one character in a film as one can in a novel. You cannot look through the eyes of one character in a film. The book of *The Comedians* was told from Brown's point of view. It is true that Brown remains on the screen more than any of the others in the film and his comments on the others are often there in his dialogue. But we still do not see others completely from his point of view as we do in the novel. For example, Martha's husband is despised by Brown in the book, but on the screen he is seen by others as a noble character."

The first shot in the film is of a blurred background on which the credits are superimposed while the voice of children are heard singing that Papa Doc is president for life. The background gradually comes into focus and is revealed as a photograph of three dead men who have been shot several times by a machine gun. As the credits end, the camera moves along the wall to show other shabby photographs, most of which have been defaced by a cross made with red pencil. Captain Concasseur (Raymond St. Jacques) enters the frame and crosses out the face of yet another fugitive who has been caught and executed by the *Tontons*. More than once Greene makes reference in the novel to these photographs, wilting on the wall of the police station in the heat; but he has made even better use of them in the film. With a single stroke the travelling shot of the photos creates the atmosphere of the police state in which the story is set, just as effectively as the shot of the police dragging off the man who spit on the lieutenant's car did at the beginning of *Our Man in Havana*.

As Concasseur marks the photograph, a ship's siren is heard screaming in the background, and this provides an auditory bridge to the scene on the ship where Brown (Richard Burton), Jones (Alec Guinness), and Mr. and Mrs. Smith (Paul Ford and Lillian Gish) are disembarking.

In order to take advantage of the melodramatic aspects of his story and make the film more visually dramatic, Greene presents directly in the film some episodes which were described only after they had happened in the novel. This is a method which he used successfully in adapting *Brighton Rock*, as we saw earlier in this chapter, and it works as well here. An example of this would be the mysterious apprehension and imprisonment of Jones, who is taken into custody as soon as he presents Concasseur with his letter of introduction to a Cabinet Minister who has been declared an enemy of the people. Jones is taken away by two *Tontons* and hurled into a cell. There is a close-up of Jones screaming in terror as we cut to Petit Pierre (Roscoe Lee Browne), the local gossip columnist, saying to Brown, "Welcome back to Haiti." The irony of the juxtaposition of these two shots is, of course, fully intended.

Greene also dramatizes Jones's later effort to con the Haitian government into buying American guns which he claims to have at his disposal. This is shown in a scene in which Jones brings all of his spurious charm to bear on the government officials at a cabinet meeting, and provides Alec Guinness with still another opportunity to fill out his deft portrayal of the character. In the novel the reader only learns what Jones has been up to after he has been found out and is escaping to Piñeda's embassy.

Greene has also written a scene into the film which dramatizes the death of Dr. Magiot, which occurs "off-stage" in the novel. On screen, Magiot's death is enacted in a harrowing scene during which the *Tontons* invade Magiot's surgery and stab him to death with a scalpel while he is in the midst of an operation. Also presented directly in the film is the incident that serves totally to disillusion the Smiths about Haiti, which, in the novel, they talk about only after it has happened. The Smiths follow a group of school children to what they

Metro-Goldwyn-Mayer

THE COMEDIANS (Metro-Goldwyn-Mayer, 1967). Jones, the confidence man (Sir Alec Guiness) improbably masquerades as a laundrywoman to escape the Haitian police. An ambassador (Peter Ustinov, left) and the expatriate hotel keeper (Richard Burton) offer their help.

think is going to be a Roman Catholic ceremony of some sort. It turns out that the whole population has been ordered to witness a public execution; and Mrs. Smith, superbly played by Lillian Gish, collapses with a moaning sob of horror when she grasps what is happening.

Some of the dialogue of the original novel has found its way into the film, though considerably condensed and rearranged, of course, for dramatic purposes. It is interesting to see how Greene can extract the pith of meaning from a long speech in the novel to make it fit into the direct dramatic presentation of a film. For example, the comment of Dr. Magiot (James Earle Jones) on Dr. Philipot's death is a neat capsulization of his discussion with Brown in the novel about theological despair. "Suicide is the clear-headed act of a mathematician,"

Magiot concludes. "So many odds against him that he thought, to live must be more miserable than to die."

When Brown accompanies Smith to visit the Minister of Social Welfare, to discuss the possibility of implementing Smith's vegetarian program, Greene slips into the scene some of the satirical remarks that Brown had made in the novel when he first listened to Smith's ideas aboard ship. As the American outlines the beneficial results of being a vegetarian, Brown says, "You've come to a vegetarian country. Ninety-five percent of the people can't afford meat and fish."

Greene has been criticized for being too moralistic in his screenplay by making his denunciation of Papa Doc's regime too explicit for a film that was not a documentary. My own reaction is that Greene more often *shows* rather than *tells* his feelings about man's inhumanity to man as concretized in the situation in Haiti. The sequence in the

THE COMEDIANS (Metro-Goldwyn-Mayer, 1967). Richard Burton and a visiting American philanthropist (Paul Ford, center) are shown Duvalierville, the already decaying ruins of what is supposed to be a model city. Their guide is the Minister of Social Welfare (Dennis Alibepeters).

Metro-Goldwyn-Mayer

Minister of Social Welfare's office begins with a close-up of a gigantic mural depicting a Negro with arms outstretched in the form of a cross, having broken the chains of servitude which bound him. In the ensuing scene Brown describes the squalor in which the people really live, while the image of the mural is still firmly impressed on the viewer's memory. The Minister of Social Welfare invites Smith and Brown to visit Duvalierville, the new city now under construction, which according to him will be a haven for the Haitian people. Smith and Brown are shown an artist's conception of the projected city, and the Minister tells Smith that it is there that he will be able to set up his vegetarian model community.

We learn in a subsequent scene in which Brown and Smith actually visit the building site that the artist's conception of Duvalierville has ludicrously idealized the reality. The site is a shambles of unfinished buildings, the cement walls of which are already beginning to crack. That Greene has presented things as they really are is clear from a remark about Duvalierville in *Time* magazine's obituary (May 3, 1971) of Papa Doc, who died on April 21, 1971, of heart disease and diabetes: "At first Duvalier was able to parlay his anti-Communist credentials into sizable aid grants from the United States. But he squandered much of the funds on grandiose prestige projects like the model city of Duvalierville, now a collection of decaying buildings overgrown by jungle."

In the novel, the visit of Duvalierville is placed after the scene in which the *Tontons* interrupt the funeral procession for Dr. Philipot, but the order of the scenes is reversed in the film. For dramatic effect, Greene arranges the incidents which cumulatively destroy Mr. and Mrs. Smith's hopes to accomplish anything in Haiti in an order in which each event is more shocking than the last. Thus, in the film we go from the visible corruption of the Duvalierville project to the vindictive cruelty of the Philipot funeral, to the climactic scene in which the Smiths witness a public execution at which even the children must be present.

In harmony with the theme of commitment which pervades the story, it is significant that, although the Smiths decide to leave Haiti, they do not plan to give up their plans for social reform, of which their vegetarian program is only a part. They move on to the Dominican Republic in the hope of trying to accomplish some good there.

THE COMEDIANS (Metro-Goldwyn-Mayer, 1967). The wife of the American philanthropist (Lillian Gish) encounters the realities of Haitian dictatorship as Richard Burton is beaten during questioning by the *Tontons Macoute*, led by Zaeks Mokae.

Metro-Goldwyn-Mayer

The Smiths are presented in what is basically a favorable light in both the novel and in the film. But the image of Piñeda in the movie is considerably improved over what it was in the book, since, as Greene has pointed out, we are not seeing Piñeda solely from Brown's point of view as we do in the novel. In the film Piñeda (Peter Ustinov) tells the young Philipot that when he heard of the disruption of Dr. Philipot's funeral he tried to organize a protest in the Diplomatic Corps, but his colleagues chose to be diplomatic and do nothing. This gesture on his part serves to make him seem something more than a cuckolded husband.

One gets the impression from the film that Piñeda is perceptive enough to guess that there is an affair going on between his wife and Brown, and that he drops subtle hints to them that they should break it off before the situation reaches a crisis. He takes the occasion to drop one such veiled hint while Brown is talking about the concept that everyone at times enacts the role of a comedian in life. "One has to play a part now and then," Piñeda remarks, "even in a good marriage." Later Martha tells her husband with more than a trace of condescension that she knows that she can lie to him and that he will always forgive her. Piñeda quite unexpectedly slaps her across the face. Ironically, this action gives Martha—and the audience—a new respect for him.

The scene in which Piñeda slaps Martha is not in the novel. Greene has made similar additions at strategic points in his screenplay which help to delineate a character's point of view for the film audience. When Brown chides young Philipot about his resolve to start an insurrection against Papa Doc, by saying that the lad carries his hope around with him everywhere he goes "like a priest with the sacrament in his pocket," Philipot replies by developing an analogy which does not appear in the novel but which perfectly reflects his commitment to his patriotic ideals. Philipot shows Brown a battered cock that has just won a cockfight: "You see this cock? I bought it just now after the fight. One eye had gone. And it couldn't see with the other because of the blood. It could hardly stand. No one would have bet a dollar on its victory. . . . Then this cock drove its beak straight into the breast of the other. Home to the heart. A brave bird. . . . 'I believe because it is impossible.' A Christian saint said that."

Whether or not any Christian saint ever expressed the sentiment with which young Philipot ends his remarks does not matter to Brown, for he replies that he is no longer impressed by such beliefs. Greene gives Brown two brief bits of dialogue elsewhere in the film, however, in which he betrays the fact that his training at the College of the Visitation has not been completely left behind. After making love to Martha, Brown almost inadvertently quotes Solomon's *Song of Songs* to Martha and adds that the Jesuits taught him that. Martha says that she suspects that Brown is a defrocked priest, but he answers, "My body has no theology." (Brown's corresponding line in the novel is: "Put your hand here. This has no theology.") In a more serious moment, Brown refuses to turn Jones over to Concasseur for $2,000. "Inflation is everywhere," he says with disdain. "It used to be only thirty pieces of silver."

Instead of betraying Jones, Brown offers to take him to his rendezvous with Philipot. While they sit in the cemetery waiting for the young revolutionary, Jones makes his confession to Brown in much the same way as in the novel, except that Brown actually gives Jones a symbolic absolution: *"Absolvo te,"* he says. Jones asks Brown what the phrase means and he replies. "It's an old Church formula which means sleep well."

From this point onward, the film departs noticeably from the book. As Greene describes it, "In the cemetery scene Concasseur manages to kill Jones before Philipot can kill Concasseur. Philipot tells Brown that he can't go back to Port-au-Prince because of his involvement with Jones. So Brown is forced to join the guerrillas in the hills and replace Jones as their leader." But, unlike the hero of Hemingway's *For Whom the Bell Tolls,* Brown does not get swept up in the cause of the insurgents once he has joined their number. Brown thus is forced to fight and probably to die for a cause in which he does not believe, and for which he does not have the slightest hope of success. "I've tried my best to keep out of your politics," Brown complains to Philipot. "You have a cause, I have none."

Then Brown turns to the men he is to lead and delivers a sardonic speech in English, which they cannot understand: "We are crazy fools. I don't know how to fight. We are going up against their Bren guns with a few old shotguns and some machetes and a garden syringe." In closing he salutes them as "you bastards, my ragged regiment." When he finishes the men applaud with enthusiasm, for only Philipot knows the nature of Brown's harangue.

Again, as in the case of the film of *Brighton Rock,* it is Greene himself who has altered the ending of the story in adapting it to the screen; but he feels that he has done so in a way that is in keeping with the spirit of the novel. "Brown is a beachcomber-type character," he explained in my interview with him. "That he had had a religious vocation and lost it is part of his beachcomber personality. He is a person who would like to be better than he is but cannot. The novel is a black comedy. Brown had been washed up on the beach in Haiti, and at the end when he becomes an undertaker he has just been washed up on another shore. In the film the ending is different but the point is the same. He does not want to join the guerrillas and he has no experience in guerrilla warfare, but he makes the best of the situation."

In the final scene of the film Martha and her husband are leaving Haiti by plane for the United States. At this point there is a bit of irony which was cut from the originally-shown version of the film, when it went into general release. We hear the stewardess say over the plane's public address system that the passengers (presumably now free of Papa Doc's jurisdiction) can unfasten their safety belts, adding that the flying time to Miami is one hour and ten minutes. As one watches the plane soar up above the mountains and into the clouds, he is suddenly struck with the realization that all of the brutality he has witnessed in the film has taken place "one hour and ten minutes" from the shores of the United States.

"To be fair," says Greene, "I must tell you that the idea of the flying time to Miami was suggested by the director, Peter Glenville." Glenville had previously directed Greene's play *The Living Room* on the stage, and they had learned to coöperate with each other at that time. "He made me more welcome on the set during the filming of *The Comedians* than I have ever been before. I hate writing a script, but it was fun with Peter Glenville. He has a quick mind. He even consulted me on the casting."

The casting in the film is excellent. Richard Burton wisely under-plays Brown throughout; and Alec Guinness gives a perfectly timed, nuanced performance as Jones, whose only virtue seems to be that he can make people laugh—no mean accomplishment in the grim world that Greene depicts. In their relatively small parts Elizabeth Taylor and Peter Ustinov as the Piñedas, and Paul Ford and Lilian Gish as the Smiths are appropriately subordinated for the good of the film as a whole. The movie really belongs to Jones; but then, so does the book, since he is the most memorable character in it.

When I asked Sir Alec Guinness if he agreed that Jones is the most interesting character in the film he said that he did not think of Jones in those terms during shooting: "The way a particular per-formance fits into a film is largely determined by the way that the film is finally edited. You have no final control over your performance in a film. This is in the hands of the editor. In any event, I wanted to play Jones because I admire Graham Greene as a novelist in general and I liked *The Comedians* as a novel when I read it."

Although *The Comedians* has several things in its favor, such as the excellent performances, it is not as satisfying as one would have ex-pected it to be. One underlying problem seems to be that the film moves along at too leisurely a pace for the kind of story it is telling, and hence a tighter editing job would have been in order. Most major

England Made Me (Atlantic Productions, 1972; released 1973). The locale of Greene's novel, pre-war Stockholm, has been moved to Nazi Germany, and Peter Finch (left) is cast as a powerful, unscrupulous industrialist and financier. The change adds historical coloration to the contrast with the young Englishman, played by Michael York (right), who discovers that there are limits to his own opportunism.

(Photo credit) Atlantic Productions.

studio films are now shot in color, and neither Glenville nor Greene probably could have succeeded in having the film shot in black-in-white, even had they wanted it. Nevertheless black-and-white would have suited the basically somber mood of the film better than color. Perhaps a good compromise would have been for Glenville to have used muted shades of color in the costumes and settings for the film more often, since the lush colors which often fill the screen work against the atmosphere which the film is striving to create.

On this point Alec Guinness says, "I would have preferred the film to have been shot in black-and-white, but ordinary people today feel a little cheated if a large-scale film like *The Comedians* isn't in color.

On the other hand, the hazy, washed-out look that one finds on some days in the tropics was nicely caught by the camera in certain scenes and contributed to the mood of the film." Eight years earlier, Carol Reed had refused to use color in shooting *Our Man in Havana*, however, when color was not as common in films as it is today, because, as he said at the time, color can give a film a hint of unreality: "Color is just not *real* enough. Perhaps it is for television, where your audience is sitting in a room with the lights on. But in a dark theater, confronted by the huge screen, I feel that it is just not convincing enough for drama."[15]

These reservations about *The Comedians* are relatively minor, however, and the film can ultimately be described as a powerful, multi-level tragi-comedy that by turns both moves and entertains us. Unquestionably Greene's adaptations of *Brighton Rock* and *The Comedians* are closer to the spirit of the novels on which they are based than are the adaptations of Greene's serious fiction that were dealt with in the previous chapter. Nonetheless, the best moments in almost any of the versions of Greene's fiction illustrate what Greene meant when he developed his concept of poetic cinema as a film reviewer back in the 1930's: moments which excite and interest us and in addition suggest the deep human values with which Greene has always been concerned, both in his entertainments and his serious novels. "The hunted man, the dangerous edge of things, psychologically and sometimes politically, these are the main obsessions of my books," he said in his BBC-TV interview. "There is a passage in Browning's *Bishop Blougram's Apology* which I always felt could have acted as an epigraph to all my books:

> Our interest's on the dangerous edge of things.
> The honest thief, the tender murderer . . .
> We watch while these in equilibrium keep
> The giddy line midway. . . ."[16]

Greene has been named a Companion of Honor by Queen Elizabeth; but he has never been overly impressed by his own accom-

---

[15]Quoted in Robert Emmett Ginna, "*Our Man in Havana*," loc. cit., p. 125.
[16]Burstall, *op. cit.*, p. 672.

plishments. The very last sentence in his *Collected Essays* says that "for a writer as much as for a priest there is no such thing as success."[17]

Yet, few novelists have gained the wide reading public that Greene enjoys; much less have any had almost their entire body of work translated to the screen. Even as I come to the end of this study of the motion pictures based on Greene's work, film makers are contemplating versions of the few remaining novels by Greene that have yet to be brought to the screen. So far, in 1972 Peter Duffell completed *England Made Me*, with Peter Finch and Michael York, in Yugoslavia, as George Cukor was finishing *Travels With My Aunt*, which I mentioned at the end of Chapter two.

So Greene's involvement in the cinema is by no means over. As he discussed the association with me in his apartment in Antibes, the afternoon turned into evening. When I was preparing to leave, I asked him one final question: How would he sum up his own attitude towards the way his work has been treated by the motion picture medium. Greene's reply came without hesitation: "Some of the films have been good and one finds them a rewarding experience. As for those that have been disappointments I can only repeat what I have said before: In the long run the smile will be on the author's face. For the book has the longer life." But I think it is a safe bet that the best of the Greene films, with *The Third Man* leading the list, will last as long as anything that he has written—a fitting tribute to a writer who has shown that the alliance of the novelist and the screenwriter can be a fruitful one, especially when, as I have maintained from the very beginning, they happen to be the same person.

[17]Graham Greene, "The Soupsweet Land," *Collected Essays*. Harmondsworth: Penguin Books, 1970; p. 345.

SELECT
BIBLIOGRAPHY

I. WORKS BY GRAHAM GREENE

Listed in order of publication

A. BOOKS

1. *The Man Within* (1929). New York: Bantam Books, 1971.

2. *Stamboul Train* (American title: *Orient Express*; 1932). Harmondsworth: Penguin Books, 1963.

3. *It's a Battlefield* (1934). With an Introduction by the Author. The Collected Edition.[1] London: The Bodley Head, 1970.

4. *England Made Me* (American title: *The Shipwrecked*; 1935). With an Introduction by the Author. The Collected Edition. London: The Bodley Head, 1970.

5. *This Gun for Hire* (British title: *A Gun for Sale*; 1936). New York: The Viking Press, 1968.

6. *Journey Without Maps* (1936). New York: The Viking Press, 1965.

7. *Brighton Rock* (1938). With an Introduction by the Author. The Collected Edition. London: The Bodley Head, 1970.

8. *The Confidential Agent* (1939). With an Introduction by the Author. The Collected Edition. London: The Bodley Head, 1971.

9. *Another Mexico* (British title: *The Lawless Roads*; 1939). New York: The Viking Press, 1968.

10. *The Power and the Glory* (1940). With an Introduction by the Author. The Collected Edition. London: The Bodley Head, 1971.

11. *The Ministry of Fear* (1943). New York: The Viking Press, 1968.

12. *The Heart of the Matter* (1948). With an Introduction by the Author. The Collected Edition. London: The Bodley Head, 1971.

13. *Why Do I Write: An Exchange of Views Between Graham Greene, Elizabeth Bowen, and V. S. Pritchett* (1948). London: Percival Marshall, 1948.

---

[1]The author has used the Collected Edition of Greene's works (1970–) for all of the novels that have thus far appeared in that series.

14. *The Third Man* and *The Fallen Idol* (1950). With Prefaces by the Author. (Greene's short story, "The Basement Room" [1935], is here published under the title of the film version, *The Fallen Idol*). New York: The Viking Press, 1950.

15. *The End of the Affair* (1951). New York: Bantam Books, 1967.

16. *The Lost Childhood and Other Essays* (1951). New York: The Viking Press, 1962.

17. *Twenty-One Stories* (1954). New York: Bantam Books, 1968.

18. *Loser Takes All* (1954, 1955). New York: The Viking Press, 1955, 1957.

19. *The Quiet American* (1955). New York: Bantam Books, 1968.

20. *Our Man in Havana* (1958). With an Introduction by the Author. The Collected Edition. London: The Bodley Head, 1970.

21. *A Burnt-Out Case* (1961). New York: Bantam Books, 1963.

22. *In Search of a Character: Two African Journals* (1961). New York: The Viking Press, 1962.

23. *Three Plays*. With an Introduction by the Author. London: Mercury Books, 1961.

24. *Introduction to Three Novels* (1962). Stockholm: Norstedt, 1962.

25. *A Sense of Reality: Four Short Stories* (1963). New York: The Viking Press, 1963.

26. *The Comedians* (1966). New York: The Viking Press, 1966.

27. *May We Borrow Your Husband? And Other Comedies of the Sexual Life* (1967). New York: The Viking Press, 1967.

28. *The Third Man* (First publication of the film script, 1968). Modern Film Scripts. New York: Simon and Schuster, 1968.

29. *Collected Essays* (1969). Harmondsworth: Penguin Books, 1970.

30. *Travels with My Aunt* (1970). New York: The Viking Press, 1970.

31. *A Sort of Life* (1971). New York: Simon and Schuster, 1971.

B. SHORTER WORKS

32. "The Middle-Brow Film." *The Fortnightly Review*. CXLV (March, 1936), 302–307.

33. Film Criticism for *The Spectator*, 1935–1940.

34. Film Criticism for *Night and Day*, 1937.

35. "Ideas in the Cinema." *The Spectator*, CLIX (November 19, 1937), 894–95.

36. "Subjects and Stories." *Footnotes to the Film*. Edited by Charles Davey. London: Lovat Dickson, 1938: pp. 57–70. Reprinted in *The Literature of Cinema* series. New York: Arno Press and The New York Times, 1970.

37. *Graham Greene On Film.* (Film criticism, 1935-1939) Edited by John Russell
    Taylor. New York: Simon and Schuster, 1972.

38. "The Lieutenant Died Last." *Collier's Magazine*, CV (June 29, 1940), 9–10,
    24.

39. "Dear Mr. Chaplin." *The New Republic*, CXXVI (October 13, 1952), 5.

40. "Last Act in Indo-China." *The New Republic*, CXXXII (May 9, 1955), 9–11.

41. "The Novelist and the Cinema: A Personal Experience." *International
    Film Annual 2.* Edited by William Whitebait. New York: Doubleday
    & Company, 1958, pp. 54–58.

42. "Greene, 'the Funny Writer,' on Comedy." *Life*, January 23, 1970, p. 10.

II. SECONDARY SOURCES

Listed alphabetically by author:

A. BOOKS

43. Baxter, John. *The Cinema of John Ford.* New York: A. S. Barnes & Co., 1971.

44. Bluestone, George. *Novels into Film.* Berkeley: University of California
    Press, 1961.

45. Boardman, Gwenn R. *Graham Greene: The Aesthetics of Exploration.* Gains-
    ville: University of Florida Press, 1971.

46. Bogdanovich, Peter. *John Ford.* London: Studio Vista, 1968.

47. Cargas, Harry, editor. *Graham Greene.* St. Louis: B. Herder Book Co., 1970.

48. De Vitis, A. A. *Graham Greene.* New York: Twayne Publishers, 1961.

49. Evans, Robert O., editor. *Graham Greene: Some Critical Considerations.* Lex-
    ington: University of Kentucky Press, 1967.

50. Geduld, Harry M., editor. *Film Makers on Film Making.* Bloomington:
    Indiana University Press, 1969.

51. Houston, Penelope. *Contemporary Cinema.* Baltimore: Penguin Books, 1969.

52. Jensen, Paul. *The Cinema of Fritz Lang.* New York: A. S. Barnes & Co., 1969.

53. Kael, Pauline. *Kiss Kiss Bang Bang.* New York: Bantam Books, 1969.

54. Knight, Arthur. *The Liveliest Art: A Panoramic History of the Movies.* New
    York: New American Library, 1967.

55. McCann, Richard Dyer, editor. *Film: A Montage of Theories.* New York:
    E. P. Dutton & Co., 1966.

56. O'Faolain, Sean. *The Vanishing Hero.* New York: Grosset and Dunlap,
    1957.

57. Pryce-Jones, David. *Graham Greene.* New York: Barnes and Noble, 1967.

58. Sarris, Andrew. *The American Cinema: Directors and Directions, 1929–68.* New York: E. P. Dutton & Co., 1968.

B. ARTICLES

59. Adamson, Judy. "Graham Greene as Film Critic." *Sight and Sound,* XLI (Spring, 1972), 104–106.

60. Burstall, Christopher. "Graham Greene Takes the Orient Express." *The Listener,* November 21, 1968, pp. 672–78. (A transcript of Graham Greene's interview on BBC-TV, November 17, 1968).

61. Dworkin, Martin S. *"Across the Bridge." The Canadian Commentator,* IV (November, 1960), 15. Reprinted from the author's article, "Ideas On Screen," *The Progressive,* XXII (January, 1958), 36–37.

62. Ginna, Robert Emmett. *"Our Man in Havana." Horizon,* II (November, 1959), 26–31, 122–26.

63. Hartung, Philip. *"This Gun for Hire." Commonweal,* XXXVI (May 29, 1942), 136–37.

———. *"Short Cut to Hell." Commonweal,* LXVII (November 15, 1957), 176.

64. Jensen, Paul. "The Career of Dudley Nichols." *Film Comment,* VI (Winter, 1970), 56–62.

65. "A New Honor and a New Novel." *Life,* February 4, 1966, pp. 43–44.

66. Nolan, Jack Edmund. "Graham Greene's Movies." *Films in Review,* XV (January, 1964), 23–35.

67. Ostermann, Robert. "Interview with Graham Greene," *The Catholic World,* CLXX (February, 1950), 356–61.

68. Raven, Simon, *"May We Borrow Your Husband?* No Laughing Matter." *The Weekend Observer* (London), April 9, 1967, section 2, p. 26.

69. Ryan, Thomas C. "A Talk with Evelyn Waugh." *The Sign,* XXXVI (August, 1957), 41–43.

70. Sarris, Andrew. "Mankiewicz of the Movies." *Show,* March 1970, pp. 27–30, 78.

71. "Shocker," *Time,* October 29, 1951, pp. 98–104.

72. Walsh, Moira. *"The Heart of the Matter." America,* XCII (December 4, 1954), 284–85.

73. Waugh, Evelyn. "Felix Culpa?" *Commonweal,* XLVIII (July 16, 1948), 322–25.

———. "The Heart's Own Reasons." *Commonweal,* LIV (August 17, 1951), 458–59.

74. Young, Vernon. "Hollywood: Lost Moments." *Accent,* IX (Autumn, 1948), 120–28.

FILMOGRAPHY

I. FILM SCRIPTS WRITTEN BY GRAHAM GREENE

1. *Twenty-One Days* (Columbia Pictures, 1939). Screenplay by Graham Greene and Basil Dean from John Galsworthy's story, "The First and the Last." Produced and directed by Basil Dean. With Laurence Olivier, Vivien Leigh. 75 minutes.

2. *The Green Cockatoo* (New World, 1940). Screenplay by Graham Greene and E. O. Berkman from the story by Graham Greene. Directed by William Cameron Menzies. Produced by William K. Howard. With John Mills, Rene Ray. 65 minutes.

3. *Brighton Rock* (Associated British Picture Corporation, 1947). Screenplay by Graham Greene from his novel. Directed by John Boulting. Produced by Roy Boulting. With Richard Attenborough, Hermione Baddeley, William Hartnell. 92 minutes.

4. *The Fallen Idol* (London Film Productions, 1948). Screenplay by Graham Greene from his short story, "The Basement Room." Produced and directed by Carol Reed. With Ralph Richardson, Michele Morgan, Bobby Henrey, Sonia Dresdel. 94 minutes.

5. *The Third Man* (London Film Productions, 1949). Original screenplay by Graham Greene. Produced and directed by Carol Reed. With Joseph Cotten, Trevor Howard, Alida Valli, Orson Welles, and Wilfred Hyde-White. 93 minutes.

6. *Loser Takes All* (J. Arthur Rank Productions, 1956). Original screenplay by Graham Greene. Directed by Ken Annakin. Produced by John Stafford. With Glynis Johns, Rossano Brazzi, Robert Morley. 88 minutes.

7. *St. Joan* (Wheel Productions, 1957). Screenplay by Graham Greene from the drama by George Bernard Shaw. Produced and directed by Otto Preminger. With Jean Seberg, Richard Widmark, Anton Walbrook, John Gielgud. 109 minutes.

8. *Our Man in Havana* (Columbia Pictures, 1959). Screenplay by Graham Greene from his novel. Produced and directed by Carol Reed. With Alec Guinness, Noel Coward, Ernie Kovacs, Burl Ives, Maureen O'Hara. 111 minutes.

9. *The Comedians* (Metro-Goldwyn-Mayer, 1967). Screenplay by Graham Greene from his novel. Produced and directed by Peter Glenville. With Richard Burton, Elizabeth Taylor, Alec Guinness, Lillian Gish, Peter Ustinov, Paul Ford. 150 minutes.

II. ADAPTATIONS OF GREENE'S FICTION BY OTHER SCREENWRITERS

1. *Orient Express* (Twentieth-Century-Fox, 1933). Screenplay by Paul Martin, William Conselman, Carl Hovey, and Oscar Levant, from Graham Greene's novel, *Stamboul Train*. Produced and directed by Paul Martin. With Heather Angel, Norman Foster, Una O'Connor. 73 minutes.

2. *Went the Day Well?* (Ealing Studios, 1942; American title: *Forty-Eight Hours*). Screenplay by John Dighton, Diana Morgan, Angus MacPhaill, from Graham Greene's short story, "The Lieutenant Died Last." Directed by Alberto Cavalcanti. Produced by Michael Balcon. With Leslie Banks, Basil Sydney, Frank Lawton. 92 minutes.

3. *This Gun for Hire* (Paramount Pictures, 1942). Screenplay by Albert Maltz and W. R. Burnett from Graham Greene's novel, *A Gun for Sale*. Directed by Frank Tuttle. Produced by Richard Blumenthal. With Alan Ladd, Robert Preston, Veronica Lake, Laird Cregar. 81 minutes.

4. *The Ministry of Fear* (Paramount Pictures, 1943). Screenplay by Seton I. Miller from Graham Greene's novel. Directed by Fritz Lang. Produced by Seton I. Miller. With Ray Milland, Marjorie Reynolds, Dan Duryea. 87 minutes.

5. *The Confidential Agent* (Warner Brothers, 1945). Screenplay by Robert Buckner from Graham Greene's novel. Directed by Herman Shumlin. Produced by Robert Buckner. With Charles Boyer. Lauren Bacall, Peter Lorre, Katina Paxinou, Wanda Hendrix. 117 minutes.

6. *The Man Within* (J. Arthur Rank Productions, 1947; American title: *The Smugglers*). Screenplay by Muriel and Sydney Box from Graham Greene's novel. Directed by Bernard Knowles. Produced by Muriel and Sydney Box. With Richard Attenborough, Michael Redgrave, Joan Greenwood, Jean Kent. 88 minutes.

7. *The Fugitive* (R.K.O. Radio Pictures, 1947). Screenplay by Dudley Nichols from Graham Greene's novel, *The Power and the Glory*. Directed by John Ford. Produced by John Ford and Merion C. Cooper. With

Henry Fonda, Dolores Del Rio, J. Carroll Naish, Pedro Armendariz, Ward Bond. 104 minutes.

8. *The Heart of the Matter* (London Films, 1953). Screenplay by Ian Dalrymple from Graham Greene's novel. Directed by George More O'Ferrall. Produced by Ian Dalrymple. With Trevor Howard, Elizabeth Allan, Maria Schell, Peter Finch. 105 minutes.

9. *The Stranger's Hand* (J. Arthur Rank Productions, 1954). Screenplay by Guy Elmes and Georgio Bassani from Graham Greene's story. Directed by Mario Soldati. Produced by John Stafford, Peter Moore, and Graham Greene. With Trevor Howard, Alida Valli, Richard Basehart, Richard O'Sullivan. 85 minutes.

10. *The End of the Affair* (Columbia Pictures, 1955). Screenplay by Lenore Coffee from Graham Greene's novel. Directed by Edward Dmytryk. Produced by David E. Rose. With Deborah Kerr, Van Johnson, John Mills, Peter Cushing, Michael Goodliffe, Stephen Murray. 105 minutes.

11. *Across the Bridge* (J. Arthur Rank Productions, 1957). Screenplay by Guy Elmes and Denis Freeman from Graham Greene's short story. Directed by Ken Annakin. Produced by John Stafford. With Rod Steiger, Marla Landi, David Knight. 103 minutes.

12. *The Quiet American* (United Artists, 1957). Screenplay by Joseph L. Mankiewicz from Graham Greene's novel. Produced and directed by Joseph L. Mankiewicz. With Audie Murphy, Michael Redgrave, Claude Dauphin, Georgia Moll. 121 minutes.

13. *Short Cut to Hell* (Paramount Pictures, 1957). Screenplay by Ted Berkman, Raphael Blau; based on a screenplay by Albert Maltz and W. R. Burnett from Graham Greene's novel, *A Gun for Sale*. Directed by James Cagney. Produced by A. C. Lyles. With Robert Ivers, Georgann Johnson, William Bishop, Jacques Aubuchon. 89 minutes.

14. *The Power and the Glory* (CBS Television, 1961). Screenplay by Dale Wasserman from Graham Greene's novel. Directed by Marc Daniels. Produced by David Susskind. With Laurence Olivier, Julie Harris, George C. Scott, Mildred Natwick, Martin Gabel, Cyril Cusack. 98 minutes. (Given theatrical release in Britain.)

15. *Travels with My Aunt* (Metro-Goldwyn-Mayer, 1972). Screenplay by Jay Presson Allen and Hugh Wheeler from Graham Greene's novel. Directed by George Cukor. Produced by Robert Fryer and James Cresson. With Maggie Smith, Alec McCowen, Lou Gossett, and Robert Stephens.

16. *England Made Me* (Atlantic Productions, 1972). Screenplay by Desmond Corey and Peter Duffell from Graham Greene's novel. Directed by Peter Duffell. Produced by Jack Levin. With Peter Finch and Michael York.

INDEX

Harris, Julie, 112
Hartung, Philip, 26, 27
Heart of the Matter, The, 15, 36, 77,
    98, 100, 106, 113–123, 129, 130,
    156
"Heart's Own Reasons, The"
    (Evelyn Waugh) 128 fn
heaven and hell, concept of,
    118–119, 152, 157, 160
Hemingway, Ernest, 182
Henrey, Bobby, 48, 52, 59
High Court of Justice (England),
    10 fn
Hitchcock, Alfred, 6, 16, 20, 55, 56,
    57, 63
    on suspense, 55, 56
"Hollywood: Lost Moments"
    (Vernon Young), 16 fn
*Hollywood, the Dream Factory: An
    Anthropologist Looks at the Movie
    Makers* (Hortense Powdermaker),
    xiv fn
*Hollywood: the Movie Colony; The
    Movie Makers* (Leo Rosten), vii
Holy office, see Church, Roman
    Catholic
homosexuality, imputation of (in
    The Third Man), 61
Hope, Anthony, 1
Hopkins, Barbara, 74
Houston, Penelope, 76, 105, 106
Howard, Trevor, 36, 62, 76, 115,
    120, 123
Howard, William K., 46
Hyde-White, Wilfred, 63

"I Call on Alfred Hitchcock" (Pete
    Mantin), 55 fn
Ibsen, Henrik, ix
Ideas in Cultural Perspective (Philip P.
    Weiner and Aaron Noland, eds.),
    xiii fn
In Search of a Character (Greene),
    99 fn
Informer, The, 110
Ingram, Rex, ix
inhumanity theme, 171, 178
Intelligence Services, British, 76, 79

International Film Annual No. 2, 4, 14
"Interview with Graham Greene"
    (Robert Ostermann), 100 fn
It's a Battlefield, 15–16, 100
Ivers, Robert, 27
Ives, Burl, 88

Jansenism, Greene and, 101, 102
Jefford, Barbara, 5
Jensen, Paul, 29, 30, 110
John Ford (Peter Bogdanovich),
    110 fn
John Player Lecture Series, 9 fn,
    61 fn
Johns, Glynis, 92
Johnson, Georgann, 27
Johnson, Van, 129
Jones, James Earle, 177
Journal of the History of Ideas
    (magazine), xiii fn
Journey Without Maps, 20, 21 fn,
    98 fn
Joyce, James, 5

Kael, Pauline, 71, 74, 89, 143–144
Karas, Anton, 73, 74
Kerr, Deborah, 126, 129
Kimpton, Lawrence A., 134
King in New York, A, 134
Kinsella, Rev. John, 10 fn
Kiss Kiss Bang Bang (Pauline Kael),
    71, 74, 89, 143–144
Knight, Arthur, 23
Knight Without Armor, 8, 9
Korda, Sir Alexander, 60
Kovacs, Ernie, 83
Krasker, Robert, 74
Kristeller, Paul Oskar, xiii
Kubrick, Stanley, 18
Kunkle, Francis, 107

*Labyrinthine Ways of Graham Greene,
    The* (Francis Kunkle), 107
Ladd, Alan, 25, 26, 27, 28, 33
Lady Vanishes, The, 20, 63

REV. GENE D. PHILLIPS, S.J. is Assistant Professor of English at Loyola University of Chicago, where he took his B.A. and M.A. degrees. He teaches courses in fiction, drama, and film, the relationships of which he had studied for his Ph.D. in English at Fordham University. He is a frequent contributor to film periodicals in the U.S. and abroad; has served as a judge or panelist at film festivals at Chicago, Cannes, and Berlin; and is a member of the Executive Board of the National Center for Film Study. He is the author of a textbook, *The Movie Makers: Artists In An Industry* (1973), and of forthcoming volumes on the films of Stanley Kubrick, and the fiction of Evelyn Waugh.